THE COMPLETE ENCYCLOPEDIA OF
SUPERFOODS

THE COMPLETE ENCYCLOPEDIA OF
SUPERFOODS

WITH 150 HIGH-IMPACT POWER-PACKED RECIPES

COOKING FOR HEALTH, ENERGY, WEIGHT LOSS AND FITNESS: A COMPREHENSIVE
GUIDE TO THE MOST POWERFUL NUTRIENT-RICH INGREDIENTS AND THEIR PROPERTIES

AUDREY DEANE

HERMES
HOUSE

© Anness Publishing Ltd 2014
Illustrations © 2014 by Anness Publishing Ltd

If you like the images in this book and would like to investigate using them for publishing, promotions or advertising, please visit our website www.practicalpictures.com for more information.

Publisher: Joanna Lorenz
Editorial Director: Helen Sudell
Project Editor: Melanie Hibbert
Design: Nigel Partridge
Production Controller: Wendy Lawson

ISBN: 978-1-4351-5288-5

Manufactured in China

10 9 8 7 6 5 4 3 2 1

Main image on front cover: Marinated salmon with avocado, page 166

Notes
• Bracketed terms are intended for American readers.

• For all recipes, quantities are given in both metric and imperial measures and, where appropriate, in standard cups and spoons. Follow one set of measures, but not a mixture, because they are not interchangeable.

• Standard spoon and cup measures are level. 1 tsp = 5ml, 1 tbsp = 15ml, 1 cup = 250m1/ 8fl oz. Australian standard tablespoons are 20ml.

• Australian readers should use 3 tsp in place of I tbsp for measuring small quantities. American pints are 16fl oz/2 cups.
• American readers should use 20fl oz/2.5 cups in place of 1 pint when measuring liquids.

• Electric oven temperatures in this book are for conventional ovens. When using a fan oven, the temperature will probably need to be reduced by about 10–20°C/20–40°F. Since ovens vary, you should check with your manufacturer's instruction book for guidance.

• The nutritional analysis given for each recipe is calculated per portion (i.e. serving or item), unless otherwise stated. If the recipe gives a range, such as Serves 4–6, then the nutritional analysis will be for the smaller portion size, i.e. 6 servings. The analysis does not include optional ingredients, such as salt added to taste. Medium (US large) eggs are used unless otherwise stated.

Important: pregnant women, the elderly, the ill and very young children should avoid recipes using raw or lightly cooked eggs.

Contents

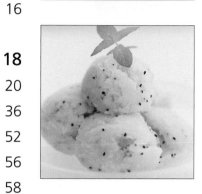

Introduction

For thousands of years, civilizations have recognized the fact that various foods have different effects on our body, and that our diet has an important role to play in keeping us healthy. In ancient times, the Chinese, Greeks, Romans and Egyptians all understood that diet was an essential part of our well-being, and this knowledge informed many of the food customs and traditions that are still in evidence today.

The scientific study of food and its impact on health is well documented and dates back to the 18th century, when learned men and physicians began to travel the world studying the effects of nutritional deficiencies. One of the best-known breakthroughs was the realization that citrus fruits could prevent scurvy among sailors. However, it was not until the late 1920s, with the discovery of vitamin C, that people fully understood what it was in the citrus fruits that kept the disease at bay. By this time the number of researchers working in the field of nutritional science had exploded, and this 'Golden Age' of nutritional analysis led to the discovery of many of the basic factors required to maintain a healthy diet and prevent disease.

Below: Drink fresh fruit juice to contribute to your 'five-a-day' intake.

This research has continued into the modern day and, with the advent of highly sophisticated techniques and scientific procedures, many new findings are being made all the time. Unfortunately, the claims of some supposed 'superfoods', traditionally well-regarded in areas such as Chinese herbal, Ayurvedic and homeopathic medicine, have not stood up to modern scientific scrutiny.

It is worth noting that, although widely used, the word 'superfood' is not a legally recognized term. The European Union are now reviewing a whole spectrum of nutritional claims with the ultimate aim of publishing a list of credible declarations.

Whether the term 'superfood' will ever become legally recognized is debatable, but it is now commonly used to describe foods with a beneficial nutritional content.

Food for Health

There are a wide range of substances found in foods, sometimes termed phytonutrients, or phytochemicals, that are reported to have beneficial effects on health and well-being. The term 'phyto' means from plants, but animal-derived foods are now emerging that are also being included in the superfoods family. While each superfood generally contains a particular beneficial nutrient, it is very important to emphasize that these benefits can't be fully exploited unless they are eaten as part of a healthy balanced diet. They will not mitigate the adverse effects of a poor diet and lifestyle, so it's no good eating a diet high in saturated fat, taking no exercise and smoking, then eating a handful of blueberries and a bowl of porridge and thinking everything is going to be just fine.

Foods High in Antioxidants:
Antioxidant-rich foods, such as blueberries, goji berries, oranges and tomatoes, are usually part of the fruit

Above: Antioxidant-rich raspberries taste great in a smoothie.

and vegetable family and indeed were probably the first group of foods to be given the name superfoods. Antioxidants are thought to be crucial for our well being due to their powerful ability to 'mop up' free radicals that circulate around the body. These free radicals may be introduced from external factors such as through smoking or come from our own bodily processes. It is thought that an excess of these may be a factor in the occurrence of cancer and this may be why a diet high in fruit and vegetables could help us to avoid a third of all cancers. Many vitamins have antioxidant activity, such as vitamin A (retinol), vitamin C (ascorbic acid) and vitamin E (tocopherol) as well as some minerals, including selenium. All have a vital role to play in keeping potentially harmful substances in check and preventing them from causing diseases such as cancer.

Foods High in Flavonoids: These substances, also known as polyphenols, are found in food and drinks such as tea, red wine and chocolate. Flavonoids have some antioxidant activity, but it is their role in cell signalling that is the basis for their reported health benefits. Studies have shown that they are able to regulate the cell signals and can affect cell growth, thus possibly influencing cancer incidence. These compounds could also reduce the risk of coronary heart disease and atherosclerosis, a condition where the arteries become clogged with fatty deposits such as cholesterol. Flavonoids may also have beneficial effects in brain disorders such as Alzheimer's and Parkinson's disease.

Foods High in Phytosterols:

These important compounds, found in wheatgerm and brown rice, may have the ability to lower blood cholesterol levels by altering the way it is metabolized by the body. Found in plant cells, phytosterols are the plant equivalent of animal cholesterol. The highest concentrations of phytosterols are found in grain and bean oils and lower amounts are found in fruit and vegetables.

Foods High in Isoflavones and Phytoestrogens:

These substances, present in foods such as soya beans, alfalfa and chickpeas, show strong antioxidant activity and also provide dietary oestrogens that have beneficial effects on some of the hormonal systems of the body. These include helping to control blood cholesterol and reducing negative effects of the menopause such as osteoporosis. They may also have a role to play in protecting the body against cancers such as those of the breast and prostate.

Foods High in Dietary Fibre:

The general population does not eat enough fibre, yet fibre is important because it helps the body with many key functions. It can help improve your gastrointestinal health and glucose metabolism, helping those suffering from Type II Diabetes. It can help reduce coronary heart disease risk factors by reducing bad blood fats and hypertension, and also

reduce the risk of developing some cancers. Eating a higher fibre diet makes us feel fuller for longer after a meal so can help with weight control.

Foods High in Healthy Fats: Fat has had a lot of bad press in recent years, with people striving for a low-fat diet. We now recognize that though many of us would benefit from lower-fat diets, the type of fats we are consuming is equally important. Generally, we should be eating fewer saturated varieties and more of the healthy fats – mono-unsaturated and polyunsaturated fat. These healthy fats, present in foods such as olive oil, oily fish, flaxseed and walnuts, are important as they influence how we control cholesterol in our bodies, an excess of which can cause problems such as narrowing of arteries, which leaves us prone to heart attack and stroke.

Healthy omega-3 fats (part of the polyunsaturated fat family) are particularly important as they have many unique roles to play in the body, ranging from brain structure and function to potentially reducing excessive inflammatory reactions such as rheumatoid arthritis.

Above: For optimum nutrition, eat a good variety of fruit and vegetables.

Variety is Key

Many other compounds have been discovered in foods and some of these are very specific in their effect on the body. What this all points to is that it is best to eat as many different types of food as possible to gain the most benefit. The value of knowing about the different types of superfoods is in enabling you to understand those foods that may be of the most benefit to you, depending on your specific needs, when included in your balanced diet. Remember to always consult with a medical professional first, especially if you suffer from chronic illness or are on prescription medicines, as a change in diet may do more harm than good.

The basic elements of a healthy diet and lifestyle are outlined in the introductory section. Following this chapter about healthy living, a detailed directory provides key information for some of the most nutrient-packed superfoods known. The directory is followed by 150 mouthwatering, nutrient-rich recipes, each containing at least one or more superfood ingredients.

Balancing good health and lifestyle

A healthy, balanced diet should be based primarily on the regular consumption of unrefined complex carbohydrate-rich starchy foods and fruit and vegetables, with a slightly lower contribution from protein-rich foods and dairy products and a restricted intake of foods high in fat, salt and sugar. These proportions should provide your body with the energy and essential nutrients that it needs to maintain optimum health.

Carbohydrates

Foods rich in carbohydrates, such as bread, pasta, potatoes and sugar, provide the body with its main energy source. The body breaks down the more starchy foods such as bread, rice and potatoes into simple sugars such as glucose, which can then be used as energy. About one third of our food intake should come from wholegrain starchy foods. This will provide about half of the body's energy requirements. Starchy foods often contain other useful nutrients including protein, vitamins and minerals.

Sugar is sometimes termed an 'empty food' or 'empty calories' as it has no nutrient value other than energy and should be restricted by those trying to control their weight. It is useful in sport and for diabetics, who need a quick energy boost, but this is short-lived as the body counteracts this rise in blood sugar with the release of the hormone insulin. For most of us, therefore, it is healthier to eat carbohydrate foods that release energy much more slowly and don't induce the spikes in blood sugar levels that we then have to process. The measure of how fast sugar is released from a food is known as its GI (Glycaemic Index) value; the fastest being pure sugar at 100 and the lowest being some of the wholegrain, high-fibre foods, such as oats, wholegrain breads, brown rice and pulses. Foods with a low carbohydrate content, for example milk, meat, eggs and green vegetables, also have low GI values so release their energy gradually.

Fibre

Another type of carbohydrate, fibre is largely indigestible by the body and its importance in the diet cannot be underestimated. There are two types of fibre: soluble and insoluble. Insoluble fibre, such as in brown rice and pasta, is associated with improving the bulk of stools as it absorbs water. This prevents constipation and could be a factor in reducing cancer of the bowel and colon. Soluble fibre, as is found in apples, oats and lentils, is quite different as it can actually be partially digested in the lower intestine and fermented by the gut's bacteria. This produces beneficial compounds that are absorbed back into the body and these help to keep the gut healthy. Wholegrain foods, like some cereals and vegetables, are high in fibre and have the added benefit of retaining the nutrient-rich germ often removed in manufacturing.

Proteins

These are essential for growth, repair and maintenance of every cell in the body. They provide the building blocks to make muscle, hormones and enzymes, and are crucial in many

THE MAIN FOOD GROUPS
The pie chart below illustrates the proportions of the five main food groups that you should be aiming to eat each day.

breads and cereals
33%

fruit and vegetables
33%

fats and sugar 7%

dairy foods
15%

protein foods
12%

metabolic processes. Proteins are made up of amino acid units, of which there are 20. Most can be made by the body itself, however eight cannot; these are termed 'essential' as we have to get them from our food. Generally, animal sources of proteins such as meat, fish and eggs contain all of the essential amino acids, whereas most plant sources are lacking in one or more of them. Some examples of plant foods containing the full complement of amino acids are soya, quinoa and buckwheat. It is important to eat a variety of protein foods to ensure that we get all of the essential amino acids that we need.

Fats and Oils

Given the amount of bad press that it gets, it may surprise you to learn that fat is essential in the diet. Modern dietary advice concentrates on the type of fats we eat. Fat is the most concentrated form of energy, releasing twice as many calories as the same amounts of carbohydrate and protein, which is why eating too much tends to make us overweight. However, fat also contains the vital fat-soluble vitamins A, D and E and provides us

Below: Cook with healthier vegetable oils rather than butter.

> **FAT TYPES**
> **Saturated**
> Meat, dairy, lard
>
> **Unsaturated**
> Monounsaturated: olive oil, groundnut oil, sesame oil
> Polyunsaturated: rapeseed oil, soya oil, fish oil

with essential fatty acids, all of which are critical to our good health.

Diets high in saturated fats have been associated with raised blood cholesterol and an increased risk of heart disease, a fact corroborated by the World Health Organization (WHO), which recommends avoiding saturated fat in order to reduce the risk of a cardiovascular disease. The body of evidence has changed opinions about dietary cholesterol and its effect on blood cholesterol. While we used to think that eating cholesterol-containing foods such as eggs and prawns could raise our blood cholesterol, we now know that the biggest influence is the amount of saturated fats that we eat. People whose diets are high in saturated fats are more likely to have raised levels

Below: Lean meat and fish are high in protein and low in saturated fat.

Above: Drink plenty of water after exercising to prevent dehydration.

of cholesterol. Unsaturated fats such as some seed oils help to restore the correct balance of the two types of cholesterol found in the body. HDL cholesterol is good, whereas LDL cholesterol is bad as high levels of LDL cholesterol are associated with an increased risk of heart disease.

Water

Our body is approximately 50 per cent water, so it is important to replenish our supplies. We continuously lose water through breathing, perspiring and getting rid of waste products. We need water to keep us cool, for transporting nutrients around the body in the blood and ensuring that the kidneys can function properly. Fluid can be taken in through our food as well as through drinking liquids, and we

> **KEEP HUNGER PANGS AT BAY**
> It is especially important at the start of the day to eat foods that have a low GI so that they release energy slowly and stop you from feeling hungry before lunchtime. Try eating a bowl of porridge or wholegrain cereal for breakfast.

need 1.5–2 litres/2½–3½ pints a day. The body is actually very good at telling us whether we are dehydrated: our urine becomes darker as our kidneys re-absorb more water back into the body, we become thirsty and we may get headaches.

Problems arise when we fail to recognize these signs and just feel unwell. Tea and coffee, while being mild diuretics, do contribute to fluid intake as does the food that we eat, so it doesn't all have to come from pure water. It is especially important to keep an eye on our fluid intake during hot weather or when we do exercise, as we lose water more rapidly and in greater quantities.

Vitamins and Minerals

Since our bodies have to get what we need from our diets, vitamins and minerals are essential to us. Foods may be rich in some vitamins and minerals but deficient in others, so it is important to eat a varied diet to ensure that we get the full range. However, vitamins and minerals can also interact with each other with positive and negative effects. We need adequate vitamin C to help iron absorption; conversely, excessive dietary calcium can reduce the

Below: Stave off hunger pangs by snacking on antioxidant-rich grapes.

EAT A RAINBOW
Remember to include as many food colours in your diet as you possibly can. This chart shows you the nutrients offered by the different colour groups.

Yellow/Orange	Orange/Red	Red/Purple/Blue	Green	White
Food sources:				
Carrots	Oranges	Blueberries	Spinach	Garlic
Sweet potato	Tomatoes	Cranberries	Kale	Leeks
Cantaloupe melon	Watermelon	Red grapes	Broccoli	Onion
Pumpkin	Pink grapefruit	Elderberries	Greens	
Super nutrients:				
B-carotene	Lycopene	Anthocyanins	Lutein	Allicin
A-carotene	B-carotene	Betacyanins	Zeaxanthin	
	Z-carotene	Proanthocyanidins	B-carotene	
			Chlorophyll	

absorption of zinc and iron. Some vitamins, like the B group and C, are water-soluble and need to be eaten every day as we cannot store them, whereas the fat-soluble vitamins A, D and E can be stored in the liver.

Fruit and vegetables are an excellent source of vitamins and minerals as well as many other fabulous nutrients. According to the World Health Organization (WHO), we should be eating at least 400g (or approximately five portions) of fruit and vegetables a day. This can include dried and canned fruit and vegetables, as well

Below: Slow-energy releasing porridge is a great way to start the day.

as fruit juice and smoothies. The WHO estimates that a low vegetable and fruit intake is one of the top ten risk factors for mortality in the world, and eating sufficient amounts could save 2.7 million lives per year. The key to getting this right is to eat as many different types of fruit and vegetable as possible. The easiest way to do this is to use colour as a guide and aim to eat a rainbow of variety. Many of the powerful phytonutrients in fruit and vegetables contribute to the food's colour, and by consuming a variety of colours you can ensure that you take in a healthy range of these nutrients. All of the superfoods in this book can make valuable contributions to health, especially when a wide variety are included in the diet. Many of the recipes in this book use combinations of these foods to help you achieve this.

Sugar

This comes in many different guises – natural, added, white, brown, corn syrup and invert. Though most of us should eat less of it, sugar in foods can be a useful energy source, particularly when it encourages the consumption of foods rich in other useful nutrients, such as fruit. There is no benefit from choosing naturally occurring sugars such as cane sugar or honey over regular table sugar.

REDUCING SUGAR AND SALT

• Slowly reduce how much sugar you add to your tea or coffee until you wean yourself off it.
• Gradually mix more unsweetened cereal with your sugary favourite cereal to get used to less sugar at breakfast.
• Reduce how much salt you add to vegetables during the cooking process.
• Choose 'no added salt and sugar' foods.
• Don't put salt on the table.

From a nutritional or chemical viewpoint, they are very similar, with no nutritional value other than providing energy (calories). Sugar intake should be limited as it is highly cariogenic, which means that bacteria in the mouth convert the sugar to acids that cause tooth decay. This is why fruit juice, which contains a lot of natural sugars, should be drunk in moderation.

Salt

Eating too much salt can increase your blood pressure, which, in turn, puts you at greater risk of suffering

Below: Include as much variety of colour in your diet as possible.

from heart disease or stroke. We can all reduce how much we add to our cooking, but it is more difficult to limit our intake from pre-prepared foods, including ready meals, which are estimated to provide around 75 per cent of the salt that we eat. Our natural 'taste' for salt can be reduced as we get used to eating less by limiting our intake of salt-rich foods, including ham, bacon, sausages, cheese, salty snacks, soups, canned vegetables, ready meals and takeaway food.

Healthy Diet and Lifestlye

The best tips for an improved lifestyle are to take regular exercise, maintain the correct weight, eat little and often throughout the day, rest and sleep well, avoid alcohol and stop smoking.

For a healthier diet, try to eat more carbohydrate-rich foods, especially wholegrain types, eat more fruit and vegetables, consume more fish, cut down on sugar, salt and saturated fat, drink plenty of fluids, and do not skip breakfast. Remember to boost your diet with superfoods and include as many colours as you can.

Above: Fruit, vegetables and juices all contribute to our water intake.

ANTIOXIDANT STRENGTH AND ORAC SCORES

The antioxidant strength of a certain food can be determined using the ORAC (oxygen radical absorption capacity) score system. This gives an indication of how well the antioxidants in a certain food can prevent oxidation and neutralize the potentially harmful effects of free radicals. The foods with the highest scores include acai berries, blueberries, cranberries and artichoke hearts, as well as beans such as kidney, red and pinto. Spices also have exceptionally high ORAC values, but as they are consumed in such small quantities, they do not contribute significantly to the diet. While still to be scientifically proven, it is thought that neutralizing free radicals can help to minimize age-related degeneration and disease.

Healthy cooking

How we cook, prepare and store food can impact on its nutritional value. Some nutrients become more useful, or bio-available, to us through cooking, whereas some nutrients become less bio-available to us, or are destroyed. All food degrades over time from the moment that it is harvested, through the supply chain and to the shop or supermarket where we buy it. Whenever possible, we should buy food that looks fresh, is in good condition and is not damaged.

Good Storage
For fresh foods, the key is to keep the 'chill chain' going, so letting food warm up and get cold again is not good for the nutritional quality or safety of foods. Transport refrigerated food home as soon as possible and place in the fridge. For frozen foods, it is the freezing process that puts the food in nutritional limbo, so if food is allowed to defrost, nutritional quality starts to decline. For store-cupboard foods, it is important to store them in a cool dry place away

Below: Decant foods from packaging into sealable jars to retain freshness.

from strong smells such as cleaning fluids, as some foods can absorb these and become tainted. Some store-cupboard foods need to be kept in a dark place to slow fat rancidity; this is especially true of nuts, seeds and oils. Highly unsaturated oils, such as flaxseed oil and walnut oil, should be kept in the fridge as the cool temperature slows rancidity. Fruit and vegetables should be kept in a cool place and out of any plastic covering that may encourage mould growth. If you spot damaged or mouldy fruit or vegetables, remove them immediately otherwise they can contaminate the other foods and speed up spoilage.

To Cook or Not to Cook?
It is true that some nutrients are lost during cooking, however some nutrients actually become more bio-available. The chopping and peeling and cooking of many fruit and vegetables releases nutrients from the cellular structure. Sometimes cooking in a little oil can help to release nutrients from the food, such as

Below: Cook carrots in just a little oil to maximize their nutrient levels.

Above: Chop up fresh greens to make them more digestible.

the beta-carotene from carrots or the antioxidant lycopene from tomatoes. Conversely, vitamin C and some B-vitamins are destroyed by heat and so eating some raw fruit and vegetables may be beneficial.

Healthy Cooking Techniques
When cooking with oil, always try to use sparingly. Grill and dry-fry foods rather than using the deep fat fryer or lots of oil. Try crushing whole spices and then dry-frying them as this releases the flavour volatiles from the spices and makes them more digestible. Many vitamins are destroyed by high cooking temperatures or by boiling in water, so steam vegetables where possible to prevent the water-soluble vitamins leaching into the water. If you do need to boil the vegetables, use as little water as possible, boil until just soft, and try to use the water to make a gravy or sauce.

Use non-stick cooking equipment where you can as this instantly cuts down on how much oil and fat you use in recipes. As well as the teflon-coated pans, baking tins (pans), grill (broiling) pans and trays that are widely available, you can now also buy many silicone bakeware products which are also non-stick.

Healthy Cooking Appliances

The most well-known and probably widely used time-saving appliance is the microwave. This versatile cooker is a feature of most modern kitchens and contributes to a healthier diet by reducing cooking times for produce such as fruit and vegetables. The added convenience of being able to defrost frozen foods more quickly means you can fill your freezer with unprocessed home cooking to enjoy when time is limited.

Recently some new appliances have appeared on the market with the specific aim of helping you to cook more healthily. These range from halogen ovens and high-tech steam cookers through to low-fat frying and grilling appliances. Some have very impressive features.

Halogen ovens: This compact yet versatile appliance is energy-efficient and offers healthy cooking options. It uses the intense heat of a halogen bulb while a fan circulates the air rapidly. Food can be cooked in half the time of conventional methods, and no added fats or oils are needed. Cooking options include roasting, baking, grilling and steaming.

Electric steam cookers: Using a water reservoir to generate the steam, these range from basic one-compartment rice-cooker-style units all the way through to very clever, multi-compartment machines, with different temperature zones that allow different steaming times. The benefits of steaming foods are mainly the reduced nutrient loss and improved texture of delicate foods such as fish and some vegetables. If you haven't space for an electric steam cooker, use a steamer pan over boiling water.

Electric low-fat grills: The healthy credentials are based on the fact that the grill (broiler) can cook the food while the fat drains away, either into the ridges of the griddle or into a drip

USEFUL EQUIPMENT FOR HEALTHY FOOD
- Steamer – ideal for cooking vegetables, as more vitamins are retained than with boiling. Also good for cooking fish.
- Liquidizer or blender – perfect for making smoothies and juices as well as for smoothing soups and sauces (great for hiding fruit and vegetables from children).
- Griddle pan – reduces the amount of fat used to cook meat and vegetables.
- Food processor – useful for pulverizing nuts and seeds and making breadcrumbs.

Right: A blender enables you to make a speedy, nutritious soup.

tray. Look out for grills with removable dishwasher-safe plates. If you don't want to buy an appliance, use your oven grill with a wire rack.

Electric low-fat fryers: This does sound impossible, but products are being launched that use very small amounts of oil to cook food such as chips (French fries). This results in chips with less than 3 per cent fat content. The unit moves the food continuously ensuring an all over 'frying' effect without the oil being soaked up. Although pricey, the results are good.

Below: Chicken browns well and the fat drains away in a halogen oven.

Below: Steaming nutritious asparagus only takes a few minutes.

Good health through life

The principles of a good diet and lifestyle apply throughout our whole life and should become the norm rather than a faddy, short-term thing. Try to form good habits that will stay with you forever, and this will also have a benefit to all those around you, particularly children, who will hopefully adopt good habits too. Nutritional requirements change throughout our lives, and having a basic understanding of these will help you to meet your body's needs. The following guidelines give an overview of these changes, but remember that this broad advice is no substitute for individual advice given by a health professional such as a GP, nurse or dietician.

Pregnancy

Being pregnant puts a huge burden on the body so it is crucial for women who are planning to conceive to ensure that they are in optimum health:

Folic Acid: Helps protect against foetal abnormalities such as neural tube defects. Good sources include dark green leafy vegetables.

Below: Optimum nutrition is more important than ever during pregnancy.

Calcium and Vitamin D: Consider both of these together as they aid efficient absorption and utilization. Vitamin D is more important for women of Asian, African and Middle Eastern origin, as these women find it harder to get the vitamin D from sunlight, and have an increased risk of the baby contracting rickets. Good food sources of vitamin D are eggs and oily fish, while calcium-rich foods include dairy products and green leafy vegetables.

Omega-3 Fatty Acids: Crucial building blocks for brain and eye tissue in the foetus, it is best to try to eat the fish form of omega-3, as the vegetarian sources, such as linseeds and some rapeseed oil, are not so easily used by the body. Good sources include oily fish and seafood. However, because of concerns over toxins, shark, marlin or swordfish should be avoided and tuna limited. For other oily fish such as salmon, herring and trout, up to two portions a week are recommended. It is also important to maintain your omega-3 intake after having your baby as this may help avoid post-natal depression.

Iron: Due to the increasing blood volume and the foetus laying down stores of iron that will see it through the first six months of life, pregnant women are at risk of anaemia. However, the body is able to cope with this by increasing the absorption rate of iron from food while mobilizing iron stores, provided the mother has sufficient iron stores initially. Eating plenty of foods rich in vitamin C will also aid this.

Fibre: Some women suffer from constipation during pregnancy, so it is important to eat lots of fruit, vegetables and wholegrains. This, coupled with good fluid intake, will help to alleviate the problem.

Foods to Avoid: Liver and liver products are best avoided due to the potentially toxic affects of vitamin A on the baby. Avoid unpasteurized products such as cheeses, milk and fresh mayonnaise. Avoid alcohol, especially in the first two trimesters. If you have allergies, try to avoid eating nuts to reduce the risk of a nut allergy in the baby.

Young Infants

Most health organizations currently recommend that a young baby is fed exclusively either breastmilk or formula up to the age of six months. Breastmilk is thought to be best, especially in the first few weeks of life, as many crucial antibodies which are important in building a healthy immune system and other protective factors are passed from mother to baby. By six months, the baby's body can adequately digest and metabolize food, which enables vital replenishment of nutritional stores.

Calcium and Vitamin D: The rapid growth rate of the skeleton ensures that calcium requirements are kept high. Babies need to have at least 600ml (1 pint) of milk a day up to 1 year. This then drops to about 350ml/12 fl oz.

Iron: Babies stock up on their iron stores from the mother in the last trimester of pregnancy, and so long as the pregnancy is full-term these stores should last until 6–9 months of age. However, introducing cow's milk, low in iron, too early into a baby's diet will mean that these stores may run out sooner.

Vitamin C: This vitamin is essential to ensure optimal absorption of iron.

Omega 3: The baby's brain will still be growing rapidly and will need supplies of omega 3 to ensure that this is optimized.

Above: Children love vitamin-packed home-made fruit smoothies.

Toddlers and Young Children

The main challenges when ensuring good nutrition for toddlers and young children are their high energy and nutrient requirements, their small stomachs and their variable appetites. There are many growth spurts during this age range, leading to spikes in appetite, and this puts extra emphasis on those nutrients required to ensure optimal growth and development.

Particular nutrients to focus on are protein, iron, calcium and vitamins A, C and D. It will be entirely normal for children to become hungry between their three meals a day, and so highly nutritious snacks will be required to ensure good nutrition and to prevent them reaching for high-fat or sugary snacks such as crisps and chocolate.

Adolescents

The need for a good balanced diet during adolescence is essential to meet the body's growth requirements.

The main human growth spurt takes place now and energy and protein needs will be increased. This is particularly true of boys who may appear to be permanently hungry, and there is a risk that under-nutrition can inhibit growth. It is important that hunger pangs are alleviated with nutritious snacks

throughout the day along with the normal meals. Breakfast cereals with milk are a good way to ensure that vitamin, mineral and calcium intakes are maintained.

Calcium: Calcium needs are high as bone growth is rapid, and much calcium is laid down in the bones that is essential for their life-long health. If calcium needs aren't met there is a greater risk of osteoporosis in later life.

Iron: Needed during growth for muscle and blood production, this is a key nutrient. It also becomes very important for girls as menstruation begins. Ensure vitamin C-rich foods are eaten to help absorption. This is particularly true for vegetarians, as iron from vegetables and pulses is more difficult to absorb.

Menopause

The main issue during the menopause is the increased risk of osteoporosis, a disease that affects up to 15 per cent of women aged 50. The best way to reduce the risk of developing osteoporosis is to ensure good bone density earlier in life and to reduce the rate of bone loss later in life.

Oestrogen helps to maintain bone density, so as oestrogen levels fall during the menopause, bones begin to lose calcium and the density decreases, heightening the risk of osteoporosis. It is important to ensure that calcium intakes are high at this time of life, and that vitamin D, which is integral to the way the body absorbs and uses calcium, is boosted.

Phytoestrogens are the plant version of our oestrogen so eating foods that contain these compounds could mimic their effect and may help to alleviate menopausal symptoms and preserve bone density.

Mature Adults

As we age, our bodies gradually wear out and we become less efficient at everything, including digestion and

absorption of food. Since appetite also tends to decrease, food needs to be increasingly nutrient-rich as we age, to ensure all the body's nutritional needs are met.

Calcium and Vitamin D: Osteoporosis is a major cause of illness in people over the age of 50, and so it is vital to maintain a good calcium intake as well as to ensure that some skin is exposed to the sun for adequate production of vitamin D. One point to note is that glass does not let the important vitamin D-yielding sunrays through, so it is not sufficient to simply sit at a window. It is probably for this reason that vitamin D deficiency is a big problem in housebound elderly.

Iron: While iron requirements may not be higher in the elderly, there are many other factors that will interfere with iron absorption, including medication. Drinking tea during meal times can also reduce iron absorption, as the tannins bind with the iron to make it non-bioavailable. Ideally, tea should be drunk between meals and water or juice drunk with meals, so long as fluid intake is not then compromised.

Below: Keeping active will help to maintain good health as you mature.

Essential minerals and vitamins

Regular intake of a wide range of minerals and vitamins is essential for good health, and the vast majority can be found in many different foods. By frequently eating enough of the correct foods, including at least five portions of fruit and vegetables per day, most people should not need to take vitamin or mineral supplements. An exception to this is vitamin B12, which is only found in animal products and yeast extracts, so if you are vegan you may need to take this in supplement form. Try to eat a variety of different types and colours of produce each day, in particular brightly coloured and dark green fruit and vegetables, to ensure that you are obtaining as wide a range of nutrients and beneficial compounds as possible. This chart describes which foods are the richest sources, the role the mineral or vitamin plays in health maintenance, and the signs that may suggest a deficiency.

MINERAL	BEST SOURCES	ROLE IN HEALTH	DEFICIENCY
Calcium	Canned sardines (with bones), dairy products, green leafy vegetables, sesame seeds, dried figs and almonds.	Essential for building and maintaining strong bones and teeth, muscle function and the nervous system.	Deficiency is characterized by soft and brittle bones, osteoporosis, fractures and muscle weakness.
Chloride	Nuts, wholegrains, beans, peas, lentils, tofu and black tea.	Regulates and maintains the balance of fluids in the body.	Deficiency is rare.
Iodine	Seafood, seaweed and iodized salt.	Aids the production of hormones released by the thyroid gland.	Deficiency can lead to sluggish metabolism, and dry skin and hair.
Iron	Meat, offal, sardines, egg yolks, fortified cereals, leafy vegetables, dried apricots, tofu and cocoa.	Essential for healthy blood and muscles.	Deficiency is characterized by anaemia, fatigue and low resistance to infection.
Magnesium	Nuts, seeds, wholegrains, beans, peas, lentils, tofu, dried figs and apricots, and green vegetables.	Essential for healthy muscles, bones and teeth, normal growth, and nerves.	Deficiency is characterized by lethargy, weak bones and muscles, depression and irritability.
Manganese	Nuts, wholegrains, beans, lentils, brown rice, tofu and black tea.	Essential component of enzymes involved in energy production.	Deficiency is not characterized by any specific symptoms.
Phosphorus	Found in most foods, especially lean meat, poultry, fish, eggs, dairy products and nuts.	Essential for healthy bones and teeth, energy production and the absorption of many nutrients.	Deficiency is rare.
Potassium	Bananas, milk, beans, peas, lentils, nuts, seeds, whole grains, potatoes, fruit and vegetables.	Essential for water balance, regulating blood pressure, and nerve transmission.	Deficiency is characterized by weakness, thirst, fatigue, mental confusion and raised blood pressure.
Selenium	Meat, fish, citrus fruits, avocados, lentils, milk, cheese, Brazil nuts and seaweed.	Essential for protecting against free radical damage and may protect against cancer – an antioxidant.	Deficiency is characterized by reduced antioxidant protection.
Sodium	Found in most foods, but comes mainly from processed foods.	Essential for nerve and muscle function and body fluid regulation.	Deficiency is unlikely but can lead to dehydration and cramps.
Zinc	Lean meat, oysters, peanuts, cheese, wholegrains, seeds, beans, peas and lentils.	Essential for a healthy immune system, normal growth, wound healing, and reproduction.	Deficiency is characterized by impaired growth, slow wound healing, and loss of taste and smell.

VITAMIN	BEST SOURCES	ROLE IN HEALTH	DEFICIENCY
A (retinol in animal foods, betacarotene in plant foods)	Animal sources: liver, oily fish, milk, butter, cheese, egg yolks and margarine. Plant sources: orange-fleshed and dark green fruit and vegetables.	Essential for vision, bone growth, and skin and tissue repair. Beta-carotene acts as an antioxidant and protects the immune system.	Deficiency is characterized by poor night vision, dry skin and lower resistance to infection, especially respiratory disorders.
B1 (thiamin)	Lean meat (especially pork), wholegrain and fortified bread and cereals, brewer's yeast, potatoes, nuts, beans, peas, lentils and milk.	Essential for energy production, the nervous system, muscles, and heart. Promotes growth and boosts mental ability.	Deficiency is characterized by depression, irritability, nervous disorders, loss of memory. Common among alcoholics.
B2 (riboflavin)	Meat (especially liver), dairy, eggs, fortified bread and cereals, yeast extract and almonds.	Essential for energy production and for the functioning of vitamin B6 and niacin, as well as tissue repair.	Deficiency is characterized by lack of energy, dry cracked lips, numbness and itchy eyes.
Niacin (nicotinic acid, also called B3)	Lean meat, fish, beans, peas, lentils, potatoes, fortified breakfast cereals, wheatgerm, nuts, milk, eggs, peas, mushrooms, green leafy vegetables, figs and prunes.	Essential for healthy digestive system, skin and circulation. It is also needed for the release of energy.	Deficiency is unusual, but characterized by lack of energy, depression and scaly skin.
B6 (piridoxine)	Lean meat, fish, eggs, wholegrain cereals, brown rice, nuts and cruciferous vegetables, such as broccoli, cabbage and cauliflower.	Essential for assimilating protein and fat, for making red blood cells, and maintaining a healthy immune system.	Deficiency is characterized by anaemia, dermatitis and depression.
B12 (cyano-cobalamin)	Meat (especially liver), fish, milk, eggs, fortified breakfast cereals, cheese and yeast extract.	Essential for growth, formation of red blood cells and maintaining a healthy nervous system.	Deficiency is characterized by fatigue, increased risk of infection, and anaemia.
Folate (folic acid)	Offal, dark green leafy vegetables, wholegrain and fortified breakfast cereals, bread, nuts, beans, peas, lentils, bananas and yeast extract.	Essential for cell division; especially needed before conception and during pregnancy.	Deficiency is characterized by anaemia and appetite loss. Linked with neural defects in babies.
C (ascorbic acid)	Citrus fruit, melons, strawberries, tomatoes, broccoli, potatoes, (bell) peppers and green vegetables.	Essential for the absorption of iron, healthy skin, teeth and bones. Strengthens the immune system and helps to fight infection.	Deficiency is characterized by increased susceptibility to infection, fatigue, poor sleep and depression.
D (calciferol)	Mainly exposure to sunlight. Also liver, oily fish, eggs, fortified breakfast cereals and fortified dairy produce.	Essential for bone and tooth formation; helps the body to absorb calcium and phosphorus.	Deficiency is characterized by softening of the bones, muscle weakness and anaemia. Shortage in children can cause rickets.
E (tocopherols)	Oily fish, seeds, nuts, vegetable oils, eggs, wholemeal bread, avocados and spinach.	Essential for healthy skin, circulation, and maintaining cells – an antioxidant.	Deficiency is characterized by increased risk of heart attack, strokes and certain cancers.

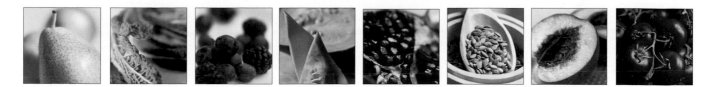

SUPERFOODS DIRECTORY

This comprehensive guide lists all the main superfoods available, from the most vibrant and nutritious fruit and vegetables through to wholesome grains, pulses, nuts and seeds, and finishing with the healthiest dairy, meat and fish choices. Included here are details on the latest health benefits associated with each superfood and these, along with buying, cooking and storage tips, will help you to gain the most from these wonderful foods.

Fruit

Perhaps the ultimate convenience food, most fruits can be simply washed and eaten and, because the nutrients are concentrated just below the skin, it is best to avoid peeling. Cooking fruit reduces some valuable vitamins and minerals, so, if you can, eat it raw. Fruit is an excellent source of energy and provides valuable fibre and antioxidants, which are said to reduce the risk of heart disease and certain cancers. Thanks to modern farming methods and efficient transportation, most fruit is available all year round, although it is generally best when home-grown, organically produced and in season.

ORCHARD FRUITS

These refreshing fruits have a long history spanning thousands of years, and offer an incredible range of colours and flavours. Orchard fruits include many favourites, from crisp, juicy apples, which are available all year round, to luscious, fragrant apricots – a popular summer fruit.

Apples

The list of apple varieties is vast, with over 7,500 known cultivars, although only a fraction are in widespread commercial use. Some of the most well-liked eating varieties are Cox's Orange Pippin, Granny Smith, Gala, Braeburn, and Golden and Red Delicious. The most familiar cooking apple is the Bramley, with its thick, shiny, green skin and tart flesh. It is perfect for baking, or as the basis of apple sauce. Less well-known varieties, many of which have a short season, are often available from farmers' markets or farm shops. 'An apple a day keeps the doctor away' is a well-known adage, which is actually corroborated by scientific evidence as well as by tradition. Apples, while relatively low in vitamins and minerals compared to some other fruit, do have high levels of phenolic phytonutrients which

Above: Try to eat apples unpeeled as most nutrients are just under the skin.

have powerful antioxidant properties. The most predominant one is quercetin, which has been shown to have protective effects against cancer and heart disease by reducing cancer cell proliferation and reducing cell oxidative stress. Other compounds such as the catechins and epicatechin help to reduce fat by increasing oxidation, and in combination with the fibre content have been shown to reduce 'bad' LDL cholesterol levels. Most apples are stored after harvest

AN APPLE A DAY

Numerous studies have shown that eating apples regularly could reduce harmful LDL cholesterol in the body. In France, 30 middle-aged men and women were asked to add 2–3 apples a day to their diet for a month. By the end of the month, 80 per cent of the group showed reduced cholesterol levels, and in half of the group the drop was more than 10 per cent. Additionally, the level of good HDL cholesterol went up. Pectin, a soluble fibre found particularly in apples, is believed to be the magic ingredient.

BAKED APPLES

Baking is a simple and nutritious method of cooking apples. Use either large cooking varieties such as Bramley or eating apples such as golden delicous or gala.

1 Preheat the oven to 180°C/350°F/Gas 4. Remove the core of the apples, then score the skin around the circumference to prevent the skin bursting. Place the apples in a baking dish with a little water.

2 Fill the cavity of each apple with a mixture of dark brown sugar, dried fruit and nuts. Top each apple with a knob (pat) of butter. Place in the pre-heated oven and bake for approximately 40 minutes or until the apples are soft.

in controlled atmospheres in order to slow ripening, but this does not appear to affect the levels or activity of these beneficial phytonutrients. The skins of red apples also contain proanthocyanidin componds, which are part of the flavonoid family. These are important in cell-signalling processes and can help to reduce coronary heart disease risk.

Apples are delicious when they are eaten raw with their skin on, where the highest concentrations of these phenolic phytochemicals are found. Lower levels are found in the flesh and when apple juice is produced the concentrations drop even lower to around 10 per cent of the original apple. So, to maximize the benefits, keep the skin on where you can, cook apples over a low heat with little or no water and keep the lid on.

Pears

The humble pear has been popular for thousands of years and was extensively cultivated by both the Greeks and the Romans. Pears come into their own in the late summer and autumn with the arrival of the new season's crops. Favourites include green and brown-skinned Conference; Williams (Bartlett), with its thin, yellow skin and sweet, soft flesh; plump Comice, which has a pale yellow skin with a green tinge.

There are also more unusual pears such as the Asian pear, which has an uncharacteristic round shape and is particularly high in fibre. Like certain apples, some types of pear are good for cooking, others are best eaten raw, and a few varieties fit happily into both camps.

Pears can be used in both sweet and savoury dishes; they are excellent in salads, and can be baked, poached in syrup, and used in pies and tarts. They are less likely to cause allergic reactions, so make a perfect weaning food for babies when cooked and puréed. This also makes them a useful food when following an exclusion diet to establish which

Above: Pears are a good source of vitamin C, fibre and potassium.

foods may be causing an allergy or intolerance. Pears are often one of the first foods introduced back into the diet. Despite their high water content, the fruit contains useful amounts of vitamin C, and they are high in both soluble and insoluble fibre and potassium.

When buying, choose firm, plump fruit that are just slightly under-ripe. Pears can ripen in a day or so and then they pass their peak very quickly and become woolly or squashy. To tell if a pear is ripe, feel around the base of the stalk, where it should give slightly when gently pressed, but the pear itself should be firm.

Apricots

The best fresh apricots are sunshine gold in colour and full of juice. They are delicious baked or used raw in salads. An apricot is at its best when truly ripe; if the velvet flesh yields a little when gently pressed you know it is ready. Immature fruits are hard and tasteless, and never seem to ripen properly and attain the right level of sweetness. Apricots are rich in vitamin C and vitamin A, which is essential for good vision, as well as beta-carotene, a closely related substance that has strong antioxidant activity and could be helpful in reducing heart disease and cancer incidence.

Apricots are widely available dried, but this preserving method does involve sulphating the fresh apricot in order to keep the golden colour. So, if you are allergic or sensitive to sulphites, buy organic ones as no sulphites are used during the drying process which explains their dark brown colour. Dried apricots are more concentrated in nutrients weight for weight versus fresh, and are a good source of calcium and iron. They are a great healthy snack that counts as another portion of fruit, and are popular with children.

Below: Fresh, ripe apricots smell wonderfully fragrant.

Plums

Ranging in colour from pale yellow to dark, rich purple, plums come in many different varieties, although only a few are available in shops. As indicated by their rich colours, plums contain anthocyanin pigments. These include phytochemicals such as proanthocyanidins which are associated with reduced heart disease risk. They can be sweet and juicy or slightly tart; the latter are best cooked in pies and cakes, or made into a delicious jam. Sweet plums can be eaten as they are, and work well in fruit salads, or they can be puréed and combined with custard or yogurt to make a fruit fool. Plums should be just firm, and not too soft, with shiny, smooth skin that has a slight 'bloom'. Store ripe plums in the refrigerator. Unripe fruits can be kept at room temperature for a few days to ripen.

Prunes

These fruits are actually dried plums and this popular dried fruit has been used for centuries in the treatment of constipation. This is due to the combination of a high fibre content

Below: High levels of phytochemicals in plums help to fight heart disease.

and the presence of a natural laxative, which makes them particularly effective. They also have a notably high level of antioxidant activity, mainly due to the presence of polyphenols and flavonoids. It takes only three prunes to count as a portion of fruit towards the five fruit and vegetable portions a day that are recommended. Prune juice is also popular, and the juicing process does not remove the natural laxatives or the soluble fibre so it is still as effective as dried prunes. Prunes also have a low GI value, making them excellent as a healthy snack that provides slow release energy. Chop up some prunes in your porridge, or just carry a few in a small bag to ease those mid-morning hunger pangs.

Cherries

There is nothing like devouring a bag of fresh ripe cherries, and knowing that these little gems are good for you is a great bonus. There are two types: sweet and sour. Sweet cherries such as the Bing cherry are best eaten raw, while the sour type, such as Morello, are best cooked. Choose firm, bright, glossy fruits that have

Below: Slow energy-releasing prunes are a good choice for breakfast.

Above: Sweet cherries make a great antioxidant-rich snack.

fresh, green stems. Discard any that are soft, or have split or damaged skin. Cherries contain Vitamin C and fibre, and more importantly, their deep red skins are a rich source of anthocyanins, which may have anti-cancer attributes as well as cardioprotective properties. The possible anti-cancer attributes of anthocyanins are currently one of the most heavily researched areas, as they are probably one of the most widely available phytonutrients in the general diet. Research is also ongoing research on the cell-signalling effects of anthocyanins and potential beneficial uses as an anti-inflammatory.

Quinces

Fragrant, with a thin yellow or green skin, these knobbly fruits, which can be either apple- or pear-shaped, are always cooked as they are unpleasant if eaten raw. Quinces are rich in soluble fibre and pectin, which means that they are not only good for you but are also excellent for making jams and jellies. In France and Spain, quinces are used to make a fruit paste that is delicious served with cheese. Fragrant quince flesh is also a lovely addition when cooking apple sauce. Always look for smooth ripe fruits that are not too soft.

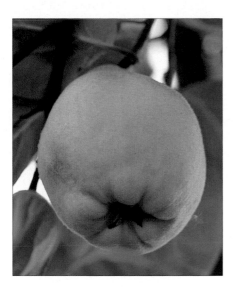

Above: High-fibre quince is delicious served with savoury dishes.

Quinces keep well and can be stored in a bowl in the kitchen or living room. They will fill the room with their aroma. They also help to calm the stomach and allay sickness.

RHUBARB
Technically a vegetable, and growing in colder climes, the fleshy stalks of the rhubarb plant are eaten as a fruit. They have an extremely tart flavour that really needs to be sweetened to make them more palatable, especially if it is being eaten for dessert. Rhubarb leaves are highly toxic, but the young pink tender stems cook in minutes and make a perfect pie or crumble filling, or a juicy compote to eat with yogurt or ice cream. Rhubarb is also a good non-dairy source of calcium, although the oxalate content does reduce its bioavailability somewhat. Due to its anthraquinone and fibre content, rhubarb is a good laxative to use if you are constipated, however, continual use causes problems for the colon. Chinese herbal medicine has used rhubarb and rhubarb root extract for many years for various intestinal complaints. It has been reported that rhubarb may have anti-cancer and anti-inflammatory properties, which may help to reduce

Above: A portion of dried fruit can count as one of your five-a-day.

blood pressure, but these research results have not been corroborated by further studies.

DRIED FRUIT
A useful concentrated source of energy and nutrients, dried fruit is higher in calories than fresh fruit, and packed with vitamins and minerals. This means that it contributes to the recommended fruit and vegetable target of five portions a day. The drying process boosts the levels of vitamin C, beta-carotene, potassium

and iron. Dried apricots are popular but dried apples, pears, bananas and pineapples are also available.

As dried fruits are so concentrated, a portion size for your five-a-day is surprisingly small. Just three dried apricots or prunes make up one portion size.

DRIED FRUIT TIPS
• Add a handful of your favourite dried fruits to your breakfast cereal for an energy-boosting start to the day.
• Keep a small snack bag of dried fruit in your bag for when you get an attack of those hunger pangs.
• Take dried fruit on a long car journey to stop you grazing on unhealthy snack foods such as crisps, cookies and sweets.
• Add your favourite dried fruit mix to bread, cakes, scones and cookies when baking.
• Add dried fruit to lunchboxes and picnics and keep some on hand for after-school snacks or a post-exercise lift.

Below: Choose thin, slender stems of rhubarb for the best flavour.

CITRUS FRUITS

Juicy and vibrant, citrus fruits, such as oranges, grapefruit, lemons and limes, are best known for their sweet, slightly sour juice, which is rich in vitamin C. They are invaluable in the kitchen for adding an aromatic acidity to many dishes, from soups and sauces to puddings and pies.

Here we concentrate on those citrus fruits that have a little more than just vitamin C to bring to the superfood arena.

Eating an orange a day should supply an adult's requirement for vitamin C, but citrus fruits also contain phosphorous, potassium, calcium, beta-carotene and fibre. Pectin, a soluble fibre found in the flesh and particularly in the membranes of citrus fruit, is known to reduce cholesterol levels. The fruits also contain flavanones, which not only have powerful antioxidant properties but are also thought to help reduce the risk of heart disease, neuro-degenerative disease and certain types of cancers.

Choosing Citrus Fruit

Look for plump, firm citrus fruit that feels heavy for its size, and has a smooth thin skin; this indicates that the flesh is juicy. Fruits with bruises, brown spots, green patches (or yellow patches on limes) and soft, squashy skin should be avoided, as should dry, wrinkled specimens. Citrus fruits can be kept at room temperature for a few days but if you want to keep them longer, they are best stored in the refrigerator and

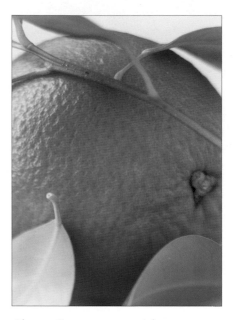

Above: Oranges are a rich source of vitamin C, pectin and folate.

eaten within two weeks. Alternatively, cut lengthways into segments and freeze. When required, just leave for five minutes at room temperature to defrost and they will be ready to use.

Oranges

Thin-skinned oranges tend to be the juiciest, and sweet varieties like Jaffa and Valencia are perfect eaten fresh. Seville, a sour orange, is cooked with sugar to make marmalade, which was the original way of preserving oranges. Famed for their vitamin C content, oranges are also a good source of pectin, a fibre found mainly in the skin around each segment, which has been shown to reduce 'bad' LDL cholesterol levels. Oranges are also a useful source of folate, which is essential if you are pregnant or are trying to get pregnant. A glass of freshly squeezed orange juice, while not retaining the pectin, is a good source of folate, thiamine and potassium and still counts as a portion of fruit. Oranges are also a useful source of flavanones such as hesperidin, which has been shown to strengthen blood vessels, and may play an important role in reducing heart disease risk and protecting

---

GRATING CITRUS RIND	CUTTING FINE STRIPS OR JULIENNE

1 For long, thin shreds of rind, use a zester. Scrape it along the surface of the fruit, applying firm pressure.	**1** Use a vegetable peeler to remove strips of orange rind. Make sure the white pith remains on the fruit.

2 For finer shreds, use a grater. Rub the fruit over the fine cutters to remove the rind without any of the white pith.	**2** Stack several strips of the citrus rind and, using a sharp knife, cut them into long, fine strips or julienne.

Above: Limes add sharpness and vitamin C to sweet or savoury dishes.

against neuro-degenerative diseases. Hesperidin is converted to hesperitin in the intestine, and this compound has neuro-protective properties as it is thought to reduce the damage caused by oxidation.

Lemons

Both the juice and the flesh of the lemon can be used to enliven vegetables, dressings, marinades, sauces and biscuits (cookies). Lemon juice can also be used to prevent some fruits and vegetables from discolouring when cut.

Also containing flavanones, in particular hesperidin, lemons are of interest to scientists researching ways of reducing neuro-degenerative risk. The best lemons should be deep yellow in colour, firm and heavy for their size, with no hint of green in the skin. A thin, smooth skin is indicative of juicy flesh.

CITRUS FRUIT TIP
Roll uncut citrus fruit firmly over a work surface or between your hands to extract the maximum amount of juice from the fruit.

GRAPEFRUIT WARNING
Some compounds present in grapefruit can interact with many prescribed drugs, reducing their effectiveness and causing other problems. If taking medication, consult with a pharmacist or medical professional before increasing grapefruit consumption.

Limes

Once considered to be rather exotic, limes are now widely available. The juice has a sharper flavour than that of lemons and if you substitute limes for lemons in a recipe, you will need to use less juice. Limes do contain the beneficial flavanones referred to earlier, but in slightly lower concentrations than oranges and lemons. This is also true of their vitamin C content. Limes are used widely in Asian cooking to flavour curries, marinades and dips. Chillies, coriander, garlic and ginger are all natural partners. Try to avoid limes with a yellowing skin as this is a sign of deterioration.

Pink and Ruby Grapefruits

The flesh of the grapefruit ranges in colour from vivid pink and ruby red to white; the pink and red varieties are sweeter and are of particular interest due to their lycopene content, which is responsible for their attractive colour. Lycopene, also found in tomatoes, is a carotenoid that has been studied extensively for its role in reducing the risk of prostate cancer in men. Many studies have shown that men whose diet is rich in lycopene show a significantly lower incidence of prostate cancer. Served juiced, halved or cut into slices, grapefruit traditionally provides a refreshing start to the day. The fruit also adds a tang to salads and makes a contrast to rich foods. Cooking or grilling mellows the tartness, but keep cooking times brief.

Above: Pink grapefruits taste sweeter than the yellow varieties.

BENEFITS OF VITAMIN C
Vitamin C and its health benefits are probably among the most researched areas in nutritional science. We know the body is unable to store vitamin C so it must rely on a daily intake from food. While found primarily in citrus fruits, vitamin C is also found in most fruit and vegetables – the highest concentrations are actually in kiwis and guavas.

A powerful antioxidant, vitamin C may help to reduce the risk of certain cancers such as of the stomach, mouth and lung. Evidence suggests that populations with vitamin C-rich diets have a reduced risk of strokes and coronary heart disease. This vitamin plays an important part in the synthesis of collagen, blood vessels and bone. It is also involved in the metabolism of cholesterol and can reduce harmful LDL cholesterol. Its role in preventing colds hasn't been scientifically proven, but it may reduce the severity.

BERRIES AND CURRANTS

These baubles of vivid red, purple and black are the epitome of summer and autumn, at the height of their season. Nowadays, these fruits are readily available all year round. Despite their distinctive appearance and flavour, berries and currants are interchangeable in their uses – jams, jellies, pies and tarts are the obvious choices. Berries are fabulous on their own or as combinations, and the benefits of including more of these in our diets cannot be ignored.

Strawberries

These are one of the favourite summer fruits and do not need any embellishment. Best served when juicy and ripe on their own, or with a

Below: Strawberries are a good source of manganese and vitamin C.

little cream or some natural yogurt. Wash gently and only just before serving, otherwise they will go mushy.

Strawberries contain a flavonoid called fisetin, which has been shown to notably improve brain function, and in one study improved the memory of rats. However, the equivalent amount of strawberries for humans would be approximately ten punnets a day, which even the most committed strawberry lover would struggle with. Fisetin is also an antioxidant and has been shown to have anti-cancer properties, and it is being researched for its effects as an anti-inflammatory for reducing allergic responses. The fisetin flavonoid is very heat-stable and does not appear to be destroyed by heat. It is well documented but often forgotten that strawberries are an excellent source of Vitamin C and are

FRUIT PURÉE

Soft berries are perfect for making uncooked fruit purées or coulis. Sweeten if the fruit is tart and add a splash of lemon juice to bring out the flavour.

1 To make a purée, place some raspberries, with lemon juice and icing (confectioners') sugar to taste, in a food processor or blender and pulse until smooth.

2 Press through a nylon sieve (strainer). Store in the refrigerator for up to two days.

also rich in manganese, which is an essential mineral for the maintenance of bone health and metabolism.

Raspberries

Soft and fragrant, raspberries are best served simply and unadulterated – maybe with a spoonful of natural (plain) yogurt. Those grown in Scotland are regarded as the best in the world. Raspberries are very fragile and require the minimum of handling, so wash only if really necessary. They are best eaten raw, as cooking can spoil their flavour and destroy vitamin C content. Raspberries are a rich source of

Above: Fresh raspberries on their own make a nutrient-rich dessert.

Above: Blackcurrants are tiny, but are packed full of vitamin C.

Above: Blueberries are bursting with cancer-fighting phytonutrients.

vitamin C and vitamin K, which is essential for blood clotting, and just like strawberries they are rich in manganese. Raspberries have one of the highest antioxidant strengths of all of the fruits; this is due to the combined effect of the high vitamin C content along with the anthocyanins and other flavonoids present in the berry. These powerful antioxidants prevent the harmful action of free radicals and may help to prevent degenerative brain diseases such as Alzheimer's. Research is being conducted into the benefits of antioxidant activity in cancer prevention and treatment. Studies into the fruit's anti-inflammatory properties have also shown promise. These factors, combined with a very high-fibre content, mean that raspberries pack a powerful nutrient punch.

Blackcurrants
As the intense dark colour suggests, these tiny berries are crammed full of anthocyanins, which have excellent antioxidant activity. Blackcurrants, like citrus fruits, are well known for their vitamin C content and you only need about 30g/1¼oz of them to get your daily requirement. As well as high

levels of anthocyanins and vitamin C, blackcurrants contain both soluble and insoluble fibre, important in maintaining good intestinal health, and may reduce the risk of certain cancers. Available fresh, frozen or as juice, blackcurrants can be quite tart but full of intense flavour. They make fabulous sorbets, smoothies and sauces, and are often a key ingredient in summer fruit combinations.

Blueberries
Dark purple in colour, blueberries have become very popular, and were probably among the first fruits to be labelled as a 'superfruit'. Their benefits came to the fore when studies revealed that they inhibited cancer cell development. These laboratory studies pointed to the blueberries' high phytonutrient content as a possible reason for these attributes. Their antioxidant activity is one of the highest ever measured in food. As well as anthocyanins, blueberries contain flavanols and tannins along with the particularly effective resveratrol, which is also found in grape skins and wine. Resveratrol is a naturally occurring anti-fungal compound produced by the plant to inhibit fungal growth on

the fruit. Other studies have pointed to beneficial effects in the battle against cognitive decline and Alzheimer's disease. The fruit is also thought to be good for lowering cholesterol and total blood fat levels. Its anti-inflammatory properties may help to reduce heart disease risk. However, it must be stressed that none of the benefits attributed to this superfood have yet been scientifically proven in human studies and further research is still needed.

Choose the berries that are plump and slightly firm, with a natural 'bloom'. Avoid any that are soft and dull-skinned, and wash and dry carefully to avoid bruising. Cultivated blueberries are larger than the wild variety, but both types are sweet enough to be eaten raw. They are good cooked in pies and muffins, can be used for jellies and jams, or made into a sauce to serve with nut or vegetable roasts. Unwashed blueberries will keep for up to a week in the bottom of the refrigerator.

Bilberries
These are from the same family as the blueberry and are sometimes referred to as the European blueberry. They are high in

anthocyanins, which are thought to help in the prevention of diseases such as heart disease, cancer and degenerative eye conditions. This has yet to be proven in humans but there is a tale of World War II pilots consuming bilberry jam specifically to improve their night vision when they went on missions. Fresh bilberries are uncommon, however, jams and conserves are more widely available.

Elderberries

Although elderberries are not commercially grown, when in season, they can easily be found growing in the wild. These large bushes are a common feature of many gardens and hedgerows, and both the flowers and berries have culinary uses. Pick the heads of the berries only when they are ripe, black and plump, as unripe berries contain a toxic alkaloid. Be sure to wash them thoroughly before use. Elderberry cordial and wine is made using the flower heads and not the berries, so it will not have the same benefits. The high levels of anthocyanins are specifically in the berries and are thought to help with the production of cell signalling compounds, which our body cells use to communicate with each other. This is a critical part of our immune response to pathogens such as bacteria, and so elderberries have been used for

Below: Anthocyanin-laden elderberries are ready to pick in the autumn.

Above: Nutrient-rich goji berries come in dried, juiced and powdered form.

many years to help with the relief of cold symptoms and for building up the immune system. As many parts of the bush have toxic compounds in them, it is advisable to cook the fruit.

Goji Berries

Also known as wolfberries, goji berries are grown in East Asia and have been used for centuries in Chinese Herbal Medicine as immune boosters and to aid circulation. Usually found in their dried form, they can be eaten like dried fruit, or they can be added to baked goods. They are also available as juices and in powdered form to add to drinks or make tea. Goji berries are good sources of many vitamins, minerals such as vitamin C, calcium and iron. They contain phytonutrients such as phytosterols, carotenoids (particularly zeaxanthin) and antioxidants, leading to many claims being made over their health benefits. These range from eyesight protection through to cardiovascular and anti-inflammatory effects as well as neuroprotective and anti-cancer properties. One must be aware that many scientific studies have been conducted to see if the claims can be proven, but to date

Above: Vitamin C-rich cranberries make a thirst-quenching juice.

they have not been conclusive. It is true, however, that the goji berry has an impressive array of nutrients, which mean its contribution to a healthy diet is substantial.

Cranberries

Mostly found frozen, dried or as a juice, the benefits of cranberries are varied. Native to North America, these little red berries have been used for many years to treat all sorts of conditions. Perhaps their best-known benefit is for urinary tract health. Compounds within the berries bind to bacteria and stop them from sticking to the wall of the urinary tract. How this actually helps during infection is yet to be fully understood. This anti-adhesion effect is thought to be why cranberry juice can also benefit oral health, as bacteria are prevented from sticking to gums and teeth.

Cranberries are also a rich source of polyphenol antioxidants and flavonoids, which have shown strong anti-cancer activity in laboratory studies; however, this effect is not proven in the human body. The dried fruits can be a little tart so try mixing them with other dried fruit or baking with them in place of raisins or sultanas. Avoid buying cranberry juices overloaded with added sugar.

GRAPES, MELONS, DATES AND FIGS

These fruits were some of the first ever to be cultivated and are therefore steeped in history. They are available in an immense variety of shapes, colours and sizes, and can be bought dried. As well as being a good source of nutrients, these fruits are high in soluble fibre.

Grapes

There are many varieties of grape, each with its own particular flavour and character, and most are grown for wine production. Eating varieties are less acidic, have a thinner skin than those used for wine-making and are more commonly seedless. Grapes range in colour from deep purple to pale red, and from bright green to almost white. Levels of anthocyanins (beneficial pigments) are higher in red grapes than in white, and this may be why more emphasis has been

Below: Black grapes have more anthocyanins than white grapes.

Above: White grapes contain heart-healthy nutrients.

placed on them; however, white grapes do still contain high levels of other flavonoids that have been shown to have beneficial effects, too.

The phytochemical content of grapes is mainly found in the skins, but grape seeds do yield tannins and, when crushed, an oil which is high in vitamin E and phytosterols. This oil can be used to cook with and is characterized by being very light, odourless and flavourless; because of

this it is often used as a carrier for other flavours. The darker the grape skin, the higher the phytochemical level. This high level of phytochemicals has led scientists to research the beneficial effects of grapes in areas such as heart health, cancer and Alzheimer's disease. Grapes contain resveratrol, a naturally occurring plant fungicide that affects how cancer cells grow and has anti-inflammatory

DRIED VINE FRUITS

Currants, sultanas (golden raisins) and raisins are the most popular dried fruits. Traditionally, these vine fruits are used for fruitcakes and breads, but currants and raisins are also good in savoury dishes. In Indian and North African cooking they are often used for their sweetness. It takes about 1.75–2.25kg/4–5lb fresh grapes to produce 450g/1lb sultanas, raisins or currants. Although high in natural sugars, which can damage teeth if eaten to excess between meals, dried fruit is a concentrated source of nutrients, including iron, calcium, potassium, phosphorus, vitamin C, beta-carotene and some of the B vitamins, and does contribute to your daily intake target of five fruit and vegetable portions.

Below: Dried raisins and sultanas all count towards your five-a-day.

properties. It is also being currently studied for its benefits to Alzheimer's patients and for treating specific cancers. Red and purple grape juices are also high in anthocyanins and polyphenols, and these have been shown in studies to reduce bad LDL cholesterol, increase good HDL cholesterol and reduce inflammation, all contributing to a reduction in heart disease risk. A particular variety, the Concord grape, has one of the highest antioxidant activity levels measured in foods, and products containing this juice are thought to be beneficial in the reduction of cholesterol levels.

Grapes are widely available and are easy to add to your family's diet. Whether as a small bunch in a lunch box with some cheese, or halved and sprinkled on a salad, grapes make a sweet, juicy addition to many savoury or sweet meal occasions.

When buying grapes, try to choose fairly firm, plump ones. The fruit should be evenly coloured and firmly attached to the stalk. Unwashed fruit may be stored in the refrigerator for up to five days.

Below: Red wine retains the heart-healthy nutrients found in grapes.

Above: The orange-fleshed cantaloupe melon is rich in beta-carotene.

Red Wine

Many of the phytochemicals found in the grape are stable enough to survive processing and fermentation during winemaking. The highly concentrated levels of phytochemicals that are found in red wine in particular has led to the coining of the phrase, 'The French Paradox'. This refers to the fact that the French population have a lower incidence of heart disease, even though their diet is relatively high in saturated fat. It is thought that, like red or purple grape juice, it is the high levels of resveratrol, polyphenols and antioxidants in red wine that contribute to this statistic. Most health professionals would not want to encourage over-consumption of alcohol and as is often the case, moderation is the key, so they often recommend one glass a day as suitable. Other commentators, however, have attributed the French paradox to the generally healthier diet and lifestyle of the French population. For example, their diet tends to include plenty of fish, olive oil and unprocessed foods, and they also generally have a less stressed approach to life.

Melons

This small family of fruits is split into two types; muskmelons and watermelons. Muskmelons include the varieties such as cantaloupe, charentais and honeydew, and usually have more flavour; watermelons, as their name suggests, have a far higher water content and so a less intense flavour. Watermelons

Below: Watermelon is rich in the anti-cancer nutrient lycopene.

Above: Figs are one of the richest non-dairy sources of calcium available.

are very low in calories because of their high water content, which is around 90 per cent. They contain less vitamin C and other nutrients than the fragrant, orange-fleshed varieties; however, watermelons are of particular interest because of their lycopene content, which is responsible for the lovely pinky red colour of the flesh. Lycopene has been shown to reduce the risk of prostate cancer, and a wedge of watermelon actually contains more lycopene than a cup of raw chopped tomato. Beta-cryptoxanthin is also found in

WATERMELON TIP
Because of its high water content, watermelon can be frozen to make healthy and refreshing ice pops – perfect for a hot summer day.
1 Slice the watermelon and remove the pips.
2 Cut each slice into long sections or fingers.
3 Pop the watermelon pieces in a plastic food container, seal and freeze overnight.

watermelon. It is a vitamin A precursor, that is a substance that the body can convert into vitamin A. The orange-fleshed varieties of melon contain useful levels of beta-carotene, also a vitamin A precursor, which is essential for a healthy immune system and normal growth and development.

When eaten on their own, melons pass quickly through the system. But, when consumed with other foods requiring a more complex digestive process, they may actually inhibit the absorption of nutrients.

Look for melons that feel heavy for their size and yield to gentle pressure at the stem end. Have a sniff of the skin and you should be able to smell the sweet flesh of the ripe melon.

Figs
The fig has been enjoyed for many thousands of years, and is thought to have been one of the first plants ever cultivated by humans. Figs are very high in fibre and are well known for their laxative properties. They are an excellent source of minerals such as calcium, magnesium, potassium and manganese. These delicate, thin-skinned fruits may be purple, brown or greenish-gold. They are very versatile: delicious raw, chopped up, added to natural yogurt and drizzled with honey for breakfast, served with soft cheese such as goat's cheese, and are a lovely complement for cured hams such as prosciutto or Parma ham. Figs can also be poached or baked lightly to make a delicious dessert. Choose unbruised, ripe fruits that yield to gentle pressure, and eat on the day of purchase. If they are not too ripe they can be kept in the refrigerator for a day or two. Figs are best eaten at room temperature, as chilling suppresses their juicy, sweet flavour. Dried figs are equally as nutritious and you only need to eat two to count as a portion of fruit. Dried figs, chopped or made into a paste, can be used in baking for a great moist addition to cakes, cookies and fruit loaves.

Above: High-fibre dates range in colour from yellow to dark brown.

Dates
Like figs, dates are one of the oldest cultivated fruits, possibly dating back as far as 50,000BC. Dates should be plump and glossy. Medjool dates from Egypt and California have a wrinkly skin, but most other varieties are smooth. They are high in soluble fibre and are very sweet. This sweetness gives them a very high glycemic index of 103, which is more than sugar at 100, so if you need an extremely fast burst of energy, eating a handful of dates will do the job. However, if you are looking to stabilize your sugar metabolism, you would be best to avoid them.

Fresh dates make a good natural sweetener for use in baking. You can purée the cooked fruit, then add this to muffin, cake or bread mixtures, or simply mix into natural yogurt to make a quick breakfast or dessert. Fresh dates can be stored in the refrigerator for up to a week. Dried dates can be kept in the store cupboard and added to cakes, cookies, scones and bread. You can also buy chopped dates and date paste, which can be used to replace some of the fat in fruit cake recipes.

TROPICAL FRUIT

This exotic collection of fruits ranges from the familiar bananas and pineapples to the more unusual papayas and guavas. The diversity in colour, shape and flavour is sure to excite the tastebuds as well as being pleasing to the eyes.

Papayas

Also known as pawpaw, these pear-shaped fruits come from South America. When ripe, the green skin turns a speckled yellow and the pulp is a glorious orange-pink colour. The ripe flesh is rich in vitamin C, folate and beta-cryptoxanthin, a type of carotenoid, which is a vitamin A precursor as well as an antioxidant. Green papaya is a good source of papain, an enzyme well known for its ability to tenderize meat and it is thought to possibly aid digestion. Papain preparations have also been used as a healing aid to treat cuts and burns by communities where papaya grows.

To eat, peel off the skin using a sharp knife or a vegetable peeler before enjoying the creamy flesh, which has a lovely perfumed aroma

Below: Vitamin-C and folate-rich, the ripe papaya tastes similar to a peach.

and sweet flavour. Ripe papaya is best eaten raw, while unripe green fruit can be used in cooking. The edible black seeds can be dried and ground. They taste like black pepper.

Mangoes

Across the family of tropical fruits, the mango accounts for approximately 50 per cent of all production, India being the largest contributor. The skin of these luscious, fragrant fruits can range in colour from green to yellow, orange or red. Their shape varies tremendously, too. An entirely green skin is a sign of an unripe fruit, although in Asia, these are often used in salads. Ripe fruit should yield to gentle pressure and, when cut, should reveal a juicy, orange flesh. This flesh has an impressive repertoire of nutrients and phytochemicals. Rich in vitamin C, vitamin A and vitamin E, its antioxidant credentials are improved further with beta-carotene, alpha-carotene and lutein, as well as an array of polyphenols. Mango also contains the essential minerals potassium and copper, and a wide range of amino acids. The

Below: Sweet mangoes have high levels of vitamins C, A and E.

skin is edible, and is a rich source of antioxidants, polyphenols and fibre. Served sliced or puréed, mango has a lovely creamy, juicy flavour which makes it an excellent base for smoothies, ice creams and sorbets.

PREPARING MANGO

Mangoes can be fiddly to prepare because they have a large, flat stone that is slightly off-centre. The method below produces cubed fruit. Alternatively, the mango can be peeled with a vegetable peeler and sliced around the central stone.

1 Hold the fruit with one hand and cut vertically down one side of the stone. Repeat on the opposite side. Cut away any remaining flesh around the stone.

2 Taking the two large slices, and using a sharp knife, cut the flesh into a criss-cross pattern down to the skin. Holding the mango skin-side down, press it inside out, and then cut the mango cubes away from the skin.

Above: A source of vitamin B6 and C, bananas make thick fruit smoothies.

Bananas

A concentrated bundle of energy, bananas are also full of valuable nutrients. The soft and creamy flesh can be blended into smooth, sweet drinks, mashed and mixed with yogurt, or the fruits can be baked and barbecued whole. Bananas also make an ideal weaning food for babies as they rarely cause an allergic reaction. Bananas are rich in dietary fibre and a variety of vitamins and minerals, especially potassium, which is important for the functioning of cells, nerves and muscles, and can relieve high blood pressure. They are also high in vitamin B6, vitamin C and manganese. Beware of banana chips, as they are actually deep fried slices of banana which are then coated in sugar or honey and so will be much higher in fat and calories. You can get dehydrated banana, but this is very leathery in texture and dark brown in colour. Choose fresh bananas that are not too green or bruised and ripen them at room temperature. Never store bananas in the refrigerator as they will quickly blacken, and always prepare immediately before serving, as they will discolour rapidly.

Kiwis

Also known as the Chinese gooseberry, a clue to its early origins, kiwi fruit was imported into New Zealand for commercialization in the early 20th century, where the population thought it tasted like a gooseberry. The name was changed to kiwi, as there were negative associations with China at the time. Kiwi fruit is extremely rich in vitamin C and the seeds have the omega-3, alpha-linoleic acid in them. It is high in fibre and this may be the reason for its usefulness as a gentle laxative. A Norwegian study has also indicated that kiwi fruit has a blood thinning effect, however, this was at quite a high level of consumption of two to three kiwi fruit a day for 28 days. The flesh also contains an enzyme called actinidin, which means it cannot be used in milk-based foods or jellies as the enzyme digests the protein. In addition, some people have a sensitivity to this compound which can cause itchiness and other allergic symptoms. The fabulous green colour of the kiwi makes it a welcome addition to fruit salads and fruit toppings, but it is just as delicious eaten on its own. Try cutting the top off, putting it in an egg cup and scooping out the flesh with a spoon, just like you would eat a boiled egg!

Below: Even the pips (seeds) in the kiwi fruit are full of essential nutrients.

BANANA TIP

A very ripe banana, past its best for eating, can be useful in another way. Ripe bananas give off a gas called ethylene, which can speed up ripening of other fruits such as pears, peaches or avocados. Simply place the under-ripe fruit into a bag or container along with the ripe banana and leave overnight at room temperature.

Acai Berries

The acai (pronounced A-sai-ee) berry is indigenous to South America and is commercially prepared as either a juice or a freeze-dried preparation of the skin and pulp. These berries contain a wide array of phytonutrients, which goes some way to explaining the vast number of conditions that they have traditionally been used to treat. Everything from heart health, elevated immune function and anti-cancer effects have been associated with acai berry consumption. Used for centuries by the South Americans, the berry has a high anthocyanin content and unusually contains fat that comprises the good mono-unsaturated and polyunsaturated fats. These, along with a moderate phytosterol content, are probably responsible for its healthy heart attributes by helping circulation, reducing blood clots, promoting good blood fats and preventing atherosclerosis. As if this wasn't enough, acai berries also have a considerably high level of antioxidants, which have been shown to reduce the proliferation of harmful cancer cells, but this has yet to be proven in humans. There have been claims about the berry's ability to promote rapid weight loss, but again there is little scientific proof of this. However, the berry's excellent nutrient profile, combined with a high fibre and omega-3 and -6 fat content, may contribute to a feeling of fullness.

The juice is popularly used for flavouring drinks and smoothies, and the fruit pulp is made into sorbets and yogurts.

Pomegranates

This ancient fruit originates from the Persian region and is now cultivated all over the Mediterranean. Underneath the leathery skin, the unusual bright red flesh-covered seeds make this a most interesting addition to any dish. Immersing the fruit in water makes it easier to remove the seeds from the outer pith and these are best eaten raw.

The juice of the pomegranate is very refreshing, not too sweet and is a good source of vitamin C. However, it is its antioxidant polyphenol content that is thought to be responsible for some of its more far-reaching health benefits. Mainly in the realm of heart health, these polyphenols can reduce risk factors such as atherosclerosis and blood pressure, as they are able to protect cells from oxidative stress. Similar to cranberry, pomegranate juice may also have anti-viral and anti-bacterial properties, especially in the mouth, and may protect against tooth decay.

Guavas

One of the more unusual tropical fruits, the pink/orange flesh of this fruit is juicy and sweet, and indeed

---

DRIED TROPICAL FRUIT TIP
It is possible to buy most of these delicious tropical fruits in a dried version. However, many of them are actually more akin to glacé (candied) fruits, as a lot of sugar is added in order to preserve the fruit. So look carefully at the ingredient list and bear in mind that sugar, glucose syrup, invert sugar syrup, glucose and sucrose are tell-tale signs of added sugar. There are dried products that do not contain these added sugars or syrups, so persevere, as it is worth it for the health of your teeth alone.

Below: Acai berry smoothie is rich in antioxidants and omega-3 and -6 fats.

Below: Pomegranate juice is full of heart-healthy polyphenols.

Below: Guava flesh and skin has a high vitamin-C content.

is often seen as an ingredient in smoothies and juices. The flesh provides a good range of vitamins and minerals and is an excellent source of vitamin C, vitamin A, folate and minerals such as potassium and copper. It has a high fibre content, which we all need to be eating more of to ensure good gut health. The high levels of vitamin C and A, along with polyphenols, contribute to a relatively high level of antioxidant activity; as usual, the darker the flesh, the higher the value will be.

A guava is ripe when the flesh yields easily if pressed gently. The whole of the guava fruit is edible and this even includes the skin, which has a high vitamin-C concentrate. The seeds can also be eaten although they can be quite hard.

Pineapples

Probably one of the most popular of the tropical fruits, the juicy sweet flesh of the pineapple is a versatile ingredient in sweet and savoury dishes as well as on its own. It is a good source of Vitamin C and manganese levels are also high. However, pineapple is unusual as it contains a unique enzyme called

Below: Sweet, juicy pineapple is delicious hot or cold.

bromelain, which has some interesting properties. Bromelain is a proteolytic enzyme, which means it can break down protein (similar to papain). It has traditional uses as a meat tenderizer where the juice can be used as a meat marinade. Bromelain has anti-inflammatory properties that have been particularly effective in the treatment of arthritis and sports injuries as well as sinusitis. However, it is doubtful that eating pineapple alone can provide enough bromelain to relieve these conditions, and so commercial preparations of bromelain are used medicinally. Canned pineapple is widely available, however, the heat processing that the fruit is subjected to destroys the bromelain content present.

Warmed pineapple tastes fabulous as the juiciness and flavours really develop and the sugars caramelize. Flash-grill (broil) or barbecue slices to heat the fruit without destroying the bromelain content.

The colour of the outer skin of a pineapple is not necessarily an indicator of ripeness. It is true that the skin does change colour as the fruit ripens, but it is also true that a green pineapple can be ripe to eat. A more accurate method is to simply sniff the base of the pineapple, and when it smells sweet and juicy it is ripe. If you are unable to smell anything, it is not yet ripe, if it smells fermented and like pear drops, it is over-ripe. You can speed up the ripening process by leaving the fruit in a warm sunny place; the heat will accelerate the breakdown of the starch contained within the flesh to form sugar and ripen the fruit.

PINEAPPLE TIP

When buying pineapples, look out for those that have fresh green spiky leaves, are heavy for their size, and are slightly soft to the touch. Always store ripe pineapples in the refrigerator.

PREPARING PINEAPPLE

1 Use a sharp knife to cut off the green leaves that form the crown and discard it.

2 With a sharp knife, remove the skin from the pineapple, cutting deeply enough to remove most of the 'eyes'.

3 Use a small knife to carefully take out any 'eyes' that remain in the pineapple flesh.

4 Cut the pineapple lengthwise into quarters and remove the core section from the centre of each piece. Chop the pineapple flesh or cut it into slices and use as needed.

Vegetables

Vegetables offer an infinite number of culinary possibilities for the cook. The choice is immense, and the growing demand for organic produce has meant that pesticide-free vegetables are now increasingly available. Vegetables are an essential component of a healthy diet and have countless nutritional benefits. They taste best and are most nutritious when freshly picked.

ROOTS AND TUBERS

Vegetables such as sweet potatoes, parsnips and carrots are comforting and nourishing, so it is not surprising that they should be popular in the winter. Their sweet, dense flesh provides sustained energy, valuable fibre, vitamins and minerals.

Parsnips

The parsnip is closely related to the carrot – not to the turnip as commonly believed. Parsnips are really just a paler, stronger-tasting version of the carrot. As they are not brightly coloured, they do not have the carotenes of the carrot, but they are still rich in vitamins C and K, folate, manganese and potassium. This vegetable has a particularly sweet, creamy flavour and is delicious roasted, puréed or steamed. Parsnips are best purchased after the first frost of the year as the cold converts their starches into sugar, enhancing their

Above: Carrots are an excellent source of vitamin A.

sweetness. Scrub before use and only peel if tough. Avoid large roots, which can be woody.

Carrots

The best carrots are not restricted to the cold winter months. Summer welcomes the slender, sweet new crop, often sold with their green, feathery tops. These are best removed after buying as they can rob the root of moisture and nutrients. Buy organic carrots if you can, because high pesticide residues have been found in non-organic ones. An added bonus is that organic carrots do not need peeling. A single carrot will supply enough vitamin A for an entire day's requirement. Some of this vitamin-A activity is derived from its precursors, alpha- and beta-carotene, which are also the antioxidants responsible for the bright orange colour. These carotenes are bound up in the structure of the carrot and are released through chopping and slicing; their availability can be improved further still by cooking in a little oil. The high levels of carotene are the reason why

Left: Creamy-tasting parsnips are rich in folate, manganese and potassium.

carrots are always cited as beneficial for healthy eyesight. Vitamin A is essential for vision, as it is a component of the visual pigments present in the retina of the eye. A deficiency of vitamin A leads to impaired vision and night blindness. The phytonutrient benefits of beta-carotene are being researched greatly in areas such as the prevention of lung cancer. There have been some conflicting results with respect to beta-carotene in isolation, and the most recent theories suggest that the best results are found when a combination of carotenoids is present. Carrots should be prepared

VIBRANT VEGETABLES

Always try to include a range of food colours in your diet and you'll ensure that you are consuming some fabulous phytonutrients. Beta-carotene is just one of the carotenoids found in green, yellow, orange and red vegetables (as well as fruit). Lycopene is another carotenoid which has a fabulous red-pink colour and is abundant in tomatoes, watermelon and pink guava. Most carotenoids are antioxidants, which slow down or prevent cell damage from free radical oxidation in the body. Vitamins C and E are other carotenoids, along with bioflavonoids. These help to enhance the immune system, which protects us against viral and bacterial infections and boosts the body's ability to fight cancer and heart disease. Chlorophyll, another antioxidant, is bright green and is therefore mainly found in green vegetables. Anthocyanin, a type of flavonoid, is responsible for the dark blues, reds and purples of beetroot, red onions and aubergines.

Above: Antioxidant- and mineral-rich beetroots act as liver cleansers.

just before use to preserve their valuable nutrients. They are delicious raw, steamed, roasted or puréed.

Beetroots (Beets)

Deep ruby-red in colour, beetroots add a vibrant hue and flavour to all sorts of dishes. They are often pickled in vinegar, but are better roasted, as this emphasizes their sweet, earthy flavour. Raw beetroot can be grated into salads or used to make relishes. If cooking the vegetable whole, wash carefully, taking care not to damage the skin, or the nutrients will leach out. Trim the stalks to 2.5cm/1in above the root. Small beetroots taste sweeter than larger ones.

Beetroot has long been considered medicinally beneficial and records show that the Romans often used it to treat fevers and as a laxative. It is an excellent liver cleanser, probably due to its high antioxidant levels. Beetroot is also a good source of folate and contains notable levels of vitamin C, manganese, potassium and magnesium. The beetroot's colour is due to the presence of betalain, a pigment compound

similar to the anthocyanin family of compounds, not to be confused with betaine, which is also found in beetroot and is quite different. Betaine is able to protect blood vessels and bone collagen from damage due to excessive levels of homocysteine in the blood, and this may protect against vascular disease and bone weakness.

Celeriac

This knobbly root is closely related to celery, which explains its flavour – a cross between aniseed, celery and

Below: Celeriac is a diuretic and also contains vitamin C, calcium and iron.

parsley. Unlike most root vegetables, celeriac is not predominantly carbohydrate and therefore has approximately half the calories per 100g/3¾oz of potatoes. It must be peeled before use, and when grated and eaten raw in salads, celeriac has a crunchy texture. It can also be steamed, baked in gratins or combined with potatoes and mashed with butter or margarine and grainy mustard. Celeriac can also be used in soups and broths. Like celery, celeriac is a diuretic. It also a good source of vitamin C, vitamin K, calcium, iron, potassium and fibre.

Swedes (Rutabagas)

Globe-shaped swedes are part of the cruciferous vegetable family. Swedes contain many phytochemicals, such as the sulphurous compounds that are believed to have antioxidant and cancer-fighting properties. Like celeriac, they are a good source of vitamin A and vitamin C as well as potassium, and are lower in calories than the potato. Swede has pale orange flesh with a delicate sweet flavour. To prepare, trim off the thick peel, then treat it in the same way as other root vegetables. You can grate swede raw into salads; dice and cook it in casseroles and soups; or steam, then mash and serve it as an accompaniment to main dishes.

Below: Swede contains antioxidants that may help to prevent cancer.

Above: Highly nutritious baby turnips taste pleasantly peppery.

Turnips

This humble root vegetable has many health-giving qualities, as it is part of the important cruciferous vegetable family. Small turnips with their green tops intact are especially nutritious. Their crisp, ivory flesh enclosed in white, green and pink-tinged skin, has a pleasant, slightly peppery flavour, the intensity of which depends on their size and the time of harvesting. Small turnips can even be eaten raw. Alternatively, steam, bake or use in casseroles and soups. The green tops are rich in beta-carotene and vitamin C.

Potatoes

The sometimes-demonized potato has been blamed by many as being the reason for weight gain. However, potatoes are not in themselves fattening – it is the added ingredients such as butter or cheese and the cooking method that can often bump up the calories. Potatoes don't count as one of our 5-a-day because they are mainly carbohydrate, but they are an enormously important starchy food for many and are in fact the largest contributor to our vitamin-C intake. Their vitamins and minerals are stored in, or just below, the skin, so they're best eaten unpeeled. New potatoes and special salad potatoes need only be scrubbed. Steam rather than boil, and bake instead of frying to retain valuable nutrients and to keep fat levels down.

Potatoes provide plenty of sustained energy, as well as vitamin B6, folate and potassium.

There are thousands of potato varieties, and many lend themselves to particular cooking methods. Small potatoes, such as Pink Fir Apple and Charlotte, and new potatoes, such as Jersey Royals, are best steamed. They have a waxy texture, which retains its shape after cooking, making them ideal for salads. Main crop potatoes, such as Estima and Maris Piper, are more suited to roasting, baking or mashing, and can be used to make chips. Discard any potatoes with green patches as these indicate the presence of toxic alkaloids called solanines.

Sweet Potatoes

A very distant relative of the potato, this bright yellow- or orange-fleshed vegetable is also known as a yam, especially in North America. However, it should not be confused with the white fleshed tuber, which is not as nutritious. Sweet potatoes can vary in shape, from short and stocky, like a traditional potato, through to long and tapered, and colour can range from yellow through to dark purple. The deeper the colour the more nutritious the vegetable will be. It is rich in the anti-oxidant beta-carotene as well as in fibre and vitamin B6, and

Below: Vitamins and minerals are stored in or just under the potato skin.

Above: Sweet potatoes are a good source of fibre and beta-carotene.

Above: Vitamin C-rich, radishes also have diuretic properties.

Above: Wasabi (Japanese horseradish) is widely available in paste form.

contains reasonable amounts of iron, calcium and vitamin C, all of which make it a valuable starchy food. Due to its nutrient credentials and unlike the potato, the sweet potato does count as a 5-a-day portion. It can be prepared in a similar way to a potato, but its sweetness lends itself to many other uses such as in desserts – as pie fillings, for example. Never store sweet potatoes in a refrigerator as this causes the flesh to harden and will affect the flavour.

Jerusalem Artichokes
This small knobbly tuber has a sweet, nutty flavour and is related to the sunflower rather than arichoke family. Jerusalem artichokes contain surprisingly high levels of iron for a root vegetable and significant levels

Below: The Jerusalem artichoke is high in vitamin C and fibre.

of potassium. Peeling can be difficult, although scrubbing and trimming is usually sufficient. Store in the refrigerator for up to one week. Use in the same way as potatoes – they make good creamy soups.

Radishes
There are several types of this peppery-flavoured vegetable, which is a member of the cruciferous family. The round ruby red variety is most familiar; the longer, white-tipped type has a milder taste. Mooli or daikon radishes are white and very long; they can weigh up to several kilos or pounds. Radishes can be used to add flavour and a crunchy texture to salads and stir-fries. A renowned diuretic, radishes also contain vitamin C.

Horseradish
This pungent root is never eaten as a vegetable. It is usually grated and mixed with cream or oil and vinegar, and served as a culinary accompaniment. Its pungency is very effective in clearing blocked sinuses. Horseradish contains sinigrin, part of the glucosinolate family of phytochemicals, and this is an important compound being studied for its potential anti-carcinogenic properties. Seek out bright, firm, unwrinkled root vegetables, which do not have any soft patches. Whenever possible, choose organically grown produce, and purchase in small

quantities to ensure freshness. As with all root vegetables, store in a cool, dark place.

Wasabi
Also called the Japanese horseradish, wasabi is a cruciferous vegetable which contains the same glucosinolates as horseradish but in higher quantities. It is very effective at stimulating the nasal passages. Available either as a root or in paste form, wasabi is a traditional accompaniment to sushi and sashimi. Many commercial paste and powder preparations actually contain horseradish, not Japanese wasabi, and so won't be as strong. Read the ingredients list carefully looking for hon-wasabi, which is real Japanese wasabi.

Below: Horseradish contains potentially cancer-fighting sinigrin.

BRASSICAS

This large group of vegetables boasts an extraordinary number of health-giving properties. Brassicas are cruciferous vegetables and range from the crinkly-leafed Savoy cabbage to the small, walnut-sized Brussels sprout. These green, leafy vegetables include spinach, spring greens and kale.

Broccoli

This highly nutritious vegetable should be a regular part of everyone's diet. Two types are commonly available: purple-sprouting, which has fine, leafy stems and a delicate head, and calabrese, the more substantial variety with a tightly budded top and thick stalk. Raw broccoli is an excellent source of vitamin C but its levels decline as it is cooked, so keep cooking to a minimum.

Broccoli is also a good source of vitamin A and a range of B vitamins, most notably folate, which is essential if you are pregnant or planning a pregnancy. Minerals are abundant in this vegetable, including manganese, phosphorus, potassium, iron and calcium. As well as its enviable nutritional profile it also boasts some valuable phytonutrients. Broccoli contains sulphur compounds, which the body can convert into sulphoraphane, which helps with the

Above: Broccoli is one of the richest vegetable sources of folate.

elimination of carcinogens from the body, thus reducing cancer risk. Other sulphur compounds have anti-viral and anti-bacterial properties. These valuable compounds will leach into cooking water after about ten minutes so it is important not to boil broccoli for any longer. Better still, steam, microwave or stir-fry broccoli for a short time only.

Choose broccoli that has bright, compact florets. Yellowing florets, a limp, woody stalk and a pungent smell are an indication of overmaturity and an inferior nutrient profile. Trim stalks before cooking, although young stems can be eaten too, or serve raw in salads or with a dip.

Cauliflowers

The cream-coloured, compact florets should be encased in large, bright green leaves. There are other more brightly coloured varieties, such as orange and purple, but the cream version is the most common. This 'whiteness' by no means diminishes the nutritional profile of the

cauliflower, as it is a rich source of vitamin C, vitamin K, folate, vitamin B6, potassium and manganese, as well as being a good source of fibre. Its phytonutrient content is comparable to broccoli, including a wide range of the sulphur containing compounds that have been associated with reduced cancer risk. They work by stimulating the enzymes involved in the elimination of carcinogens.

Below: Cauliflower is a good source of cancer-fighting phytochemicals.

PREPARING BROCCOLI

Trim the stalks from the broccoli and divide it into florets. The stems of young broccoli can be sliced and eaten, too.

To get the most nutrients from a cauliflower, eat it raw in salad, bake with a cheese sauce or steam lightly. Cauliflower has a mild flavour and is delicious tossed in vinaigrette dressing or combined with tomatoes and spices in a curry. Overcooked cauliflower is unpleasant, has a sulphurous taste and is reduced to mush. Avoid cauliflowers that have black spots or yellowing leaves.

Cabbages

This is another member of the cruciferous family of vegetables. Many people have had a bad experience with cabbage, usually due to overcooking the vegetable to a sloppy mush that smells sulphurous and unpleasant. Cabbage is best eaten raw, or cooked until only just tender. There are several different varieties: Savoy cabbage has substantial, crinkly leaves with a stronger flavour and is perfect for stuffing or gently steaming; firm white and red cabbages can be shredded and used raw in salads or for pickling, while pak choi (bok choy) is best cooked in stir-fries or eaten with noodles.

All varieties are excellent sources of fibre, vitamins A, C, B6 and K as well as folate, manganese, potassium and magnesium. Cabbage is also an

Below: Eat vitamin-rich cabbage raw or steamed for optimum nutrition.

MIXED CABBAGE STIR-FRY

Stir-frying is a quick method of cooking that retains much of the vitamins and minerals that are lost during boiling; it remains crisp and keeps its vivid colour.

15ml/1 tbsp groundnut or
  sunflower oil
1 large garlic clove, chopped
2.5cm/1in piece fresh root
  ginger, chopped
450g/1lb/5 cups mixed cabbage
  leaves, such as Savoy, white,
  curly kale or pak choi (bok
  choy), finely shredded
10ml/2 tsp soy sauce
5ml/1 tsp runny honey
5ml/1 tsp toasted sesame oil
  (optional)
15ml/1 tbsp sesame
  seeds, toasted

1 Heat the oil in a wok or large, deep frying pan, then sauté the garlic and ginger for about 30 seconds. Add the cabbage and stir-fry for 3–5 minutes until tender, tossing frequently.

2 Stir in the soy sauce, honey and sesame oil and cook gently for 1 minute. Sprinkle with sesame seeds and serve.

excellent source of beneficial sulphur-containing compounds, which, as well as showing effective anti-cancer activity, can also reduce inflammation by tempering the activity of white blood cells. This may explain why cabbage leaves have long been used to treat inflammation such as engorged, sore breasts in women who are breast-feeding. Raw or juiced cabbage is particularly potent and also has antiviral and antibacterial qualities. Again, the quicker you can cook cabbage the better, as this will retain the most nutrients. When choosing, you should select cabbages that have a heavy heart, and Chinese cabbages should be compact and heavy for their size with bright, undamaged leaves.

Above: Brussels sprouts contain plant sterols – natural cholesterol reducers.

Brussels Sprouts

These are basically miniature cabbages that grow on a long, tough stalk, and they have a strong nutty flavour. They have one of the highest concentrations of sulphurous compounds including those that the body converts to sinigrin, which in research has been shown to destroy pre-cancerous cells and may be able to prevent colon cancer. They are excellent sources of fibre, vitamins A, B6, C and K, as well as folate, potassium and manganese. Their folate content may also contribute to their anti-cancer properties, as it is involved in DNA repair in the cell.

PREPARING BRUSSELS SPROUTS

1 Peel off any outer damaged leaves from the Brussels sprouts.

2 Before cooking, cut a cross in the base of each sprout, so that they cook quickly and evenly.

Brussels sprouts also contain plant sterols, which are natural cholesterol reducers. The best are the small ones with tightly packed leaves – avoid any that are very large or turning yellow or brown. Sprouts are sweeter when picked after the first frost. They are best cooked very lightly, so either steam or, better still, stir-fry to keep their green colour and crisp texture, as well as to retain their vitamins and minerals.

GREEN LEAFY VEGETABLES

For years we have been told to eat up our greens and now we are beginning to learn why. Research into their health benefits has indicated that eating dark green leafy vegetables, such as spinach, spring greens, chard and kale, on a regular basis may protect us against certain forms of cancer. These quite fragile, green, leafy vegetables do not keep well – up to 2 or 3 days at most. Eat soon after purchase to enjoy them at their best. Look for brightly coloured, undamaged leaves that show no signs of yellowing or wilting.

Spinach

This dark, green leaf is a superb source of cancer-fighting antioxidants and has an impressive vitamin and mineral content. It contains about four times more beta-carotene than broccoli and also has very high levels of lutein and zeathanthin, which are both found in the lens of the human eye. This has provoked some interesting studies of which results suggest that people who had high intakes of lutein and zeathanthin largely from spinach were up to 50 per cent less likely to have cataract problems. Spinach does contain good levels of iron, but it is in a form that is not easily absorbed – spinach contains oxalic acid, which inhibits the absorption of iron and binds any calcium present. However, eating spinach with a vitamin C-rich food will increase absorption. Spinach contains an immense amount of

Above: Iron-rich spinach tastes great in salads or added to hot dishes.

vitamin K, essential for the blood clotting process and is a good source of vitamins A, C and E, folate and riboflavin. Other minerals present in good amounts are magnesium, potassium and manganese. Nutritionally, it is most beneficial when eaten raw in a salad or steamed lightly, as boiling can halve the levels of folate.

Watercress

The hot, peppery flavour of watercress complements milder tasting leaves and is classically combined with fresh orange or fruit. Watercress is a member of the

Below: The lutein and beta-carotene in watercress are strong anti-oxidants.

cruciferous family and shares its cancer-fighting properties due to the presence of sulphur containing compounds. Watercress also contains beta-carotene and lutein, both of which are powerful antioxidants. It is rich in vitamins A, C and K, and also in calcium, manganese and potassium. Watercress can be used fresh in salads, where it adds a peppery zing, or it can be used to make soups or sauces. It does not keep well and is best refrigerated and eaten within two days of purchase.

Spring Greens (Collard Greens) and Curly Kale

These leafy, dark green young cabbage leaves are all very similar and are all the same cultivar. Rich in vitamin A, C and especially K, spring greens have an excellent beta-carotene, lutein and zeathanthin profile, giving them exceptional antioxidant credentials. They are also rich in a wide range of sulphur-containing compounds including indole-3-carbinol, which in studies has been shown to affect oestrogen metabolism and may therefore be of use in preventing reproductive organ cancers, although this is unproven in humans. The availability of these compounds can be increased by chopping up spring greens, releasing the sulphur compounds and essential enzymes required to convert them into their active forms. Keeping cooking times to a minimum will also help to retain all of the nutrients, stir-frying or steaming being the best options.

Swiss Chard

Part of the same family as beetroot, this vegetable is grown for its highly nutritious leaves. Similar to spinach, Swiss chard has a more robust, slightly bitter flavour and is best eaten when the leaves are young and tender. Swiss chard is very rich in antioxidants such as vitamins A and C and a variety of flavonoids. It contains one of the highest

Above: Kale contains chlorophyll, iron, calcium and vitamins A and C.

concentrations of vitamin K known. The leaves are quite fragile and do not keep well, so should be eaten as soon

Above: Swiss chard is one of the best sources of vitamin K.

as possible, either in a salad or wilted in a steamer. The stalks are edible, but need to be cooked for longer.

IMPORTANCE OF PHYTOCHEMICALS

Cruciferous vegetables, such as broccoli, cabbages, kohlrabi, radishes, cauliflowers, Brussels sprouts, watercress, turnips, kale, pak choi (bok choy), spring greens (collards), chard, and spinach, are particularly valuable because of the cocktail of phytochemicals that are found in them. This mix includes the antioxidant vitamins A, C and E, folate, fibre, phytosterols, glucosinolates, isothiocyanates, phenols, chlorophyll, lignans, flavonoids and minerals such as selenium and potassium. This heady mix of powerful compounds may be particularly effective in eliminating carcinogens from the body before they can go on to damage DNA. Additionally, some cell-signalling pathways could be altered to prevent cells becoming cancerous. While no specific intake guidelines for this family of vegetables exist, some tests have suggested that adults should aim for at least five portions of cruciferous vegetables a week to get the most potential benefit.

Below: Choose smaller pak choi varieties with firm stalks and leaves.

Below: Both the leaves and the bulb of the kohlrabi can be eaten.

VEGETABLE FRUITS
In cultivation and use, tomatoes, avocados and peppers are all vegetables, but botanically they are actually classified as fruit. Part of the nightshade family, it is only relatively recently that they have become appreciated for their health-giving qualities.

Aubergines (Eggplants)
A good source of folate and fibre, aubergines also contain moderate amounts of potassium, manganese and B vitamins. The dark-purple, glossy-skinned aubergine is the most familiar variety and, as its skin colour suggests, is a rich source of anthocyanins. These flavonoid compounds are potent antioxidants.

The small, ivory-white, egg-shaped variety is probably responsible for its name 'eggplant' in the USA, and is not such a rich source of anthocyanins. There is also the bright-green pea aubergine that is used in Asian cooking, and a pale-purple Chinese aubergine. Known in the Middle East as 'poor man's caviar', aubergines give substance and flavour to spicy casseroles and

Below: The dark-purple skin of the aubergine is rich in antioxidants.

tomato-based bakes, and are delicious roasted, griddled and puréed for garlic-laden dips. It is not essential to salt aubergines to remove any bitterness; however, this method prevents the absorption of excessive amounts of oil during frying. When buying, look for small to medium aubergines, which have sweet, tender flesh. Large specimens with a shrivelled skin are over-mature and are likely to be bitter and tough. Aubergines can be stored in the refrigerator for up to two weeks.

Tomatoes
These widely consumed fruits vary in colour, shape and size according to which of the vast number of varieties are available. All share one major benefit; they are an excellent source of lycopene. This powerful antioxidant has been the subject of much research in the field of cancer prevention, especially that of the prostate. Studies of populations suggest that diets high in lycopene have up to a 20 per cent lower risk of prostate cancer. About 80 per cent of our lycopene intake comes from tomatoes, so it is an important source. You should note, however, that the cooking and processing of tomatoes increases the bioavailability of lycopene, with tomato paste being the most concentrated source. So, in this case it is better to make tomato soup or sauces to maximize your lycopene intake. However, raw tomatoes are still important as they are good sources of other vitamins and minerals, as well as fibre.

Plum tomatoes are perfect for cooking as they have a rich flavour and a high proportion of flesh to seeds – but they must be used when fully ripe. Too often, shop-bought tomatoes are bland and tasteless because they have been picked too young. Vine-ripened and cherry tomatoes are sweet and juicy and are good in salads or uncooked sauces. Large beefsteak tomatoes have a good flavour and are also excellent

PEELING AND SEEDING TOMATOES
Tomato seeds can give sauces a bitter flavour. Removing them and the tomato skins will also give a smoother end result.

1 Immerse the tomatoes in boiling water and leave for about 30 seconds – the base of each tomato can be slashed to make peeling easier.

2 Lift the tomatoes out of the bowl using a slotted spoon, rinse in cold water to cool slightly, and peel off the skin.

3 Halve the tomatoes, then scoop out the seeds and remove the hard core. Dice or roughly chop the flesh according to the recipe.

Above: Juicy vine-ripened tomatoes are rich in vitamin C.

Above: Capsaicin, found in chillies, may have anti-cancerous properties.

for salads. Sun-dried tomatoes add a rich intensity to sauces, soups and stews. Look for deep-red fruit with a firm, yielding flesh. To improve the flavour of a slightly hard tomato, leave it to ripen fully at room temperature. Avoid refrigeration because this stops the ripening process and adversely affects the taste and texture of the tomato.

Chillies

Native to the Americas, this member of the capsicum family now forms an important part of many cuisines, including Indian, Thai, Mexican, South American and African. Chillies do actually contain more vitamin C weight for weight than an orange, although we only eat them sparingly because of the heat factor. They also contain notable concentrations of vitamins K and B6, as well as folate, potassium and manganese. Chillies contain beta-carotene and a unique family of phytochemicals called capsaicinoids, of which capsaicin is the heat-producing compound predominantly found in the seeds and flesh. These stimulate the release of endorphins by binding to heat sensors on the tongue. This sends a message to the brain causing an increased heart rate and the release of endorphins, which are the body's natural painkiller. Chillies stimulate the body and improve circulation, but if eaten to excess can irritate the stomach. Capsaicin may also have other effects such as the ability to kill cancer cells, reduce LDL cholesterol, alleviate stomach ulcer symptoms and contribute toward pain relief. There are more than 200 different types of chilli, ranging from the long, narrow Anaheim to the lantern-shaped and incredibly hot Habañero.

Red chillies are not necessarily hotter than green ones – but they will probably have ripened for longer in the sun. The heat-inducing capsaicin is found mainly in the seeds, white membranes and, to a lesser extent, in the flesh. Chillies range in potency from the mild and flavourful to the blisteringly hot. Dried chillies tend to be hotter than fresh. Smaller chillies, such as bird's eye chillies, contain proportionately more seeds and membrane, which makes them more potent than larger ones. Always handle chillies with care and wash your hands afterwards as they can irritate the skin and eyes. Choose unwrinkled, bright, firm chillies and store in the refrigerator.

Olives

Originating from the Mediterranean region, along with olive oil, these little gems have become iconic because of the phenomenon of the 'Mediterranean Diet'. High levels of monounsaturated fat and low levels of saturated fat, among other factors, have contributed to a low incidence of heart disease in the region. Olives are also high in the fat-soluble vitamins A and E, as well as in copper and calcium.

Traditionally, black olives were those that were allowed to ripen fully on the tree; they are sometimes known as natural black olives. It is far more common, however, to see olives that have been processed to become black. These black olives start as green olives from the tree which are then held in tanks to oxidize and turn black; they are then allowed to cure in a salted brine before packing. Green olives are picked before they have a chance to

Below: Olives offer a good source of vitamins A and E, calcium and copper.

PEELING PEPPERS

1 Roast the peppers under a hot grill for 12–15 minutes, turning regularly until the skin is charred and blistered. Alternatively, you can place on a baking tray and roast in an oven preheated to 200°C/400°F/Gas 6 for 20–30 minutes, until the skin is blackened and blistered.

2 Put the peppers in a plastic bag and leave until cool – the steam will encourage the skin to peel away easily.

3 Peel off the skin, then slice in half. Remove the core and scrape out any remaining seeds. Slice or chop according to the recipe.

Above: Sweet and vibrant, peppers are rich in vitamin C.

ripen and are then cured and packed. This serves two purposes; it reduces the bitterness of a freshly picked olive and it enables the olive to be preserved. Green olives tend to taste slightly bitter and have a stronger flavour than black olives. Chop up olives and add to your favourite salad or pizza topping.

Peppers
Like chillies, sweet or bell peppers are also members of the capsicum family. They range in colour from green through to orange, yellow, red and even purple. Green peppers are fully developed but not completely ripe, which can make them difficult to digest. They have refreshing, juicy flesh with a crisp texture. Other colours of peppers are more mature, have sweeter flesh, and are more digestible than less ripe green peppers. Peppers are very high in vitamin C and the carotenoids b-cryptoxanthin and lycopene, all of which exhibit powerful antioxidant activity. They are also a good source of fibre, vitamins A, K and B6, as well as potassium and manganese. Roasting or chargrilling peppers will enhance their sweetness. They can also be stuffed, sliced into salads or steamed. Always try to choose

peppers that are firm and glossy with an unblemished skin, and store in the refrigerator for up to a week.

Avocados
Although avocados have a high fat content, most of the fat is monounsaturated; these healthier fats are thought to help lower bad LDL cholesterol levels in the body without affecting the good HDL fats. Avocados also contain valuable amounts of a host of other vitamins and minerals; in particular, they are high in vitamins C, K and B6, niacin, folate and pantothenic acid as well as notable amounts of potassium, copper, magnesium and manganese. Avocados have one of the highest fibre contents of all of the fruits, and this comprises both insoluble and soluble fibre, with one avocado providing around 9g/1¼oz of fibre. Those on diets high in fibre have consistently been shown to have lower coronary heart disease risk and lower incidence of Type II diabetes.

Once cut, avocados should be brushed with lemon or lime juice to prevent discoloration. Usually eaten raw, avocado halves can be dressed with vinaigrette, or filled with sour cream or hummus and sprinkled with cayenne pepper. In Mexico, where

Below: Fibre-rich avocados are good for reducing coronary risk.

they grow in abundance, guacamole is the most common dish, but avocados are also used in soups and stews.

MUSHROOMS

Thanks to their rich earthiness, mushrooms add substance and flavour to all sorts of dishes. There are more than 2,000 edible varieties but only a tiny proportion are readily available. These fall into three camps: common cultivated mushrooms, like the button (white); wild varieties that are now cultivated, such as the shiitake; and the truly wild types that have escaped cultivation, such as the morel. Mushrooms have been used for their medicinal properties over thousands of years and have been the subject of great scientific break-throughs, such as the discovery of modern-day statin drugs for the treatment of high cholesterol. Much revered in ancient times, mushrooms have been researched extensively and it is thought to be their complex polysaccharide structure, containing beta-glucan, that is partly responsible for their properties.

The shiitake and the maitake mushrooms have the highest concentrations of beta-glucan compounds, and this sets them apart from the hundreds of other mushrooms available. In general, mushrooms are a low-fat, high-fibre food that are integral to many of our favourite dishes.

Button (White), Cap and Flat Mushrooms

The most common cultivated variety of mushrooms, these are actually the same variety in various stages of maturity. The button mushroom is the youngest and has a tight, white button-like cap. It has a mild flavour and can be eaten raw in salads. Cap mushrooms are slightly more mature and larger in size, while the flat mushroom is the largest and has dark, open gills. Flat mushrooms are the most flavoursome and are good

grilled or baked on their own, or stuffed. Researchers at Pennsylvania State University in the USA found these common white mushrooms to have extremely high levels of the powerful antioxidant, L-Ergothioneine.

Shiitake Mushrooms

The shiitake mushroom is native to China and has been grown in that region for hundreds of years. Used widely in Chinese, Japanese and Korean cuisine since ancient times, it has been recognized that they are not just a nutritious food source but also that they possess medicinal properties.

The shiitake mushroom contains high concentrations of lentinan, a particular type of beta-glucan. This highly purified extract, has been researched extensively as an anti-tumour agent and for its immune regulation properties. It is an approved cancer drug in Japan, but has yet to reach this status elsewhere.

These mushrooms have also been shown to reduce cholesterol levels and are thought to have anti-viral and anti-fungal properties. They are available fresh or dried, the latter being more intense in flavour and a more concentrated source of the active agents. The dried mushrooms

Below: Shiitake mushrooms have particularly high levels of beta-glucan.

DRIED MUSHROOM TIP

When soaking dried mushrooms, remember to keep the liquid and add to the sauce or stock later, thus retaining more of the nutrients and flavour.

need to be re-hydrated by soaking before they are added to dishes such as soups, risottos or pies. These mushrooms have a strong, almost meaty, flavour.

Maitake Mushrooms

The maitake mushroom grows in a wonderful cluster formation and is often found at the base of an oak tree. It can grow to as large as 60cm/24in in diameter. As well as being rich in many minerals, maitake mushrooms contain the beta-glucan compounds thought to be an immune system stimulator, and which recent research has shown to have anti-cancer properties. Often available only in supplement form, if you are lucky enough to come across the maitake mushroom, use it like any other mushroom, lightly steamed or added to soups or risottos.

CLEANING MUSHROOMS

Wipe mushrooms with damp kitchen paper and trim the stems. Wild mushrooms often harbour grit and dirt so may need to be rinsed briefly under cold, running water, but dry thoroughly. Mushrooms don't usually need to be peeled.

THE ONION FAMILY

Onions and garlic are highly prized as two of the oldest remedies known to man. What is more, these versatile vegetables are indispensable in cooking. The wide variety of onions can be enjoyed raw or cooked and, with garlic, add flavour to a huge range of savoury dishes.

Garlic

For centuries, this wonder food has been the focus of much attention, and is praised for its medicinal powers, which range from curing toothache to warding off evil demons. Garlic is rich in organosulphur compounds, which are converted to allicin when the clove is chopped or crushed. These compounds have been shown to decrease the production of cholesterol by liver cells, have anti-inflammatory effects, prevent clogging and act as vasodilators of arteries. All of these properties will contribute in some way to a reduced risk of cardiovascular disease. Allicin can also affect the metabolism of carcinogens in the body by inhibiting certain enzymes that activate these

Below: Garlic's properties are thought to be due to the potent compound allicin.

Above: Chopping onions releases the beneficial compounds.

carcinogens, thus potentially reducing cancer risk. Population studies suggest that a high intake of garlic may protect against gastric and colorectal cancer. Allicin also shows some antibacterial and antifungal qualities. This is most effective, however, when used raw in an ointment preparation rather than taken internally. The flavour of garlic is milder when whole or sliced; crushing or chopping releases the oils, making the flavour stronger. Slow-cooking also tames the pungency of garlic, although it still affects the breath. Most garlic is semi-dried to prolong its shelf life, yet the cloves should still be moist and juicy. Young garlic, which is available in early summer, has a long green stem and soft white bulb. It has a fresher flavour than semi-dried garlic, but can be used in the same ways. Pungency varies, but the general rule when buying garlic is the smaller the bulb, the more potent the flavour. If stored in a cool, dry place and not in the refrigerator, garlic will keep for up to about eight weeks. If the air is

damp, garlic will sprout, and if it is too warm the cloves will eventually turn to grey powder.

Onions and Shallots

Every cuisine in the world includes onions in one form or another and, along with garlic, they are often the first thing that is cooked. Like garlic, chopping the onion releases the organosulphur compounds that are then converted to allicin. Onions are an essential flavouring, offering a range of taste sensations, from the sweet and juicy red onion and powerfully pungent white onion to the light and fresh spring onion (scallion).

GARLIC TIP

In order to loosen the skin and make the garlic cloves far easier to peel, push down on each clove with the heel of a large chopping knife.

Above: Red onions are packed with antioxidant flavonols.

Pearl onions and shallots are the babies of the family. Tiny pearl onions are generally pickled, while shallots are stronger in flavour and are good roasted with their skins on, when they develop a caramel sweetness. Spring onions are the only onions that are generally eaten raw, as they are not so strong as the other varieties. Yellow onions are the most common and are highly versatile. As well as being a good source of allicin, all onions, and red onions in particular, are a good source of flavonols such as quercetin, a very active compound which has been shown to have anti-inflammatory and anti-cancer properties as well as being a potent antioxidant. Shallots show the highest antioxidant activity and the greatest concentrations of these flavonoid polyphenols. When buying, choose onions that have dry, papery skins and are heavy for their size. They will keep for 1–2 months when stored in a cool, dark place.

Leeks

Like onions and garlic, leeks have a very long history. They grow in all sorts of climates and are known to have been eaten and enjoyed by the ancient Egyptians, Greeks and Romans. Leeks are very versatile, having their own distinct, subtle

Above: Shallots have particularly potent quercetin levels.

flavour. They are less pungent than onions but are still therapeutically beneficial. Leeks have the same active constituents as onions, but in smaller amounts. They are an excellent source of vitamins A, C and K as well as vitamin B6 and folate. They contain considerable amounts of iron and manganese as well as calcium, magnesium and copper. Much of the nutritional goodness is in the green part of the leek, so don't discard too

Below: Avoid leeks without their roots, as they deteriorate more rapidly.

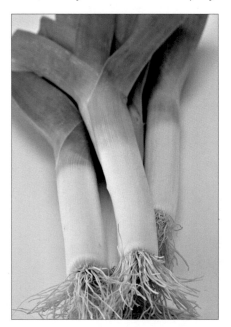

much of this. Excellent in soups and casseroles, leeks can also be used as a pie filling or in flans, or simply steamed and served hot with a light, creamy sauce, or cooled slightly and dressed with a vinaigrette. They are also delicious sliced or shredded and then stir-fried with garlic and ginger. Choose firm leeks with bright green leaves. Leeks will keep for up to a week in the refrigerator.

CLEANING LEEKS

Leeks need meticulous cleaning to remove any grit and earth that may hide between the layers of leaves. The following method should ensure that the very last tiny piece of grit will be washed away.

1 Trim off the root, and then trim the top of the green part and discard. Remove any tough or damaged outer leaves.

2 Slash the top green part of the leek into quarters then rinse the leek well under cold running water, separating the layers to remove any hidden dirt. Slice or leave whole, depending on the recipe.

PUMPKINS AND SQUASHES

Widely available in the USA, Africa, Australia and the Caribbean, pumpkins and squashes come in a tremendous range of shapes, colours and sizes. Squashes are broadly divided into summer and winter types, of which butternut squash and pumpkins are winter examples.

Butternut Squashes

Also known as a type of winter squash, the bright orange flesh of the butternut makes a very attractive addition to many dishes. Its natural sweetness makes this a popular vegetable with children, and it can spruce up plain mashed potato with its flavour and colour. As its bright orange colour might suggest, it is packed full of carotenoids, which not only have vitamin A activity but are also strong antioxidants. As with carrots, the availability of these carotenoids is increased by chopping or mashing, which releases them from the cell structure; a little oil also helps. Butternut squash also contains a decent amount of vitamin C and

Above: Roasted butternut squash is a rich source of vitamin A.

manganese, which have antioxidant properties, and also potassium, which plays an important role in muscle function, especially that of the heart. Roasting butternut squash will concentrate its flavour and sweetness. Alternatively, simply boiling it and adding to a soup mix will give added body and creaminess without the need to add any cream.

Pumpkins

Another winter variety, pumpkins are rich in all of the carotenoids, which include alpha-carotene, beta-carotene and beta-cryptoxanthin, all powerful antioxidants. Pumpkins also contain lutein and zeathanthin; both of these carotenoids are found in the eye and may protect against age-related macular degeneration. They are native to the USA, where they are synonymous with Thanksgiving and Halloween celebrations. Small pumpkins have sweeter, less fibrous flesh than the large ones. Deep orange in colour, pumpkin can be used in both sweet and savoury dishes, such as pies, soup, casseroles and souffles. When cooking pumpkin, you should avoid boiling it as it can become waterlogged and soggy.

ROASTING SQUASH

1 Preheat the oven to 200°C/400°F/Gas 6. Cut the squash in half, scoop out the seeds and place the squash cut-side down on an oiled baking tray.

2 Bake for 30 minutes or until the flesh is soft. Serve in the skin, or remove the flesh and mash with butter.

PEELING PUMPKIN

1 Cut the pumpkin in half using a large sharp knife and scoop out the seeds and fibrous parts with a spoon.

2 Cut the pumpkin into large chunks, then cut off the skin using a sharp knife.

SHOOT VEGETABLES

This collection of vegetables refers to those plants that bear perennial fruit above the ground, ranging from the aristocratic asparagus to the flower bud-like globe artichoke. A wide range of flavours, shapes and textures are represented, but all are highly prized vegetables with some interesting credentials.

Fennel

Florence fennel is closely related to the herb of the same name. The short, fat bulbs have a similar texture to celery and are topped with edible feathery fronds. Fennel has a mild aniseed flavour, most potent when eaten raw. Cooking tempers the flavour, giving it a delicious sweetness. Fennel contains a complex compound called anethole, thought to be responsible for its carminative effects, having a soothing effect on the intestines and reducing flatulence. There are also studies suggesting that anethole may have beneficial effects on inflammation in the body. When using fennel raw, slice it thinly or chop roughly and add to salads. Alternatively, slice or cut into wedges and steam, or brush with olive oil and roast or cook on a griddle. Choose bulbs that are firm, without splitting or bruising. Fennel is at its best when fresh and should be eaten as soon after harvesting as possible as its flavour diminishes with time. It can, however, be stored in the refrigerator for a few days.

Globe Artichokes

These vegetables have a particularly good mineral profile, which includes very high levels of magnesium, manganese, copper and potassium. They are also a good source of folate and vitamin K. The fibre content of the artichoke is one of the highest in the vegetable family, and this has many health benefits, such as maintaining good cholesterol levels and general bowel health.

Cooked artichoke leaves are eaten with the fingers by dipping them into garlic butter or a vinaigrette dressing then drawing each leaf through the teeth and eating the fleshy part. The leaves of the globe artichoke contain an interesting substance called cynarin. This bitter-tasting compound has

Below: Fennel provides an excellent source of the essential vitamin K.

long had associations with liver health and is reputed to assist regeneration of liver cells; it is also involved in cholesterol metabolism. Cynarin also stimulates gallbladder activity and has been shown to have benefits in digestive health. To date, however, clinical trials are inconclusive on the areas of liver function and cholesterol metabolism.

Asparagus

Highly valued since Roman times, asparagus has been cultivated commercially since the 17th century. There are two main types: white asparagus is picked just before it sprouts above the surface of the soil, while green-tipped asparagus is cut above the ground and develops its colour when it comes into contact with sunlight. It takes three years to grow a crop from seed, which may account for its expense.

Asparagus is very rich in vitamin K and the B-vitamins, folate and riboflavin. Folate is essential for the healthy development of the foetus as it has a crucial role in DNA synthesis. To prepare asparagus for use, first scrape the lower half of the stalk with a vegetable peeler and then trim off the woody end. Asparagus tastes best when it is lightly steamed or boiled. If boiling, try to use a tall pan so that the tips are out of the water and are able to steam-cook while the tougher stalks can cook in the boiling water.

Below: Lightly steam asparagus to retain all the valuable minerals.

PREPARING GLOBE ARTICHOKES
1 Hold the top of the artichoke firmly and, using a sharp knife, remove the stalk and trim the base so that the artichoke is able to sit flat.

2 Using a sharp knife or scissors, trim off and discard the tops of the leaves and cut off the pointed top.

3 Cook the artichokes in a pan of lightly salted boiling water for 35–45 minutes, until a leaf can be pulled out easily. Carefully drain the artichokes upside down.

4 Pull out the central leaves, then scoop out the hairy choke with a teaspoon and discard.

Herbs

Herbs have been highly prized by natural practitioners for centuries because, in spite of their low nutritional value, they do contain phytonutrients that possess numerous reputed healing qualities. Many of these phytonutrients are found in the essential oils of these plants, which give them their amazing pungency. These essential oils have high levels of antioxidant activity and many herbs feature in the top 50 foods with the highest ORAC scores. In cooking, herbs can make a significant difference to the flavour and aroma of a dish and they have the ability to enliven the simplest meals. Fresh herbs can be easily grown at home in the garden, or in a pot or window box.

Basil

One of the most popular fresh herbs in the kitchen, sweet basil is used extensively in Mediterranean cooking and complements tomato dishes especially well. The essential oils

Below: Herbs can be grown easily in flowerbeds, pots and window boxes.

Above: The beta-carophyllene in basil has anti-inflammatory qualities.

of sweet basil leaf are of particular interest as they are potent antioxidants and therefore of interest in cancer research. There have also been studies into a compound called beta-carophyllene (BCP), a natural anti-inflammatory compound also found in oregano but better known as a constituent of cannabis. The BCP in basil and oregano has

PESTO
Freshly made pesto, spooned over warm pasta or spread over bread and topped with a round of goat's cheese, makes a perfect quick supper. It is usually made with basil, but other herbs, such as rocket, coriander (cilantro) or parsley, can be substituted. The pine nuts can also be replaced with walnuts, cashew nuts or pistachio nuts.

50g/2oz/1 cup fresh basil leaves
2 garlic cloves, crushed
40g/1½oz/½ cups pine nuts
120ml/4fl oz/½ cup olive oil, plus extra for drizzling
60ml/4 tbsp freshly grated Parmesan cheese
salt and black pepper

1 Place the basil, garlic and pine nuts in a food processor or blender and process until finely chopped.

2 Gradually add the olive oil and then the Parmesan, and blend to a coarse purée. Season to taste. Spoon into a lidded jar, then pour over the extra olive oil to cover. Use immediately, or store in the refrigerator for 3–4 days.

BOUQUET GARNI

Combining the wonderful aromatic flavours of some fabulous herbs, a bouquet garni is essentially a bunch of mixed herbs, tied together with string or wrapped in muslin (cheesecloth). Classic combinations include sage, thyme and bay but its not unusual to see parsley, tarragon or rosemary with a few black peppercorns. Many savoury recipes call for a base sauce or stock to be flavoured with a bouquet garni. The bouquet is boiled with the base liquid and is then removed prior to serving the dish.

Right: A bouquet garni can contain whatever herbs you have to hand.

anti-inflammatory properties without the mood-altering effects of cannabis. Basil leaves do bruise easily and begin to turn brown, so always use immediately and towards the end of the cooking time.

Below: Fresh lemon balm has anti-viral and anti-bacterial properties.

Lemon Balm

The fragrant broad leaves of this herb are particularly good for making a refreshing herbal tea and go well with mint. Lemon balm can be added to any sweet or savoury dish that uses lemon juice or mint and can also be used to replace citrus peel in recipes. Lemon balm is said to have some calming and mild sedative attributes and could be beneficial for those suffering from stress or nervous exhaustion. It also has antibacterial and antiviral qualities, due to its eugenol and tannin content. It is also claimed to make a good mosquito repellent when rubbed on the skin.

Mint

The most familiar types are spearmint and peppermint, but there are other distinctly flavoured varieties, such as apple, lemon and pineapple mint, which are worth looking out for, and make a refreshing drink when infused in boiling water. Mint contains the essential oil menthol, which is a traditional cure for nausea and indigestion, and is also effective as a decongestant when you are suffering from a cold, especially if you inhale the steam of the mint infusion.

FREEZING HERBS

This is an excellent method of preserving fresh delicate herbs such as basil, chives, dill, tarragon, coriander (cilantro) and parsley. The herbs will lose their fresh appearance and texture when frozen, but are still suitable for use in cooking. They will keep for up to 3 months in the freezer.

• Half-fill ice-cube trays with chopped herbs and top up with water. Freeze, then place the cubes in freezer-bags. The frozen cubes can be added to soups, stews and stocks, and heated until they melt.

• Place whole sprigs or leaves, or chopped herbs in freezer bags, expel any air and tightly seal.

• Freeze herb sprigs or leaves on trays. When the herbs are frozen, transfer them carefully to freezer-bags, expel any air, seal tightly and return to the freezer.

• Pack chopped fresh herbs in plastic pots and freeze. Sprinkle into soups and stews straight from the freezer.

Mint is used as a flavouring in a wide variety of dishes, from stuffings to fruit salads, and as a sauce with lamb dishes. Mint is a vital ingredient in the Middle Eastern salad tabbouleh, and is also mixed with natural yogurt to make raita, a soothing accompaniment to hot curries.

Oregano
The oregano plant is actually a species of mint and is a perennial herb used extensively in Mediterranean cooking. It goes well with vegetable and meat dishes and even spicy foods. Its potential benefits to health are linked to its high phenolic and flavonoid content, which is associated with very high antioxidant activity. Try adding the chopped fresh or dried leaves to tomato dishes, sprinkle on grilled meats or mix with olive oil and lemon juice for a classic Greek dressing.

DRYING HERBS
Bay, rosemary, sage, thyme and marjoram all dry well. However, other more delicate herbs, such as basil, coriander (cilantro) and parsley, are better used fresh. Pick herbs before they flower, preferably on a sunny morning after the dew has dried. Avoid washing them – instead, brush with a pastry brush or wipe with a dry cloth. Tie the herbs in bunches and hang them upside down in a warm, dark place. The leaves should be dry and crisp after a week. Leave the herbs in bundles or strip the leaves from the stems and store in airtight jars.

Above: Mint's essential oil, menthol, is used to treat nausea and indigestion.

Rosemary
Wonderfully aromatic, rosemary is traditionally used in Mediterranean cuisine, particularly for meat dishes, but it can also add a smoky flavour to hearty bean and vegetable dishes. Rosemary has a high antioxidant content from a wide range of compounds such as rosmarinic acid and carnosic acid. This antioxidant activity may protect the body

Below: Oregano is a good source of antioxidant phenols and flavonoids.

USING DRIED HERBS
Although fresh herbs have the best flavour and appearance, dried herbs can be a convenient and useful alternative, especially in the winter months when some fresh herbs are not available.
• A few herbs such as basil, dill, mint and parsley do not dry well, losing most of their flavour.
• Oregano, thyme, marjoram and bay retain their flavour when dried and are useful substitutes for the fresh herbs.
• Dried herbs have a more concentrated flavour than fresh, so much less is required – usually a third to half as much as fresh.
• When using dried herbs in cooking, always allow sufficient time for them to rehydrate and become soft.
• Dried herbs do little for uncooked dishes, but are useful for flavouring marinades, soups and slow-cooked stews.
• When buying dried herbs, they should look bright, not faded and, because light spoils their flavour and shortens shelf-life, store in sealed, airtight jars in a cool, dark place.

from free-radical damage, and the antioxidant carnosic acid has been studied for its potential benefits in the field of brain degenerative diseases; results suggest that it may offer some protection to the brain. This could go some way to explaining its traditional reputation for memory improvement. Add sprigs of rosemary to roasted dishes or strip the small green leaves from the woody stem if adding to stocks or soups.

Sage
Native to the Mediterranean region, the silver-grey or purple leaves of this herb have a potent aroma and only a small amount is needed. Sage is

commonly added to meat dishes but, if used discreetly, it is delicious with beans, cheese, lentils and in stuffing. Interestingly, the Latin name for sage, *Salvia*, actually means 'healing', and gives us an insight into the heritage of this herb as a far-reaching healing aid throughout the centuries. In more recent times, sage has been found to contain a variety of phytosterols and flavonoids, which may explain its potential use in relieving menopausal symptoms. Other areas which have been studied more extensively are its effects on reducing excessive sweating and saliva production, as a tonic for the stomach and possibly as an aid to Alzheimer's disease management. The essential oils in sage also have antibiotic and antiviral properties, and are good for external use on insect bites and skin infections.

Thyme

This robustly flavoured aromatic herb tastes good in tomato-based recipes, and also goes well with roasted vegetables, lentils and beans. It is also an essential ingredient in a bouquet garni. Thyme contains a compound called thymol, which is

a powerful antiseptic and is widely used in mouthwash formulations. Tinctures of thyme have traditionally been used to relieve symptoms of sore throats and coughs. Because thyme is more of a robust woody herb, it delivers its flavour far better if added at the beginning of the cooking process.

Above: Sage contains beneficial phytosterols and flavonoids.

Below: Rosemary contains the active antioxidant rosmarinic acid.

Below: Thyme's antiseptic properties make it an excellent mouthwash.

MAKING HERBAL INFUSIONS

Infusions, or tisanes, are made by steeping fresh herbs in boiling water. Infusions can be used as a refreshing healthy drink or a medicinal gargle. Peppermint tea drunk after a meal is an excellent remedy for indigestion.

To make peppermint tea: pour boiling water over fresh peppermint leaves. Cover and leave to stand for about ten minutes, then strain the liquid into a cup and drink.

Sea vegetables

Western societies have only relatively recently acknowledged the amazing variety and remarkable benefits of sea vegetables, which have been an essential part of the Asian diet for centuries. Versatile sea vegetables can be used as the main component of a dish, to add texture and substance, or as a seasoning. They are usually sold in dried form and will keep for months.

Health Benefits
The health benefits of sea vegetables have been recognized for centuries, and range from improving the lustre of hair and clarity of the skin to reducing blood cholesterol levels. Sea vegetables have significant amounts of the major minerals, such as iron, calcium, magnesium, potassium and phosphorus, and useful amounts of trace elements, such as selenium and zinc. They are particularly high in the essential mineral, iodine, which helps efficient thyroid function. They are also rich in the antioxidant beta-carotene and contain some of the B-complex vitamins.

The rich mineral content of sea vegetables benefits the nervous system, helping to reduce stress. It also boosts the immune system, aiding metabolism. Research shows that alginic acid found in some seaweeds, notably kombu, arame, hijiki and wakame, binds with heavy metals, such as cadmium, lead, mercury and radium, in our intestines and can help to eliminate them.

Above: A bowl of nori flakes.

Nori
This useful sea vegetable has a delicate texture and mild flavour. It is sold in thin purple-black sheets, which turn translucent green when toasted or cooked. It is one of the few sea vegetables that does not require soaking. In Japanese cooking, nori sheets are used to wrap small parcels of vinegared rice and vegetables that are eaten as sushi. Toasted nori is used as a garnish.

Laver
A relation of nori which grows outside Japan, laver is commonly found around the shores of Britain. It is used in traditional regional cooking – particularly in Wales, Scotland and Ireland. It is cooked to a thick purée, which can be spread on toast or mixed with oatmeal to make laverbread. It can also be added to sauces and stuffings. Available ready-cooked in cans, laver has a particularly high concentration of vitamins and minerals.

Wakame
This sea vegetable is often confused with its relative, kombu, because it looks very similar until it is soaked, when it changes colour from brown to a delicate green. Wakame has a mild flavour and is one of the most versatile of sea vegetables. Soak briefly, then use it in salads and soups, or toast, crumble and use it as a condiment. It is rich in calcium and vitamins B and C.

Kombu
Also known as kelp, kombu is a brown sea vegetable that is most commonly sold in dried strips. It has a strong flavour and is used in slowly cooked dishes, soups and stocks. Kombu is an essential ingredient in the Japanese stock, dashi. It is richer in iodine than other sea vegetables, and is also rich in calcium and potassium, as well as iron.

Arame
Sold in black strips, arame has a mild, slightly sweet flavour. It needs to be soaked before using in stir-fries or salads, but if using in moist or slow-cooked dishes, such as noodles and soups, it can be added straight from the packet. Arame is rich in iodine, calcium and iron, and is used to treat high blood pressure.

Carrageen
This fern-like seaweed, also known as Irish moss, is found along the Atlantic coasts of North America

TOASTING NORI
Nori sheets can be toasted over an electric or gas hob until they turn crisp. Be careful not to scorch the nori – or your fingers.

1 Hold a sheet of nori with a pair of tongs about 5cm/2in above an electric hot plate or gas hob for about 1 minute, moving it around so it toasts evenly and turns bright green and crisp.

2 Leave the nori sheet to cool, then crumble. Add to stir-fries or sprinkle over salads and soups.

and Europe. Like agar-agar, it has gelling properties but produces a softer set, making it useful for jellies and mousses and as a thickener in soups and stews. Carrageen is used for treating colds and bronchial ailments as well as digestive disorders.

Hijiki
This sea vegetable looks similar to arame but is thicker and has a slightly stronger flavour. Once soaked, hijiki can be sautéed or added to soups and salads, but it needs longer cooking than most sea vegetables. Hijiki expands greatly during soaking, so only a small amount is needed. It is particularly rich in calcium and iron.

Dulse
A purple-red sea vegetable, dulse has flat fronds, which taste spicy when cooked. It needs to be soaked until it turns soft before adding to salads, noodle dishes, soups and vegetable dishes. It can also be toasted and crumbled for a nourishing garnish.

Below: Hijiki strands will expand greatly on soaking, so use sparingly.

Dulse is rich in several important minerals, including iodine, potassium, phosphorus, manganese and iron.

Agar-agar
The vegetarian equivalent to the animal-derived gelatine, agar-agar has a neutral taste and can be used as a setting agent in both sweet and savoury dishes. It can be bought as flakes or strands, both of which need to be dissolved in water before use. Agar-agar is more effective than gelatine, so only a small amount is needed. It is also said to be an effective laxative.

Chlorella
A type of green algae and a relative of seaweed, chlorella is a good source of protein, vitamins and minerals. In the past it was considered to be the answer to the world's food production problems in the light of rapidly growing populations, but large-scale production difficulties meant that it did not fulfil its potential.

Chlorella has many reputed health benefits and has been clinically proven to help reduce blood pressure and blood cholesterol levels. There is also evidence that it could help our immune response and speed up wound-healing. Available as tablets or in powdered form, chlorella can be added to food and drink or taken as a supplement.

Below: Marsh samphire has a salty flavour that complements fish dishes.

Above: Agar-agar is an extremely good source of dietary fibre.

Spirulina
Also an algae, spirulina has an unusually high concentration of protein. It contains a good range of essential fatty acids including the omega-3 family, and has an excellent vitamin and mineral profile. It is high in antioxidants such as beta-carotene. Its reputed health benefits include lowering cholesterol and improving heart health. Its concentrated nutritional profile could make it a useful food source for the future.

Available in tablet and powdered form, spirulina has a slightly bitter flavour. The powder can be added to drinks such as juices or smoothies.

Marsh Samphire
Also known as sea asparagus, this unusual plant grows in coastal areas on the mud flats of salt marshes. It resembles a mini cactus, and its succulent flesh is a delicacy. Growing close to the sea, it shares many of the same characteristics as seaweed, being a rich source of chlorophyll and minerals, such as iodine and zinc.

Marsh samphire is not readily available in shops but can be found at your local fishmonger. Alternatively, at the start of the season in June, visit the sea shore at low tide and forage for yourself. Steam it gently and serve with a little butter or olive oil. Eat by pulling off the juicy flesh with your teeth.

Sprouted seeds, grains and pulses

Sprouts are quite remarkable in terms of nutritional content. Once the seed (or pulse or grain) has germinated, the nutritional value rises dramatically. There are almost 30 per cent more B vitamins and 60 per cent more vitamin C in the sprout than in the original seed, pulse or grain. The sprouting process also results in an increase in the activity of many enzymes that remain dormant in the dry seed, grain or pulse. This enhanced enzyme activity is then able to break down carbohydrates, proteins and fats into simpler compounds and new compounds, making them more bio-available to us. Supermarkets and health food shops sell a variety of sprouts. If you can, choose fresh, crisp sprouts with the seed or bean still attached. Avoid any that are brown, slimy or musty-looking, or have a strange odour. Sprouts are best eaten on the day they are bought but, if fresh, they will keep,

Above: Alfalfa beansprouts are an excellent source of phytoestrogens.

wrapped in a plastic bag, in the refrigerator for 2–3 days. Rinse thoroughly and pat dry before use. It is also easy to grow them at home – all you need is a jar, some muslin (cheesecloth) and an elastic band.

Mung Beansprouts

These widely available beansprouts, are popular in Asian cooking, where they are used in soups, salads and stir-fries. They are fairly large and crunchy, with a delicate flavour. If you are cooking them, do so for only a few seconds to retain some crunch.

Above: Mung beansprouts

Lentil Sprouts

These sprouts have a slightly spicy, peppery flavour and thin, white shoots. You should use only whole lentils, as split ones will not sprout.

Alfalfa Sprouts

These tiny, wispy white bean-sprouts have a mild, nutty flavour and are related to the pea.

Above: Lentil sprouts

WARNING

People with weakened immune systems, as well as the very old and the very young, should not eat raw sprouts.

TIPS ON SPROUTING

• Use whole seeds and beans, as split ones will not germinate.
• Regular rinsing with fresh water and draining is essential when sprouting, to prevent the beans from turning rancid and mouldy.
• Cover the sprouting jar with muslin (cheesecloth) to allow air to circulate and water in and out.
• After two or three days, the jar can be placed in sunlight to encourage the green pigment chlorophyll and increase the sprout's magnesium and fibre content.

SPROUTING SEEDS, PULSES AND GRAINS

Larger pulses, such as chickpeas, take longer to sprout than small beans, but they are all easy to grow and are usually ready to eat in three or four days. Store sprouts in a covered container in the refrigerator for 2–3 days.

1 Wash 45ml/3 tbsp seeds, pulses or grains thoroughly in water, then place in a large jar. Fill the jar with lukewarm water, cover with a piece of muslin (cheesecloth) and fasten securely with an elastic band. Leave in a warm place to stand overnight.

2 The next day, pour off the water through the muslin and refill the jar with water. Shake gently, then turn the jar upside down and drain thoroughly. Leave the jar on its side in a warm place, away from direct sunlight.

3 Rinse thoroughly three times a day until they reach the desired size. Remove the contents from the jar, rinse and remove any ungerminated beans.

These sprouts contain phytoestrogens, which have a mild oestrogen-mimicking effect in the body, and have been used to alleviate menopausal symptoms. They are best eaten raw to retain their crunchiness.

Aduki Beansprouts
These fine wispy sprouts have a sweet nutty taste and are particularly good in salads and stir-fries.

Wheat Berry Sprouts
Sprouts grown from wheat berries have a crunchy texture and sweet flavour and are excellent in breads. If they are left to grow, the sprouts will become wheatgrass, a powerful detoxifier that is usually made into a juice.

Chickpea Sprouts
These sprouts are grown from chickpeas and have a wonderful nutty flavour. These sprouts will add a crunchy texture and some substance to your salads and side dishes.

Above: Aduki beansprouts

Above: Wheat berry sprouts

Right: Chickpea sprouts

HOW TO USE BEANSPROUTS
• Sprouted pulses and beans have a denser, more fibrous texture, while sprouts grown from seeds are lighter. Try using a mixture of all three to vary the tastes and textures.
• Sprouted grains are good in breads, adding a pleasant, crunchy texture. Knead them in after the first rising, before shaping the loaf.

• Mung beansprouts are often used in Asian cooking, particularly in stir-fries, and require very little cooking.
• Chickpea and lentil sprouts are ideal for use in casseroles and bakes.
• Alfalfa sprouts are good as part of a sandwich filling as well as in salads. They are not suited to cooking.

CEREAL GRAINS

Grains have been cultivated throughout the world for hundreds of years. The seeds of cereal grasses are packed with concentrated goodness and are an important source of complex starchy carbohydrates, protein, vitamins and minerals. When eaten as wholegrains they offer us the most health benefits, and many health organizations have guidelines that recommend we eat at least three portions of wholegrain a day. The most popular types of grain, such as wheat, rice, oats, barley and corn or maize, come in various forms, from wholegrains to flours. Inexpensive and readily available, these grains are incredibly versatile and should form a major part of our diet.

Wheat

The largest and most important grain crop in the world, wheat has been cultivated since 7,000BC. The wheat kernel comprises three parts: bran, germ and endosperm. Wheat bran is the outer husk, while wheat germ is the nutritious seed from which the plant grows. The endosperm, the inner part of the kernel, is full of starch and protein and forms the basis of wheat flour. In addition to flour, wheat comes in various other forms. Wheat is most nutritious when it is unprocessed and in its

Below: Wheat berries

wholegrain form. Indeed, when milled into white flour, wheat loses a staggering 80 percent of its nutrients.

Wheat Berries

These are whole wheat grains with the husks removed, and they can be bought in health food shops. Wheat berries may be used to add a sweet, nutty flavour and chewy texture to breads, soups and stews, or can be combined with rice or other grains. Wheat berries must be soaked overnight, then cooked in boiling salted water until tender. If they are left to germinate, the berries sprout into wheatgrass, possibly a powerful detoxifier and cleanser (see opposite).

Wheat Flakes

Steamed and softened, berries that have been rolled and pressed are known as wheat flakes or rolled wheat. They are best used on their own or mixed with other flaked grains in porridge (oatmeal), as a base for muesli, or to add nutrients and substance to breads and cakes.

Wheat Bran

The outer husk of the wheat kernel, wheat bran is a by-product of white flour production. It is very high in insoluble dietary fibre, which makes it an effective laxative as it increases bulk. It is an extremely good source of almost all of the B vitamins – only B_{12} is absent – as well as all the essential minerals except sodium, although the phytate content of the bran can reduce the absorption of

COOKING WHEAT BERRIES
Wheat berries make a delicious addition to salads, and they can also be used to add texture to breads and stews.

1 Place the wheat berries in a bowl and cover with cold water. Soak overnight, then rinse thoroughly and drain.

2 Place the wheat berries in a pan with water. Bring to the boil, then cover and simmer for 1–2 hours until tender, replenishing with water when necessary.

calcium and iron quite considerably. Wheat bran makes a healthy addition to bread doughs and breakfast cereals, as well as cakes and biscuits.

Below: Wheat flakes

Grown from the whole wheat grain, wheatgrass has been recognized for centuries for its general healing qualities. However, this has not been proven within the realms of modern scientific research. It does contain a good range of B vitamins, including vitamin B_{12}, which is unusual in a non-meat source, as well as vitamins A, E, and a little vitamin C. Its vibrant green colour comes from chlorophyll, which may be able to bind with harmful toxins and help the liver to eliminate them, although this has not been scientifically proven. Once it is juiced, wheatgrass must be consumed within 15 minutes, preferably on an empty stomach.

Wheat Germ

The nutritious heart of the whole wheat berry, wheat germ is an excellent source of protein, the B vitamins (except B_{12}) and all of the essential minerals. It is higher in

Below: Bulgur wheat

fat than wheat bran, but this is a polyunsaturated oil, and includes both omega-3 and omega-6 essential fatty acids. Wheat germ is one of the richest sources of phytosterols, which can reduce the total cholesterol and the 'bad' LDL cholesterol in the blood, and therefore reduce heart disease risk. It is is used in much the same way as wheat bran and is available toasted or untoasted, lending a nutty flavour to breakfast cereals and porridge. Because of its higher oil content, store wheat germ in an airtight container in the refrigerator, as it can become rancid if kept at room temperature.

Cracked Wheat

This is made from crushed wheat berries and retains all the nutrients of wholewheat. Often confused with bulgur wheat, cracked wheat can be used in the same way as wheat berries (although it cooks in less time), or as an alternative to rice and other grains. When cooked, it has a slightly sticky texture and pleasant crunchiness. Serve it as an accompaniment, or use it in salads.

Bulgur Wheat

Unlike cracked wheat, this grain is made from cooked wheat berries, which have the bran removed, and are then dried and crushed. This light, nutty grain is simply soaked in water for 20 minutes, then drained – some manufacturers specify cold water but boiling water produces a softer grain. It can also be cooked in boiling water until tender. Bulgur wheat is the main ingredient in the Middle Eastern salad tabbouleh, where it is mixed with chopped parsley, mint, tomato, cucumber and onion, and dressed with lemon juice and olive oil.

Above: Wheat germ

COELIAC DISEASE

Distinct from a wheat allergy or intolerance, this auto-immune condition is triggered by an intolerance to gluten, a type of protein found in many cereals, but most commonly wheat. It damages the lining of the small intestine and reduces the ability to absorb nutrients properly. Unfortunately, the intolerance is permanent and the only way to manage the disease is to avoid gluten-containing foods totally. It often manifests itself with abdominal discomfort or weight loss, but less severe symptoms are very common too and it can go undiagnosed for some time.

This diagnosis is critical and diagnostic blood tests can be used to indicate intolerance, however, a trained practitioner should carry this out, as false positives are common.

Sometimes a more invasive gut biopsy may also be necessary. A gluten-free diet is a major undertaking as such a great proportion of the western diet includes wheat. Expert advice from your GP or dietician should be sought, to ensure that no further dietary issues arise when excluding such a large food group from the diet.

RICE

Throughout Asia, a meal is considered incomplete without rice. It is a staple food for over half the world's population, and almost every culture has its own repertoire of rice dishes, ranging from risottos to pilaffs. What is more, this valuable food provides a good source of vitamins and minerals, as well as a steady supply of energy.

Choosing the Rice

Which rice you choose will depend largely on the meal you intend to cook. Basmati, with its wonderful fragrance and flavour, is for many the only rice to serve with an Indian meal. For a Chinese, Thai or Indonesian meal, Thai fragrant rice, with its pleasant aroma and slightly sticky texture (important if you intend to use chopsticks) is excellent, while the versatile American long grain rice is great for stir-fries, pilaffs, jambalayas and gumbos.

There are a few instances where only a specific type of rice will do – risottos, for example, can only be made successfully with risotto rice – but in general, providing you know a little about the qualities of the rice, there are no hard and fast rules. Although tradition demands rice puddings be made with a short grain rice, there's no reason why you

Below: Brown rice contains more nutrients than refined white rice.

Above: Rice is the main energy source for much of the world's population.

shouldn't use long grain. Basmati and even Thai fragrant rice make delicious puddings, too.

Storing Rice

Raw (uncooked) rice can be kept in a cool, dark place for up to three years in the unopened packet or in an airtight container. It should be kept perfectly dry; if the moisture content creeps up, the rice will turn mouldy. If the rice is very old, it may need more water or longer cooking. Check the packet for 'best before' dates. Cooked rice can be stored for up to 24 hours if cooled, covered and kept in the refrigerator. You can also freeze the cooled rice; reheat it in a covered casserole in the oven or thaw it and use it for fried rice or in a salad. The rice should should be piping hot all the way through and should only be reheated once.

Brown Rice

Brown rice is a valuable source of complex carbohydrates and insoluble fibre. This whole rice form contains a higher proportion of B vitamins than white rice because the bran and germ have not been removed. The starch in brown rice is absorbed more slowly, keeping blood sugar levels on an even keel and making it an important food for diabetics. Brown rice and rice bran contain a

COOKING LONG GRAIN RICE

There are many methods and opinions on how to cook rice. The absorption method is one of the simplest and retains valuable nutrients, which would otherwise be lost in cooking water that is drained away.

Different types of rice have different absorption powers, but the general rule of thumb for long grain rice is to use double the quantity of water to rice. For the following method, use 1 cup of brown long grain rice to 2 cups of water. 200g/7oz /1 cup long grain rice is sufficient for about four people as a side dish.

1 Rinse the rice in a sieve (strainer) under cold, running water. Place in a heavy-based pan and add the measured cold water. Bring to the boil, uncovered, then reduce the heat and stir the rice. Add salt, to taste, if you wish.

2 Cover the pan with a tight-fitting lid. Simmer for 25–35 minutes, without removing the lid, until the water is absorbed and the rice tender. Remove from the heat and leave covered for 5 minutes before serving.

COOK'S TIPS
- Always leave cooked rice to stand for 5 minutes after draining and before serving, to 'rest' it and complete the cooking process.
- Remember that rice absorbs water as it cooks. If you use too much water or cook the rice for too long, it will become soggy.
- If rice is still a little under-cooked after cooking, cover it tightly and set aside for 5–10 minutes. It will continue to cook in the residual heat.

polyphenol called g-oryzanol which has been extracted and studied for its effects in people with high cholesterol levels; the results show that it could reduce total cholesterol in these people. It is also gluten free.

Basmati Rice

This is a slender, long-grain rice, which is grown in the foothills of the Himalayas. It is aged for a year after harvest, giving it a characteristic light, fluffy texture and aromatic flavour. Its name means 'fragrant'. Both white and brown types of basmati rice are available. Choose brown basmati as it contains more nutrients, and has a slightly nuttier flavour than the

Below: The short grains of risotto rice are also good for rice puddings.

white variety. Widely used in Indian cooking, basmati rice has a cooling effect on spicy curries. It is also excellent for rice salads, when you want very light, fluffy separate grains.

Risotto Rice

For risotto, you need to use a special, fat, short grain rice. Arborio rice is the most widely sold variety. When cooked, most rice absorbs around three times its weight in water. Risotto rice can absorb nearly five times its weight, which results in a creamy grain that retains a slight bite.

Camargue Red Rice

This rice comes from the Camargue region in France and has a distinctive chewy texture and a nutty flavour. It is an unmilled brown rice that is unusually hard, which, although it takes about an hour to cook, retains its shape. The red-coloured outer bran is a good source of fibre, vitamins and minerals. This type of rice also has a lower glycaemic index than white rice, so it is good for slow-release energy. Cooking intensifies its red colour, making it a good addition to salads and stuffing.

Wild Rice

This is not a true rice but an aquatic grass grown in North America. It has dramatic, long, slender brown-black

Below: High in fibre, wild rice actually belongs to the grass family.

grains that have a nutty flavour and chewy texture. It takes longer to cook than most types of rice – 35–60 minutes, depending on whether you prefer it chewy or tender – but you can reduce the cooking time by soaking it in water overnight. Wild rice is extremely nutritious. It contains all eight essential amino acids and is particularly rich in lysine. It is a good source of fibre, is low in calories and gluten-free. Use in stuffings, or mix with other rices in pilaffs and salads.

Rice Bran

Like wheat and oat bran, rice bran comes from the husk of the grain kernel. It is high soluble dietary fibre and useful for adding texture and substance to bread, cakes and biscuits (cookies) as well as to stews.

QUICK WAYS TO FLAVOUR RICE

- Cook brown rice in vegetable stock with sliced dried apricots. Sauté an onion in a little oil and add ground cumin, coriander and fresh chopped chilli, then mix in the cooked rice.

- Add raisins and toasted almonds to saffron-infused rice.

OTHER GRAINS

Wheat, oats and rice are undoubtedly the most widely used grains, yet there are others such as barley, quinoa and buckwheat, that should not be ignored, because they provide variety in our diet, are packed with nutrients and are classed as wholegrains. The versatile grain comes in many forms, from whole grains to flour, which are used widely in baking, breakfast cereals and many cooked dishes.

Oats

Available in many different guises, all oats have slightly different attributes and uses. One thing is true of all variations: the oat is a very healthy food to eat for a number of reasons. As well as being high in B vitamins, vitamin A and iron and manganese, it is one of the only foods to have satisfied both the American FDA and the UK FSA rules on health claims for its benefits for heart health. This is because oats contain a high level of soluble fibre, one of which is called beta-glucan, which has been proven to reduce overall cholesterol levels. One other effect of the soluble fibre is to slow down the energy release from the oat food and therefore make you feel fuller for longer. Most oat-based foods will have a good glycaemic index.

Below: Pearl barley makes a tasty low-glycaemic index risotto.

Rolled Oats and Oatmeal

This popular product is made when whole oats are hulled, removing the hard outer husk leaving a whole kernel. This can then either be cut into smaller pieces or rolled under heavy rollers. This process retains the bran and the germ and all of the nutrients associated with them. Quick-cooking rolled oats have been pre-cooked in water and then dried, deactivating the enzymes that can cause oats to go rancid. It is a popular grain in northern Europe, particularly Scotland, where they are commonly turned into porridge, oatcakes and pancakes. Medium oatmeal is best in cakes and breads, while fine is ideal in pancakes, as well as for fruit- and milk-based drinks.

Oat Bran

If the oat groat is rolled several times, the oat bran eventually separates out, leaving oat flour. High in soluble fibre and retaining a good proportion of the vitamins and minerals, the oat bran can then be sprinkled over breakfast cereals and mixed into plain or fruit yogurt to boost the fibre content. For best results, oat bran should be eaten daily at regular intervals. It can be a useful way to ease constipation and generally ensure that we are getting enough fibre in our diets.

Below: Add beta-glucan-rich oatmeal to dishes for slower-release energy.

CAN COELIACS EAT OATS?

This is a very common query for coeliac sufferers. It is important to note that oats do still contain a type of protein called avenin, which is similar to gluten and can cause a reaction in coeliacs, so oats should not automatically be considered as gluten-free.

Barley

Believed to be the oldest cultivated grain, barley is still a fundamental part of the everyday diet in Eastern Europe, the Middle East and Asia. Pearl barley, the most usual form, is husked, steamed and then polished to give it its characteristic ivory-coloured appearance. It has a mild, sweet flavour and chewy texture, and can be added to soups, stews and bakes. It is also used to make old-fashioned barley water. Pot barley is the whole grain with just the inedible outer husk removed. It takes much longer to cook than pearl barley. Pot barley is more nutritious than pearl barley, because it contains the extra soluble fibre, phosphorus, iron, magnesium, zinc and B vitamins, especially thiamin from the whole grain. More recently, studies have shown that its soluble fibre is the same as that found in oats – beta-glucan – and can have the same effect on reducing blood cholesterol levels. Barley flakes made from rolled whole barley are also available and make a good porridge or can be added to home-made muesli. Barley and barley-containing foods also have a good glycaemic index as they release their energy slowly.

Quinoa

Hailed as a true supergrain, quinoa (pronounced 'keen-wa') was called 'the mother grain' by the Incas, who cultivated it for hundreds of years. Quinoa's supergrain status hails from its rich nutritional value. Unlike other grains, quinoa contains a high level of

Above: Quinoa is a useful source of protein for vegetarians and vegans.

Above: Boil millet in milk for a sweet iron- and vitamin-B-rich porridge.

Above: Amaranth seeds contain an impressive list of nutrients.

protein, with a good balance of all of the essential amino acids, unusual for a food of vegetable origin. It is an excellent source of manganese, magnesium, copper, phosphorus, iron and zinc as well as B vitamins and insoluble fibre. It is particularly valuable for people with coeliac disease, as it is gluten-free. The tiny, bead-shaped grains have a mild, slightly bitter taste and firm texture. It is cooked in the same way as rice, but the grains quadruple in size, becoming translucent. Quinoa is useful for making stuffings, pilaffs, bakes and breakfast cereals.

Millet
Although millet is usually associated with bird food, it is a highly nutritious grain. It once rivalled barley as the main food of Europe and remains a staple ingredient in many parts of the world, including Africa, China and India. Millet is an easily digestible grain. It contains more iron than other grains and is a good source of manganese, copper, phosphorus, magnesium, and B vitamins, notably thiamin and niacin. Millet is gluten-free, so it is a useful food for people with coeliac disease. Its mild flavour makes it an ideal accompaniment to spicy stews and curries, and it can be used as a base for pilaffs or milk puddings. The tiny, firm grains can also be flaked or ground into flour. The flour can be used for baking, but

needs to be combined with high-gluten flours to make leavened bread; alternatively, it can make good flat bread. Toast the millet grain for an extra nutty flavour.

Buckwheat
In spite of its name, buckwheat is not a type of wheat, but is actually related to the rhubarb family. It is also very nutritious, containing all of the essential amino acids, minerals and B vitamins, especially niacin. Buckwheat also contains rutin, a flavonoid and antioxidant which has the ability to strengthen blood vessels and may help people with circulation problems. Buckwheat is gluten-free, and so is useful for people who suffer from coeliac disease.

The grain is available plain or toasted and it has a nutty, earthy flavour. It is a staple food in Eastern Europe as well as Russia, where the triangular grain is milled into a speckled-grey flour and used to make blini pancakes. Buckwheat pancakes are popular in parts of the USA and France. The whole grain, which is also known as kasha, makes a fine porridge or a creamy pudding. Buckwheat pasta made from buckwheat flour tastes nutty and is darker in colour than wholewheat pasta. Buckwheat noodles, of which soba noodles are the best-known type, are a much darker colour than wheat noodles –

almost grey. In Japan, soba noodles are traditionally served in soups or stir-fries with a variety of sauces.

Amaranth
This plant, which is native to Mexico, is unusual in that it can be eaten as both a vegetable and a grain. Like quinoa, amaranth is considered a supergrain due to its excellent nutritional content. Although its taste may take some getting used to, its nutritional qualities more than make up for it. Amaranth has more protein than pulses and is rich in all essential amino acids, particularly lysine. It is also high in B-vitamins, manganese, magnesium, phosphorus iron and zinc. Amaranth also contains calcium, but the high oxalic acid levels bind this and make it largely bio-unavailable. Amaranth is a natural source of plant stanols, which are chemically similar to phytosterols and have the same effect of reducing levels of the 'bad' LDL cholesterol, which may aid heart health. The tiny pale seed or 'grain' has a strong and distinctive, peppery flavour. It is best used in stews and soups or to make a porridge, but can also be ground into flour to make bread, pastries and cookies. The flour is gluten-free and has to be mixed with wheat or another flour that contains gluten to make leavened bread. Amaranth leaves are similar to spinach, but are less widely available,

LEGUMES

Extremely important in agriculture, legumes have the ability to fix nitrogen from the air and replenish the soil's nitrogen levels, which reduces the need for expensive fertilizers. Pulses are the seeds of these leguminous plants and are nutritionally vital, especially where meat production is limited or communities are vegetarian or vegan. Lentils and beans provide the cook with a diverse range of flavours and textures. They have long been a staple food in India, South America, the Middle East and the Mediterranean, and there is hardly a country that does not have its own favourite legume-based dish, from Boston baked beans in the USA to lentil dhal in India. In Mexico, they are spiced and used to make refried beans, while in China they are fermented for black bean sauces. Low in fat and high in complex carbohydrates, vitamins and minerals, legumes are also an important source of protein for vegetarians and, when eaten with cereals, easily match animal-based sources. The phytonutrient content of legumes is varied and the combined effect of this makes them a very valuable food to us – so much so

Below: High-fibre brown lentils take longer to cook than split varieties.

that the American dietary guidelines include a specific recommendation to consume as many as six portions of legumes per week.

Lentils

The humble lentil is one of our oldest wholefoods. It originated in Asia and North Africa and continues to be cultivated in those regions, as well as in France and Italy. Lentils have an impressive range of nutrients, including B vitamins, and are especially rich in folate; they also contain many essential minerals, including manganese, phosphorus, zinc, magnesium and copper. Lentils are one of the richest plant sources of iron, and even though it is in a form that is not easily absorbed, the high levels still make it a valuable contributor, especially in vegetarian and vegan diets. Extremely low in fat and richer in protein than most pulses, lentils contain both insoluble and soluble fibre. This insoluble fibre content aids the functioning of the bowels and colon and the soluble fibre reduces the 'bad' LDL cholesterol in the body. The fibre also slows down the rate at which sugar enters the bloodstream, providing a steady supply of energy, which could help reduce the risk of Type II diabetes. Lentils are not a complete source of protein as they do not contain all of the essential amino acids, but if they are served with a grain such as rice, this will make the dish a complete source. Phytonutrients present in lentils include flavonoids, isoflavones, phytosterols and lignans, all of which combine to make lentils a well-qualified superfood. This potent combination could be the reason why those with diets high in legumes have a lower incidence of Type II diabetes and cardiovascular disease. Lentils are hard even when fresh, so they are always sold dried. Unlike most other pulses, they do not need soaking. Although lentils can be kept for up to a year, they do toughen with time. Buy from shops with a

fast turnover of stock and store in airtight containers in a cool, dark place. Look for bright, unwrinkled pulses that are not dusty and always rinse well before use.

COOKING SPLIT RED AND YELLOW LENTILS

Lentils are easy to cook and do not need to be soaked beforehand. Split red and green lentils cook down to a soft consistency, while whole lentils retain their shape when cooked, but take longer to prepare.

1 Place 250g/9oz/generous 1 cup split lentils in a sieve (strainer) and rinse under cold running water. Transfer to a pan.

2 Cover with 600ml/1 pint/2½ cups water and bring to the boil. Simmer for 20–25 minutes, stirring occasionally, until the water is absorbed and the lentils are tender. Season to taste.

Above: Fibre-dense green lentils absorb flavours such as garlic well.

> **LENTIL TIP**
> Avoid adding salt to the water when cooking lentils as this prevents them softening. Instead, season after they are cooked.

Red Lentils

Orange-coloured red split lentils, sometimes known as Egyptian lentils, are the most familiar variety. They cook in just 20 minutes, eventually disintegrating into a thick purée. They are ideal for thickening soups and casseroles and, when cooked with spices, make a delicious dhal. In the Middle East, red or yellow lentils are cooked and mixed with vegetables and spices to form balls known as kofte.

Yellow Lentils

Less well-known, yellow lentils taste very similar to the red variety and are used in much the same way and break down to a purée. Like red lentils, yellow lentils are split and therefore will not sprout.

Green and Brown Lentils

Sometimes referred to as continental lentils, these disc-shaped pulses retain their shape when cooked. Green and brown lentils contain

Below: Red lentils have less fibre than green varieties but cook faster.

30 per cent fibre, far higher than the 11 per cent found in red and yellow varieties. This means that they will take longer to cook than split lentils – about 40–45 minutes – and are ideal for adding to warm salads, casseroles and stuffings.

Puy Lentils

These tiny, dark, blue-green, marbled lentils grow in the Auvergne region of central France. They are considered to be far superior in taste and texture than other varieties, and they retain

Below: Iron-rich Puy lentils are a great accompaniment to fish dishes.

their bead-like shape during cooking, which takes around 25–30 minutes. Puy lentils are a delicious addition to simple dishes such as warm salads, and are also good braised in wine and flavoured with fresh herbs.

> **CREAMY RED LENTIL DHAL**
> This makes a tasty and satisfying winter supper for vegetarians and meat eaters alike. Serve with naan bread, coconut cream and fresh coriander (cilantro) leaves. The coconut cream gives this dish a really rich taste.
>
> **Serves 4**
> 15ml/1 tbsp sunflower oil
> 500g/1¼lb/2 cups red lentils
> 15ml/1 tbsp hot curry paste
> salt and ground black pepper
>
> **1** Heat the oil in a large pan and add the lentils. Fry for 1–2 minutes, stirring constantly, then stir in the curry paste and 600ml/ 1 pint/2½ cups boiling water.
>
> **2** Bring the mixture to the boil, then reduce the heat to a gentle simmer. Cover the pan and cook for 15 minutes, stirring occasionally, until the lentils are tender and the mixture has thickened.
>
> **3** Season the dhal with plenty of salt and ground black pepper to taste, and serve piping hot.

PULSES

Including chickpeas and a vast range of beans, these are the edible seeds from plants belonging to the legume family of pulses. They are packed with protein, vitamins, minerals and fibre, and are also extremely low in fat. Pulses count towards part of your target of eating five portions of fruit and vegetables a day. The protein contained in them is extremely good quality as it contains all of the essential amino acids, which is particularly valuable for vegetarian and vegan diets. Pulses are also rich in phytonutrients such as flavonoids, phytosterols and lignans, and studies show that people with diets rich in these nutrients have lower incidences of cardiovascular disease and Type II diabetes.

For the cook, their ability to absorb the flavours of other foods means that pulses can be used as the basis for an infinite number of dishes.

HOW TO PREPARE AND COOK PULSES

There is much debate as to whether soaking pulses before cooking is necessary, but it certainly reduces cooking times, and can enhance flavour by starting the germination process.

First, wash pulses under cold running water, then put in a bowl of fresh cold water and leave to soak overnight. Discard any pulses that float to the surface, drain and rinse again. Place the pulses in a large pan and cover with fresh cold water. Boil rapidly for 10–15 minutes, then reduce the heat, cover and simmer until tender.

Using a pressure cooker to cook pulses also reduces the cooking time by about two-thirds. Soak first as per usual, then follow your appliance's instructions. Timings are usually only about 20 minutes.

PULSE TIPS

Many people are put off eating beans due to their unfortunate side effects. The propensity of beans to cause flatulence stems from the gases they produce in the gut. Following these guidelines can reduce this:
• Never cook pulses in their soaking water as it contains indigestible sugars.
• Skim off any scum that forms on the surface of the water during cooking.
• Add digestive spices, such as dill, asafoetida, ginger, cumin and caraway, to the cooking water.

Most pulses require soaking overnight in cold water before use, so it is wise to plan ahead if using the dried type or alternatively, if you are pushed for time, many are available canned.

Black Beans

These shiny, black, kidney-shaped beans are often used in Caribbean cooking and are sometimes known as the black turtle bean. They are packed with nutrients, and are a very rich source of folate, which is particularly important if you are thinking of becoming or are pregnant, as it reduces the risk of neural tube defects in babies. Black beans are an

Above: Chickpeas are an excellent provider of protein and B-vitamins.

excellent source of all the B vitamins, which are essential for energy release and required for healthy nerves and muscles. They also contain good levels of all of the essential minerals, while remaining low in sodium. They do contain iron and calcium, but these will be bound with phytates and are less bioavailable. The beans have a sweetish flavour, and their colour adds a dramatic touch to soups, salads or casseroles.

Chickpeas

Also known as garbanzo beans, robust and hearty chickpeas resemble shelled hazelnuts, and have a delicious nutty flavour together with a creamy texture. As with black beans, the protein in chickpeas is very high quality and contains all of the essential amino acids. Chickpeas are an extremely rich source of folate, and the other B-vitamins are also well represented. They have a valuable array of essential minerals, including a modest amount of calcium, useful if you don't or can't have dairy products in your diet. They are a good source of insoluble fibre, improving bulk and preventing

Left: Black beans are a good source of folate and other B vitamins.

constipation, which could reduce the risk of colon cancer. This fibre content also contributes to a good glycaemic index, which can help manage diabetes and may even reduce cholesterol levels. They do need lengthy cooking if you are using dried chickpeas, however, canned ones are available which are more convenient. Chickpeas taste excellent in curries, and make a wonderful creamy hummus dip which can be flavoured with ingredients such as pesto, coriander (cilantro), lemon or roasted peppers.

Red Kidney Beans
Glossy, mahogany-red kidney beans retain their colour and kidney shape when cooked. They are not quite a

Above: High in protein and fibre, kidney beans add colour to cooking.

complete protein as some essential amino acids are missing; however, combining with a cereal or grain food will complement the profile and make it complete. Red beans and rice is one such classic combination. They contain high levels of folate, manganese, phosphorus and iron and are a good source of both soluble and insoluble fibre, both of which reduce cardiovascular risk by lowering cholesterol and improving the glycaemic index of food. Kidney beans have a soft, 'mealy' texture and are much used in South American cooking. An essential ingredient in spicy chillies, they can also be used to make refried beans (although this dish is traditionally made from pinto beans).

Cooked kidney beans can be used to make a variety of salads, but they taste especially good when combined with red onion and chopped flat leaf parsley and mint, then tossed in an olive oil dressing.

It is essential to follow cooking guidelines when preparing dried kidney beans. You should always boil them vigorously for 10–15 minutes in order to destroy the harmful substances called lectins, which cause a severe food-poisoning reaction of nausea, vomiting and diarrhoea as

COOKING KIDNEY BEANS
Most types of beans, with the exception of aduki beans and mung beans, require soaking for 5–6 hours or overnight and then boiling rapidly for 10–15 minutes to remove any harmful toxins. This is particularly important for kidney beans, which can cause serious food poisoning if not treated in this way.

1 Wash the beans well, then place in a bowl that allows plenty of room for expansion. Cover with cold water and leave to soak overnight or for 8–12 hours, then drain and rinse.

2 Place the beans in a large pan and cover with fresh cold water. Bring to the boil and boil rapidly for 10–15 minutes, then reduce the heat and simmer for 1–1½ hours, until the beans are tender. Drain and serve.

THE MANTECA BEAN
The American space programme NASA is involved in research into flatulence-free foods. One such food is the manteca bean, also known as the Jersey yellow bean, discovered in Chile by British scientist Dr Colin Leakey. This small, yellow bean is flatulence-free and easy to digest. The bean is now being grown both in Cambridgeshire, England, and the Channel Islands, and should become more widely available.

they damage the cell lining of the gut. Canned kidney beans have already been cooked, so they can be used safely from the can and either heated up or served cold.

SOYA BEANS

These small, oval beans vary in colour from creamy-yellow through brown to black. In China, they are known as 'meat of the earth' and were once considered sacred. Soya beans are the most nutritious of all the beans, being rich in high-quality protein. This wonder-pulse contains all of the essential amino acids that cannot be synthesized by the body but are vital for the renewal of cells and tissues. They are high in insoluble fibre, ensuring regular bowel movements, while the soluble fibre and the soya phytoestrogens associated with the protein have been found to lower blood cholesterol, thereby reducing the risk of heart disease and stroke. They are a good source of vegetarian omega-3 and a-linolenic acid, which is an important source if you do not include fish in your diet.

The phytoestrogen content has also been associated with reducing the symptoms of the menopause, but this effect has not been scientifically proven. The combination of many

USING CANNED BEANS

Canned beans are convenient store-cupboard standbys, as they don't require soaking or lengthy cooking. Choose canned beans that do not have added sugar or salt, and rinse well and drain before use. The canning process reduces the levels of vitamins and minerals, but canned beans still contain reputable amounts. Canned beans tend to be softer than cooked, dried beans, so they are easy to mash, which makes them good for pâtés, stuffings, croquettes and rissoles, but they can also be used to make quick salads. They can, in fact, be used for any dish that calls for cooked, dried beans: a drained 425g/15oz can is roughly the equivalent of 150g/5oz/¾ cup dried beans. Firmer canned beans, such as kidney beans, can be added to stews and re-cooked, but softer beans such as flageolet should be merely heated through.

BEAN TIPS

• If you are short of time, the long soaking process can be speeded up. First, cook the beans in boiling water for 2 minutes, then remove the pan from the heat. Cover and leave for about 2 hours. Drain, rinse and cover with plenty of fresh cold water before cooking.
• Cooking beans in a pressure cooker will reduce the cooking time by around three-quarters.
• Do not add salt to beans while they are cooking, as this will cause them to toughen. Cook the beans first, then season with salt and pepper. Acidic foods such as tomatoes, lemons or vinegar will also toughen beans, so only add these ingredients once the beans are soft.

excellent nutritional factors in the soya bean makes this food of great value and interest to us. It is also processed into other foods that retain these benefits and make it a more versatile, bioavailable food. Soya beans are extremely dense and need to be soaked for 12 hours before cooking or, to save time, can be cooked in a pressure cooker in larger batches and then frozen. They combine well with robust ingredients such as garlic, herbs and spices, and they make a healthy addition to soups, casseroles, bakes and salads.

The Goodness of Soya

The American FDA among others have approved a heart-health claim stating that 25g/1oz of soya protein per day, as part of a diet low in saturated fat and cholesterol, may reduce the risk of heart disease.

Green Soya Beans

These differ from the light creamy brown variety only in age. These are the young beans, picked before they fully ripen to become mature

Above: Phytonutrient-rich soya beans can be eaten whole in their pods.

soya beans. Traditionally in Japan the whole pod is picked, boiled and then served with salt. This dish is known as 'edamame' and is a popular snack food. More recently, these green soya beans, which are sometimes known as edamame beans, have become available as a fresh or frozen bean. They can be eaten as an alternative to other green vegetables such as peas or broad beans. They are highly nutritious and are an excellent source of high-quality protein, containing all of the essential amino acids; however, unfortunately, they do not contain many vegetarian omega-3 fats, unlike their older soya bean siblings. They do enjoy the same advantage of containing the isoflavones group of phytonutrients, which are responsible for the highly researched area of cholesterol reduction and the subsequent benefits to heart health. Thus, the inclusion of these little green beans can significantly contribute to your diet if you are trying to reduce cholesterol levels.

Green soya beans are quite firm and so will require boiling for a little longer than other beans or peas. Their firmness, however, makes them perfect for including in salads and cold dishes as they do not turn at all mushy. They even taste delicious on their own, dressed simply with a little vinaigrette.

QUICK COOKING AND SERVING IDEAS FOR PULSES

• To flavour beans, add an onion, garlic, herbs or spices before cooking. Remove whole flavourings before serving.

• Dress cooked beans with extra virgin olive oil, lemon juice, crushed garlic, diced tomato and fresh basil.

• Mash cooked beans with olive oil, garlic and coriander (cilantro), and pile on to toasted bread. Top with a poached egg.

• Spoon spicy, red lentil dhal and some crisp, fried onions on top of a warm tortilla, then roll it up and eat immediately.

• Mix cooked chickpeas with spring onions (scallions), olives and chopped parsley, then drizzle over olive oil and lemon juice.

• Roast cooked chickpeas, which have been drizzled with olive oil and garlic, for 20 minutes at 200°C/400°F/Gas 6, then toss in a little ground cumin and sprinkle with chilli flakes. Serve with chunks of feta cheese and wam naan bread.

• Gently fry cooked red kidney beans in olive oil with chopped onion, chilli, garlic and fresh coriander (cilantro) leaves.

SOYA BEAN PRODUCTS

The soya bean is the most nutritious of all the beans and these credentials are mostly preserved when the bean is used to make other products that can be used in cooking. Examples of these products include tofu, tempeh, textured vegetable protein, flour, miso and a variety of sauces. Some of these are produced by a process of fermenting the soya beans, which actually enhances the phytonutrient bioavailability. All of these products do still contain soya protein, which importantly has the soya isoflavones associated with them. This has the approval of the FDA and other similar organizations to carry the health claim: '25g of soya protein per day, as part of a diet low in saturated fat and cholesterol may reduce the risk of heart disease'. Vegetarian omega-3 fats are still found in soya products – the amount varies according to the fat content of the food.

Tofu

Also known as beancurd, tofu is made in a similar way to soft cheese. The beans are boiled, mashed and sieved (strained) to make soya 'milk', and the 'milk' is then curdled using a

Below: Firm tofu provides good amounts of vegetarian omega-3 fats.

coagulant. The resulting curds are drained and pressed to make tofu, and there are several different types to choose from. All varieties of fresh tofu can be stored in the refrigerator for up to one week.

Firm Tofu

This type of tofu is sold in blocks and can be cubed or sliced and used in vegetable stir-fries, kebabs, salads, soups and casseroles. Alternatively, firm tofu can be mashed and used in bakes and burgers. Tofu is a good source of vegetarian omega-3 fats, and sometimes calcium sulphate is used as a firming agent, which makes it a good source of calcium. The bland flavour of firm tofu is improved by marinating, because its porous texture readily absorbs flavours and seasonings. Firm tofu should be kept covered in water, which must be changed regularly. Freezing tofu is not recommended because it alters the texture.

Silken Tofu

Soft with a silky, smooth texture, this type of tofu is ideal for use in sauces, dressings, dips and soups. It is a useful dairy-free alternative to cream, soft cheese or yogurt, and

Below: Silken tofu has fewer omega-3 fats than firm, but has plenty of protein.

TOFU FRUIT FOOL

1 Place a packet of silken tofu in the bowl of a food processor. Add some soft fruit or berries – for example, strawberries, raspberries or blackberries.

2 Process the mixture to form a smooth purée, then sweeten to taste with a little honey, maple syrup or maize malt syrup.

can be used to make creamy desserts. As it has a lower fat content, it is not as good a source of vegetarian omega-3 fats as firm tofu. Silken tofu is often available in long-life vacuum packs, which do not have to be kept in the refrigerator and have a much longer shelf life.

Other Forms of Tofu

Smoked, marinated and deep-fried tofu are all readily available in health food stores and Asian shops, as well as in some supermarkets. Deep-fried tofu is fairly tasteless, but it has an interesting texture. It puffs up during cooking and underneath the golden, crisp coating the tofu is white and soft, and easily absorbs the flavour of other ingredients. It can be used in much the same way as firm tofu and, as it has been fried in vegetable oil, it is suitable for vegetarian cooking.

Tempeh

This Indonesian speciality is made by fermenting cooked soya beans with a cultured starter forming a soya 'cake'. This concentrated soya product is high in protein, B-vitamins and minerals and retains its level of vegetarian omega-3 fats. It is much more easily digested due to the fermentation process, and is a complete protein source containing all the essential amino acids we need to maintain health. Many consider it to be an excellent alternative to meat, as the firmer texture of tempeh means that it can be used in pies and casseroles. Tempeh is similar to tofu but has a nuttier, more savoury flavour. It can be used in the same way as firm tofu and also benefits from marinating. Tempeh is available from health food stores. Chilled tempeh can be stored in the

Below: Textured vegetable protein (TVP) is a versatile meat replacement.

refrigerator for up to a week. Frozen tempeh can be left in the freezer for one month; defrost before use.

TVP
Textured vegetable protein, or TVP as it is commonly referred to is a useful meat replacement usually bought in mince form or as dry chunks. Made from processed soya beans, TVP is very versatile and readily absorbs the strong flavours of ingredients such as herbs, spices and vegetable stock. It is very high in protein and low in fat and sodium; however, it is not a good source of vegetarian omega-3 fats as it is virtually fat-free. TVP is inexpensive and is a convenient store-cupboard item. It does need to be rehydrated in boiling water or vegetable stock, and can be used in stews and curries, or as a filling for pies.

Miso
This thick paste is made from a mixture of cooked soya beans, rice, wheat or barley, salt and water which is then left to ferment for up to three years. This concentrated soya product has a good nutrient profile containing the all-important soya isoflavones as well as good levels of B vitamins and minerals. However, it is very high in sodium and so should be used sparingly. It is reputed that, in the past, miso has helped people with radiation sickness and may have some cancer-reducing properties, but this has not been conclusively proven. Miso is primarily used as a flavouring to add a savoury flavour to soups, stocks, stir-fries and noodle dishes, and is a staple food in Asia. There are three main types: kome, or hite miso, is the lightest and sweetest; medium-strength mugi miso, which has a mellow flavour and is preferred for everyday use; and hacho miso, which is a dark chocolate colour, and has a thick texture and a strong flavour. Miso can be stored for several months, but should be kept in the refrigerator once it has been opened.

Soya Milk and Soya Milk Produce
Soya milk and soya milk products are the most widely used alternatives to milk and dairy products. Made from pulverized soya beans, soya milk is suitable for both cooking and drinking and is used to make cheese, yogurt and cream. Soya milk is very similar in nutritional value to cow's milk, and is an excellent source of protein, iron, magnesium, phosphorus and vitamin E. Unlike cow's milk, however, it is also a good source of soya isoflavones. The 'milk' is low in calories and contains no cholesterol. The calcium naturally present in the soya milk is largely bio-unavailable, bound up by phytates; however, many soya milks are fortified with calcium to compensate for this. Soya milk is often used as a milk alternative, especially among sufferers of lactose intolerance. Soya cream is made from a higher proportion of beans than that in soya milk, which gives it a richer flavour and thicker texture. It has a similar consistency to single cream and can be used in the same ways. Most soya milks and creams are sold in long-life cartons, so they do not require refrigeration until opened. Try to buy unsweetened soya milk if possible.

Below: Soya milk is often fortified with calcium and vitamin D.

Nuts

With the exception of peanuts, nuts are the storage fruits of trees and are therefore full of nutrients and oils, being particularly rich in B vitamins, vitamin E, potassium, magnesium, calcium, phosphorus and iron. Nuts are also a good source of fibre and phytosterols, and most contain mainly unsaturated fat. There is mounting evidence that the regular consumption of nuts (25g/1oz, five times or more a week) is associated with a reduced risk of cardiovascular disease due to the effect on 'bad' LDL cholesterol, and Type II diabetes due to their low glycaemic index. Nuts are particularly important for vegetarians and vegans because of their abundance of nutrients, although they contain a hefty number of calories. The quality and availability of fresh nuts can vary with the seasons, although most types are sold dried, either whole or prepared ready for use. Always buy nuts in small quantities from a shop with a high turnover of stock, because if kept for too long, they can turn rancid. Nuts in their shells should feel heavy for their size. Store nuts in airtight containers in a cool, dark

Below: Eating a handful of mixed nuts is an ideal nutritious snack.

NUT ALLERGY
Any food has the potential to cause an allergic reaction, but peanuts, as well as walnuts, Brazil nuts, hazelnuts and almonds are also known to be allergens. In cases of extreme allergy, nuts can trigger a life-threatening reaction known as anaphylaxis. Symptoms include facial swelling, shortness of breath, dizziness and loss of consciousness, so it is essential that sufferers take every precaution to avoid nuts.

place or in the refrigerator and they should maintain their freshness for at least three months.

Almonds
There are two types of almonds, sweet and bitter. Sweet almonds are not actually sweetened but are so called as a way of differentiating them from bitter almonds, which are used to make essences and oil. Bitter almonds should never be eaten raw as they contain a poisonous acid. Almonds are a very good source of fibre, phytosterols and unsaturated fat and, as well as being a good

Above: Almonds provide an excellent source of calcium.

source of B vitamins, are packed with all of the essential minerals, especially manganese, magnesium and copper. Studies have shown that eating almonds regularly can increase 'good' HDL cholesterol and reduce 'bad' LDL cholesterol, and therefore may reduce heart-disease risk. Ground almonds can be used as a substitute for part of the flour content of cake and biscuit (cookie) recipes, and because they have almost no carbohydrate content, will reduce the glycaemic index and release energy more slowly. Sweet almonds are widely available as ground, flaked, toasted flaked, blanched (skins off), slithers and whole forms. Each form has its own traditional use, from making marzipan with ground almonds to topping cakes and biscuits with flaked almonds.

Brazil Nuts
These are, in fact, seeds, and are grown mainly in the Amazon regions of Brazil and other neighbouring countries. Between 12 and 20 Brazil nuts grow, packed snugly together in a large brown husk, hence their three-cornered wedge shape. They have a very high fat content at around 70 per cent, contain the largest amount of saturated fat of all of the nuts,

MAKING NUT BUTTER
Shop-bought nut butters often contain unwanted hydrogenated oil and can be loaded with sugar. To avoid additives, make your own butter using a combination of peanuts, hazelnuts and cashew nuts.

1 Place 75g/3oz/½ cup shelled nuts in a food processor or blender and process until finely and evenly ground.

2 Pour 15–30ml/1–2 tbsp of sunflower oil into the processor or blender and process to a coarse paste. Store in an airtight jar.

and will go rancid very quickly. They have an extraordinarily high level of selenium, one of the highest levels known in foods. Selenium is not just an essential mineral but a powerful antioxidant that has been studied extensively in the area of cancer prevention. Selenium is involved in many metabolic processes including eliminating potentially damaging free radicals, which is especially significant in areas such as the protection of developing sperm in men. Selenium is also involved in ensuring that the

Above: Brazil nuts are one of the best known sources of selenium.

immune system functions properly, and may also help to prevent cancer, because populations with low selenium intake have higher cancer death rates for diseases such as prostate cancer. More evidence is needed, however, to prove any connection with a higher selenium consumption and the prevention of cancer. Brazil nuts have quite an earthy flavour and work well in baked items such as cookies, but can also be used to make pesto or nut butters.

Chestnuts
Not to be confused with the horse chestnut (conker) variety, the sweet chestnut is edible and surprisingly, unlike other nuts, chestnuts are very low in fat (about 1 per cent). Sweet chestnuts are an autumnal crop and it is not uncommon to see people foraging for these. Out of season, chestnuts can be bought dried, canned or puréed. Raw chestnuts are not recommended as they are not only unpleasant to eat but also contain tannic acid, which inhibits the absorption of iron. However, antioxidant-rich chestnuts taste excellent when roasted, which complements their soft, floury texture. Try adding whole chestnuts to winter stews, soups, stuffings or pies, or even cakes. Chestnuts are preserved in syrup to make the famous marrons glacé.

Above: Surprisingly, chestnuts contain only 1 per cent fat.

Peanuts
Not strictly a nut, but a member of the pulse family, peanuts bury themselves just below the earth after flowering – hence their alternative name, groundnuts. Peanuts are particularly high in fat but it is mainly of the monounsaturated and

ROASTING AND SKINNING NUTS
The flavour of most nuts, particularly hazelnuts and peanuts, is improved by roasting. It also enables the thin outer skin to be removed more easily.

1 Place the nuts in a single layer on a baking sheet. Bake at 180°C/350°F/Gas 4 for 10–20 minutes, or until the skins begin to split and the nuts are golden.

2 Transfer the nuts to a dish towel and rub to loosen and remove the skins.

polyunsaturated types. They are a good source of vitamin E and the B vitamins, especially niacin and folate, and are an excellent source of all of the essential minerals. Their vitamin E content, along with polyphenols such as coumaric acid, contributes to an excellent antioxidant profile, rivalling that of many fruits and vegetables. More recently, it has been discovered that peanuts also contain a high concentration of phytosterols, notably resveratrol. This compound has been shown in animal studies to reduce both cancer and cardiovascular disease risk, and may have an impact on the ageing of the body; however, research in humans is inconclusive at the moment. Buy unsalted peanuts for use in cooking as salted peanuts will be much higher in sodium, which could counteract any potential heart-health benefits. Peanuts are good in both sweet and savoury dishes, and can be made into sauces or put into stews.

Pistachio Nuts
Incredibly moreish when served as a snack, pistachio nuts have pale green flesh and thin, reddish-purple skin. Sold shelled or in a split shell, these mild nuts are often used chopped as a colourful garnish or sprinkled over both sweet and savoury foods. As with most nuts they are high in fat;

Below: Protein-packed peanuts make a handy on-the-go snack.

Above: Pistachio nuts are high in the antioxidant vitamin E.

however, they also have high levels of antioxidants such as lutein, beta-carotene and tocopherol (vitamin E). This antioxidant content has caught the eye of researchers who are investigating the potential for pistachios to help reduce the 'bad' LDL cholesterol and therefore reduce the risk of heart disease.

Check before buying pistachio nuts for cooking, as they are often sold salted, which would potentially negate any positive benefits. Traditionally used in many sweet dishes, especially those of Arabic origin, pistachios have a fabulous green colour which is unusual in sweet dishes. Pistachios can also be used in savoury dishes such as

Below: Walnuts have the highest vegetable omega-3 levels of all nuts.

stuffing and on salads, ground up and sprinkled on dishes as a garnish or just eaten as a snack.

Walnuts
Most walnuts are imported from France, Italy and California, but they are also grown in the Middle East, Britain and China. They are the only nut with significant quantities of vegetarian omega-3 and are also high in antioxidants. These two factors are thought to contribute to the cardio-protective properties of walnuts; they have been shown to reduce inflammation of arteries and reduce the oxidative stress on the artery wall, leading to less tissue damage. Walnuts also contain a high proportion of arginine, an amino acid that the body uses to produce chemicals that keep blood vessels flexible, also contributing to heart health. Walnuts have also been studied for their effects on Alzheimer's disease, where walnut extracts have been shown to reduce the presence of 'plaques' in the brains of sufferers, and this may delay the onset of the disease. Walnuts are an excellent source of folate, thiamin and vitamin B_6 as well as containing an excellent range of minerals in significant quantities. Dried walnuts have a delicious bittersweet flavour, and can be bought shelled, chopped or ground. They can be used to make excellent cakes and biscuits (cookies) as well as rich pie fillings, but are also good added to savoury dishes such as stir-fries and salads – the classic Waldorf salad mixes whole kernels with celery and apples in a mayonnaise dressing.

Cocoa
The cocoa bean originates from the Amazon basin, where the indigenous populations have consumed cocoa for many hundreds of years, recognizing its benefits to health. In more recent years, it has been revealed that cocoa has high levels of antioxidants as well as containing

HOW MUCH COCOA IS IN CHOCOLATE?

Chocolate products should indicate on their labels the percentage of cocoa solids that they contain. The higher the percentage, the more cocoa the product contains and the darker and more bitter the chocolate.

Percentages greater than 75 per cent are usually termed 'continental chocolate' and are excellent for baking and melting for sauces or toppings. Products at 45 per cent or less are usually cheaper milk chocolate products and are best for eating, as they are not strong enough to impart a good chocolate flavour in recipes. Chocolate with up to 90 per cent cocoa solids is available, which is very strong and bitter.

some very interesting amine compounds and tryptophan. These compounds are metabolized into neurotransmitters, which may be the reason why eating chocolate makes you feel good, or why it is a common comfort food, as they may have anti-depressant effects. Cocoa is also a good source of polyphenols similar to those found in red wine, and has been shown to reduce the 'bad' LDL cholesterol and raise the 'good' HDL cholesterol in the body. This, along with high levels of antioxidant activity, could contribute to a reduced cardiovascular risk. It is important to note, however, that the studies have been carried out on cocoa, not

Above: Add pure cocoa powder to recipes to boost antioxidant power.

chocolate, and so to get the most potential benefit, it is best to use a high cocoa solids product which is far more bitter than milk chocolate. Eating too much chocolate could lead to excess energy intake and therefore obesity.

Coconuts

These versatile nuts grow all over the tropics. Their white dense meat, or flesh, is made into desiccated coconut, blocks of creamed coconut and a thick and creamy milk.

Coconut flesh is over 50 per cent fat, most of which is saturated. It is the nature of this saturated fat that has been the subject of much interest and research. The saturated fat molecules in coconut are smaller than in most other saturated fats, and are known as medium chain triglycerides, or MCT's for short. These fats are absorbed into the body without having to go through the metabolism and breakdown that the larger saturated fat molecules do. This characteristic has led researchers to try to understand their impact on fat metabolism in the body. They have suggested that they may even help mobilize existing fat stores for energy and therefore actually lead to weight loss, which could help to combat the rise of obesity in the developed world. When buying a coconut, make sure that there is no sign of mould or a rancid smell. Give it a

Above: Coconut fat is more easily metabolized than most other fats.

shake – it should be full of liquid. Keep coconut milk in the refrigerator or freezer once opened. Store desiccated coconut in an airtight container, but don't store it for too long as its high fat content means that it is prone to rancidity.

COCONUT MILK

Available in cans or long-life cartons, coconut milk or cream is also easy to make at home: pour 225g/8oz/2⅔ cups desiccated coconut into a food processor, add 450ml/¾ pint/ scant 2 cups boiling water and process for 30 seconds. Leave to cool slightly. Pour into a sieve (strainer) lined with muslin (cheesecloth) and placed over a bowl. Gather the ends of the cloth. Twist the cloth to extract the liquid, then discard the spent coconut. Store the coconut milk in the refrigerator for 1–2 days, or freeze.

Seeds

They may be very small, but seeds are nutritional powerhouses, packed with vitamins and minerals, as well as beneficial oils and protein. They can be used in a huge array of sweet and savoury dishes, and will add an instant, healthy boost, pleasant crunch and nutty flavour when added to rice and pasta dishes, salads, stir-fries, soups and yogurt. All seeds are high in polyunsaturated fat, but being a healthier fat it means that they can go rancid more quickly, so keep in an airtight container in a cool dark place.

Sunflower Seeds

These are the seeds of the sunflower, a symbol of summer, and an important commercial crop throughout the world. The impressive, golden-yellow flowers are grown mainly for their seeds, which are then either processed for food use or pressed for their oil, which contains essential omega-6 fatty acids. The seeds are particularly rich in vitamin E and thiamin, and are a good source of B vitamins and the minerals manganese, copper, magnesium and selenium. These all contribute to sunflower seeds having a good level of antioxidant activity and, along with the phytosterols present, they

can have a positive influence on cholesterol levels, which may lead to improved heart health. Sunflower seeds are also a good source of tryptophan, an essential amino acid required by the body to make, among other things, serotonin and melatonin. These are important chemicals in the brain that affect how we control our mood and metabolism. The pale-green, tear-drop-shaped seeds have a semi-crunchy texture and an oily taste that is much improved by dry-roasting or toasting. Sprinkle sunflower seeds over salads, rice pilaffs and couscous, or use in bread dough, muffins, casseroles and baked dishes.

Pumpkin Seeds

Richer in iron than any other seed and an excellent source of manganese, magnesium and phosphorus, pumpkin seeds make a nutritious snack eaten on their own. They also contain the essential omega-6 and omega-3 fats, both important for heart health. Tryptophan is found in high levels, and this is essential for the production of serotonin and melatonin, which control mood and influence our sleep patterns.

Below: Sweet, nutty pumpkin seeds contain high amounts of tryptophan.

Below: A sprinkling of seeds adds an extra nutritional boost to smoothies.

ROASTING SEEDS

The flavour of seeds is much improved by 'roasting' them in a dry frying pan. Black poppy seeds won't turn golden brown, so watch them carefully to make sure that they don't scorch.

1 Spread out a spoonful or two of seeds in a thin layer in a large, non-stick frying pan, and heat them gently.

2 Cook over a medium heat for 2–3 minutes, tossing the seeds frequently, until they all turn golden brown.

In traditional medicine such as that of the Native Americans, pumpkin seeds were used to cure problems of the urinary tract. It is still not known how this may work, but clinical studies have given some credence to this attribute. This is also the case with pumpkins seeds' reputed ability to kill off intestinal parasites such as tapeworm. One particular area of ongoing research has focused on the steroid content of pumpkin seeds and their role in treating conditions such as prostate disorders. Pumpkin seeds are delicious lightly toasted, tossed in a little toasted sesame seed oil or soy sauce, or stirred into salads.

Flax seeds

Also known as linseeds, these small golden seeds are packed full of goodness. They are one of the best vegetarian sources of omega-3 fats.

Above: Crushing hemp seeds makes the nutrients more bioavailable to us.

Above: Flax seeds offer one of the best sources of vegetarian omega-3 fats.

Above: Heart-healthy psyllium is a very concentrated source of fibre.

They are very high in fibre and contain lignan, a type of phytoestrogen, which is converted by bacteria in the lower intestine into active compounds. These oestrogen-like compounds play an important role in cell signalling, which affects the way that the body controls areas such as bone density, hormonal processes and reproductive processes. Eating foods rich in lignans is consistently associated with a lower incidence of heart disease, and it is thought that it is the collective effect of all of the cardioprotective nutrients, rather than one in particular, that is responsible. Flax seeds have a very resistant outer hull, so in order to gain the most benefit, use ground flax seed to ensure that the body can absorb the goodness, otherwise the seeds will pass through it unaffected. Flax seeds have a pleasant nutty taste but, due to their high oil content, must be stored in a sealed container, preferably in the refrigerator, to prevent the oil from going rancid.

Hemp Seeds
These small round seeds have quite a hard shell. They can be bought whole or ground into a meal, the latter being more favourable as the shell can be difficult to eat. Their nutty flavour can be enhanced by roasting them carefully in a dry frying pan, and if you then grind them up, they can make a tasty topping or crust for

almost anything sweet or savoury. Hemp seeds contain an excellent array of amino acids, making them one of the most complete vegetarian sources of protein. The seed also contains all of the essential fatty acids required to maintain health, including vegetarian omega 3.

Psyllium
It is the seed husk of psyllium that is of most interest, as this is the highly fibrous part that contains the active components. The fibre is soluble in water and is able to absorb large quantities, making it useful for counteracting diarrhoea or helping with constipation. Indeed, it is found as the base ingredient in many over-the-counter-preparations. There have also been studies showing that psyllium can reduce total cholesterol, including 'bad' LDL cholesterol in the blood, thus helping to reduce the risk of heart disease. In the US, the FDA has approved a health claim to this effect when psyllium is used as part of a diet low in saturated fat and cholesterol, and this now appears on many 'fortified' products such as breakfast cereals. It is available in powdered form, which makes it easier to add to foods; however, due to its massive water-absorption capacity, it must be eaten with liquids or extra liquid must be added to the recipe. In a similar way to oats, psyllium can also slow energy release from foods

and not cause insulin spikes. This can help diabetics to improve control of the disease, but psyllium must be taken with the advice of a medical professional due to its laxative effects.

> **QUICK IDEAS FOR SEEDS**
> • Sprinkle over breads, cakes and biscuits (cookies) just before baking.
> • Combine with dried or fresh fruit, chopped nuts and natural yogurt to make a delicious and nutritious breakfast.
> • Add to flapjacks, wholemeal scones or pastry for a nutty taste.
> • Add a spoonful of your favourite seeds to rissoles, casseroles or vegetable burgers.
> • Mix with rolled oats, flour, butter or margarine, and sugar to make a sweet crumble topping. To make a savoury topping, omit the sugar and combine with chopped fresh or dried herbs.
> • Use sunflower or pumpkin seeds in place of pine nuts to make pesto.
> • Sprinkle seeds over a mixed green salad.
> • Add an instant nutritional boost to vegetable stir-fries or noodle dishes, by sprinkling a handful of seeds over the top before serving.

Spices

Highly revered for thousands of years, spices – the seeds, fruit, pods, bark and buds of plants – have been valuable commodities, often traded as a currency. In addition to their ability to add flavour and interest to the most unassuming of ingredients, the evocative aroma of spices stimulates the appetite. Today spices are still prized for their reputed medicinal properties and culinary uses, and they play a vital role in creating healthy and appetizing cooking. Their health benefits are often attributed to the intense aromatic, volatile oils they contain. Similarly to herbs, these compounds have very high antioxidant activity, and spices have some of the highest recorded ORAC scores on record. Buy spices in small quantities from a shop with a regular turnover of stock. Aroma is the best indication of freshness, as this diminishes when the spice is stale. Store in airtight jars in a cool place away from direct light.

Ginger

This spice is probably one of the oldest and most popular herbal medicines, being cited in many remedies for nausea, colic and intestinal cramps. Ginger contains volatile phenols that give it its

---

PREPARING FRESH GINGER

1 Fresh root ginger is most easily peeled using a vegetable peeler or a small, sharp paring knife.

3 Grate ginger finely – special graters are available, but a box grater will do the job equally well.

2 Chop ginger using a sharp knife to the size specified in the recipe.

4 Freshly grated ginger can be squeezed to release the juice.

---

characteristic scent and flavour and contribute toward its phytonutrient activity. Gingerol is the active volatile involved in helping to prevent nausea. It is best to eat fresh ginger for nausea, as it is converted to zingerone and shogaol when cooked, which are less effective against nausea. These compounds are more useful for treating diarrhoea. Gingerol has also been shown to have some anti-inflammatory activity. The fresh root, which is spicy, peppery and fragrant, is good in both sweet and savoury dishes, adding a hot, yet refreshing, flavour to marinades, stir-fries, soups, and fresh vegetables. It also adds warmth to poached fruit, pastries and cakes. Ground ginger is the usual choice for flavouring cakes, cookies and other baked goods, but finely grated fresh ginger can also be used and is

equally good. Pink pickled ginger is finely sliced ginger that has been pickled in sugar and vinegar and is served as an accompaniment to Japanese food.

Below: The gingerol in fresh ginger helps to alleviate nausea.

GINGER TEA
This soothing tea is comforting for those suffering from nausea, colds, flu and stomach upsets.

1 To make ginger tea, roughly chop a 2.5cm/1in piece of fresh root ginger. Place in a cup and pour in boiling water.

2 Cover and leave for 7–10 minutes. Strain or drink as it is – the ginger will stay in the bottom of the cup.

Stem ginger is preserved in a thick sugar syrup and sold in jars. This sweet ginger can be chopped and used in desserts, or added to cake mixtures, steamed puddings, scones, shortbread and muffins. Fresh root ginger should look firm, thin-skinned and unblemished. Avoid withered, woody-looking roots, as these are likely to be dry and fibrous. Store in the refrigerator or freeze. Ground ginger should smell aromatic; keep in a cool, dark place.

Cardamom

Belonging to the ginger family, cardamom is often used in Middle Eastern and Indian cooking. It contains a volatile oil called cineole, which has the ability to help relieve congestion in the chest and alleviate cold symptoms. Cardamom also contains many other volatile oils, which contribute to its distinctive aroma and flavour and has been used for many years, chewed whole, to freshen the breath and calm indigestion. Cardamom is best bought whole in its pod, as it soon loses its aromatic flavour when ground. The pod can be used whole, slightly crushed, or for a more intense flavour, the seeds can be ground. This flavourful spice tastes superb in both sweet and savoury dishes. It can be infused in milk used

Below: The cineole in cardamom may help to reduce cold symptoms.

Above: Cinnamon helps to maintain healthy blood sugar levels.

to flavour rice pudding or ice cream, and is often added to curries and other Indian dishes.

Cinnamon

This warm, comforting spice is available in sticks (quills) and in ground form. As the bark is difficult to grind, it is useful to keep both forms in the store cupboard. Cinnamon sticks can enhance both sweet and savoury dishes and are widely used to flavour pilaffs, curries, and dried fruit compotes, but remember to remove before serving. Ground cinnamon adds a pleasing fragrance to cakes, cookies and fruit. Recently evidence has emerged that cinnamon may help people with Type II diabetes. The active components may help the insulin to metabolize sugar more efficiently and keep the blood sugar levels low and safe. It also has some effect on blood fats, reducing the 'bad' LDL cholesterol, and while it has not been shown to increase 'good' HDL cholesterol, the positive effect on the overall ratio is beneficial to diabetics.

Cumin

Extensively used in Indian curries, cumin is also a familiar component of Mexican, North African and Middle

Above: Dry-fry cumin seeds before crushing to release the essential oils.

Eastern cooking. The seeds have a robust aroma and slightly bitter taste, which is tempered by dry-roasting. Black cumin seeds, which are also known as nigella, are milder and sweeter, and are reputed to have

GRINDING SPICES

Whole spices ground by hand provide the best flavour and aroma. Grind as you need them and do not be tempted to grind too much, as they tend to lose their potency and flavour. Some spices such as mace, fenugreek, cloves, turmeric and cinnamon are difficult to grind at home and are better bought ready-ground. Grind whole spices in a mortar using a pestle – or use an electric coffee grinder if you prefer.

Above: Grated nutmeg enriches the flavour of dishes and aids digestion.

Above: The citral in lemongrass may help to combat cancerous cells.

Above: Mustard stimulates circulation and rids the body of harmful toxins.

anti-inflammatory properties. This is thought to be due to a type of quinone found only in the seed, and has been associated with alleviating joint pain in arthritis.

The flavonoids in cumin do contribute to its antioxidant activity and may have anti-cancer properties. Traditionally, cumin preparations have been used to stimulate digestion and production of bile, helping to alleviate flatulence and indigestion. Ground cumin can be harsh, so it is best to buy the whole seeds and grind them just before use to ensure a fresh flavour. Cumin is good in tomato- or grain-based dishes, and its digestive properties mean that it is also ideal for adding to with beans.

Nutmeg and Mace
When it is picked, the nutmeg seed is surrounded by a lacy membrane called mace. Both are dried and used as spices. Nutmeg and mace taste similar, and their warm, sweet flavour enlivens white sauces, cheese-based dishes and vegetables, as well as custards, cakes and biscuits (cookies). Freshly grated nutmeg is far superior to the ready-ground variety, which loses its flavour and aroma with time. Although it is a hallucinogen if eaten in excess, when consumed in the small quantities that are needed in recipes, nutmeg can improve both appetite and digestion.

Lemon Grass
This long, fibrous stalk has a fragrant citrus aroma and flavour when cut and is a familiar part of South-east Asian and particularly Thai cooking, where it is used in coconut-flavoured curries. Lemon grass contains citral, which gives it its characteristic lemon scent. Citral also shows powerful antioxidant activity and has been shown in research to prevent and reduce cell damage by scavenging free-radicals. This property could have a role in cancer treatments of

PREPARING LEMON GRASS
Remove the tough, woody outer layers, trim the root, then cut off the lower 5cm/2in and slice into thin rounds, or pound in a mortar using a pestle. Bottled, chopped lemon grass and lemon grass purée are also available.

the future. Citral also contains antiseptic, anti-fungal, anti-microbial and anti-inflammatory properties.

Mustard
This spice comes from the fabulous brassica family, and is therefore cruciferous, which accounts for its beneficial value to us. There are three different types of mustard seed, white, brown, and black, which is the most pungent.

The strength of the mustard flavour is totally dependent on how the seed is prepared. Seeds soaked in cold water prior to processing produce the strongest mustards. The characteristic English mustard is made from white and brown seeds and is very strong. Dijon mustard is made from brown and black seeds and is strong. American-style mustard is usually made with a lower level of mustard, is often coloured with turmeric and paprika, and tastes very mild.

The flavour and aroma is only apparent when the seeds are crushed or mixed with liquid. If fried in a little oil before use, the flavour of the seeds is improved. As the intensity of mustard diminishes with both time and cooking; it is best added to dishes toward the end of cooking, or just before the dish is served. Like many hot spices, mustard is traditionally used as a stimulant, cleansing the body of toxins and helping to ward off colds and flu.

Fenugreek

This spice, also known as methi, is commonly used in commercial curry powders, along with cumin and coriander. On its own, however, fenugreek should be used in moderation because its bittersweet flavour, which is mellowed by dry-frying, can be quite overpowering. The seeds contain many active agents such as volatile oils which have been reported to have interesting effects on the body. Fenugreek has traditionally been used to induce childbirth and also to stimulate milk production in breastfeeding women, so pregnant women should be very careful with fenugreek. It has a hard shell and is difficult to grind, but can be sprouted and then makes a good addition to mixed leaf and bean salads, as well as sandwich fillings.

Turmeric

Also a member of the ginger family, turmeric is useful for its yellow colour and earthy, peppery flavour. This intense colour derives from curcumin, a polyphenol which has been the subject of much research in the field of cancer prevention and shows

promising results in the treatment of colo-rectal cancer. Curcumin has also been shown to prevent the formation of plaques in the brain and therefore could slow the progression of Alzheimer's disease; more research is taking place in this area. Curcumin has anti-inflammatory properties; however, robust scientific studies on inflammatory conditions such as rheumatoid arthritis is inconclusive at the moment. Turmeric is mainly available as a powder and only needs to be used in small amounts, as its flavour and colour are so intense.

Paprika

This spice is made from grinding up dried chilli fruit such as the bell pepper or red chilli. It is a milder relative of cayenne and can be used more liberally, adding flavour as well as heat. Like chillies, paprika is very high in vitamin C and contains similar antioxidants. It also contains the stimulating capsaicins, but levels will vary according to the heat of the paprika. This vibrant spice is a digestive stimulant and has antiseptic properties. It can also improve blood circulation, but take care, because if

eaten in large quantities it may irritate the stomach. The chillies are sometimes dried by smoking, and this gives the smoked paprika variety its distinctive taste and aroma. Paprika is used in many cuisines and adds fabulous colour as well as heat and flavour.

DRY FRYING OR TOASTING SPICES
This process enhances the flavour and aroma of spices and is believed to make them more digestible.

Put the spices in a dry frying pan and cook over a low heat, shaking the pan frequently, for 1 minute, or until the spices release their aroma.

Below: The active oils in fenugreek may help to induce childbirth.

Below: The curcumin in turmeric has powerful anti-inflammatory properties.

Below: Paprika contains vitamin C and stimulating capsaicins.

Oils

There is a wide variety of cooking oils and they are produced from a number of different sources: from cereals such as corn; from fruits such as olives; from nuts such as walnuts, almonds and hazelnuts; and from seeds such as rapeseed, safflower and sunflower. They can be extracted by simple mechanical means such as pressing or crushing, or by further processing, usually heating. Virgin oils, which are obtained from the first cold pressing of the olives, nuts or seeds, are sold unrefined, and have the most characteristic flavour. They are also usually the most expensive, but used sparingly they will go a long way.

OLIVE OIL
Indisputably the king of oils, olive oil varies in flavour and colour, depending on how it is made and where it comes from. Climate, soil, harvesting and pressing all influence the end result – generally, the hotter the climate the more robust the oil. One crucial factor remains the same, though; olive oil is rich in monounsaturated fat, which in many studies has been found to reduce

Below: Cook with oil rather than butter as it is lower in saturated fat.

'bad' LDL cholesterol, and its polyphenol content exerts some anti-inflammatory effects as well as keeping blood vessels elastic. Olive oil also contains vitamin E, a natural antioxidant that can help fight off free radicals, which damage cells in the body. All of these contribute to reducing the risk of heart disease and stroke. Characteristic of the Mediterranean diet, populations that consume olive oil as their main source of fat do show a reduced incidence of cardiovascular disease.

Extra Virgin Olive Oil
This premium olive oil has a superior flavour as it comes from the first cold pressing of the olives and has a low acidity – less than 1 per cent. It contains the highest concentration of polyphenols of all the types of olive oil. Extra virgin olive oil is not recommended for frying, as heat impairs its flavour, but it is good in salad dressings, especially when combined with lighter oils. It is delicious as a sauce on its own, stirred into pasta with chopped garlic and black pepper, or drizzled over steamed vegetables.

ESSENTIAL FATS
We all need some fat in our diet. It keeps us warm, adds flavour to our food, carries essential vitamins A, D, E and K around the body, and provides essential fatty acids, which cannot be produced in the body but are vital for growth and development and may reduce the risk of heart attacks. What is more important is the type and amount of fat that we eat. Some fats are better for us than others, and we should adjust our intake accordingly. It is recommended that fat should make up no more than 35 per cent of our diet.

Above: The lighter in taste an olive oil is, the more it has been refined.

Virgin Olive Oil
Also a pure first-pressed oil, this has a slightly higher level of acidity than extra virgin olive oil, and can be used in much the same way.

Pure Olive Oil
Refined and blended to remove impurities, this type of olive oil has a much lighter flavour than virgin or extra virgin olive oil and is suitable for all types of cooking. It can be used for shallow-frying.

Rapeseed Oil
Also known as canola oil in North America, this is one of the most widely used oils in the world although you may not be aware of it. Many years ago there was a problem with rapeseed oil, where a high level of erucic acid caused an issue. This has since been eliminated and in order to lose the negative associations, the name was not used and rapeseed oil came under the umbrella term 'vegetable oil'. Most vegetable oil labels have the yellow flower of oil seed rape and this is how to best identify it. In a similar way to hemp and flaxseed oils, rapeseed oil also has both essential

fatty acids; omega-6 and omega-3 types are present in favourable ratios. It is this ratio that enables rapeseed oil to be included in many commercially produced spreads which are marketed as being an important part of eating a heart-healthy diet, as they reduce the amount of saturated fats we eat and increase the amount of polyunsaturated fats in our diet.

SPECIALITY OILS
As well as the light, all-purpose oils that are used for everyday cooking, there are several richly flavoured oils that are used in small quantities, often as a flavouring ingredient in salad dressings and marinades, rather than for cooking.

Flax Seed Oil
The oil of the flax seed is sometimes more commonly known as linseed oil for wood sealing; however, the food-grade oil is a cold-pressed oil which

---

QUICK IDEAS FOR MARINADES
• Mix olive oil with chopped fresh herbs such as parsley, chives, oregano, chervil and basil. Add a splash or two of lemon juice and season with salt and pepper.
• Combine groundnut (peanut) oil, toasted sesame oil, dark soy sauce, sweet sherry, rice vinegar and crushed garlic. Use as a marinade for tofu or tempeh.

• Mix together olive oil, lemon juice, sherry, honey and crushed garlic, and use as a marinade for vegetable and halloumi kebabs.

---

has not been subjected to harsh solvent extraction processes. The oil no longer contains the lignans or the fibre of the original seed but does still have the vegetarian omega-3 fat alpha-linolenic acid. Flaxseed oil is one of the richest sources of alpha-linolenic acid and contains approximately 50 per cent omega-3 fat. Alpha-linolenic acid undergoes a small degree of conversion to the more bioavailable long-chain omega-3 fats in the body. These have been associated with many health benefits such as reducing inflammation, assisting brain development and function, and also reducing heart disease risk. As for the flax seed, the oil is prone to rancidity and so should be purchased in a dark bottle that does not let light in and should be stored in the refrigerator to prevent degradation. It does have quite a strong flavour, so should be used in salad dressings or to partially replace other oils in a baking recipe. It should never be used as a frying oil as it can catch light easily.

Hemp Seed Oil
Usually cold-pressed for food use, hemp seed oil is a green colour with a subtle nutty, grassy flavour. It contains all of the essential fatty acids in the ideal ratio for the human body to maintain health; these include linoleic acid, an omega-6 fat, and alpha-linolenic acid, an omega-3 fat. Getting this ratio correct is thought to be the key to reducing the incidence of certain conditions. Too much omega-6 fat in our diet may contribute to over-production of inflammatory compounds and exacerbate conditions such as arthritis, high blood pressure and skin conditions. Reducing omega-6 and increasing omega-3 fats may level out this situation and temper the inflammatory response, thus alleviating symptoms. Like flaxseed oil, hemp seed oil should not be used for frying and should be kept in a dark cool place to maximize its

Above: Heart-healthy walnut oil makes tasty marinades and dressings.

shelf-life; it can even be stored in the freezer as it doesn't solidify and doesn't need defrosting.

Walnut Oil
This is an intensely flavoured oil that is delicious in salad dressings and marinades. Walnut oil retains many of the benefits of the walnut. It is an excellent source of the essential omega-3 fats as well as a good source of antioxidants, all of which boost its credentials as a heart-healthy oil.

Walnut oil should not be used for frying, as heat destroys much of the antioxidant activity and diminishes its rich taste (it is also far too expensive to use in any great quantity). Instead, drizzle a little of the oil over roasted or steamed vegetables, use it to make a simple sauce for pasta, or stir into freshly cooked noodles just before serving. It can be used in small quantities, in place of some of the fat or oil in a recipe, to add flavour to cakes and cookies, especially those that contain walnuts. Walnut oil does not keep for long and, after opening, should be kept in a cool, dark place to prevent it from turning rancid. Walnut oil can be stored in the refrigerator, athough this may cause the oil to solidify.

Coffee, teas, tisanes and sweeteners

Coffee, teas and tisanes have been popular reviving and healing drinks for centuries. Tea comes in many different forms, from traditional teas such as green tea, oolong tea and black tea to fragrant tisanes and fruit infusions. Their health benefits have been well documented and used for thousands of years to treat and prevent all manner of illnesses and conditions.

Coffee

There are many compounds in coffee that have an effect on the body, including caffeine, which is a well-known stimulant. Less well known are the phenols that are found in the coffee bean, such as chlorogenic acid. These phenolic compounds have antioxidant properties that are similar to those found in tea and cocoa. The antioxidant activity of coffee increases as the bean is roasted due to the production of other compounds which exhibit antioxidant activity also.

TEA

The latest research shows that drinking between three and five cups of tea a day may help to reduce the risk of heart attack, and it may also reduce the risk of stroke and certain cancers. These benefits have been attributed to a group of polyphenols

Below: Black tea is packed full of powerful flavonoids.

found in tea, called flavonoids. The type and proportion of the different polyphenols in tea is dependent on how the tea is processed once it has been picked. All of these teas start out life as two leaves and a bud picked from the *Camellia sinensis* tea bush. The longer a tea leaf is allowed to wilt the darker it will become, as it oxidizes in much the same way as an apple goes brown. Hence, black tea is highly fermented and white tea is not fermented at all. As well as flavonoids, tea also contains fluoride, which can protect the teeth against decay. On the downside, tea can reduce the absorption of iron if drunk after a meal, and it contains caffeine (although less than coffee), which is a well-known stimulant.

Black Tea

This is the most widely available tea and is made by fermenting withered tea leaves, which are then dried. It produces a dark brown brew that has a more assertive taste than green tea. It contains fewer epicatechins but a higher proportion of theaflavins and thearubins, both powerful flavonoids that also show anti-cancer activity in cell studies.

White Tea

The difference between white and green tea is the age of the leaf that

Below: Fragrant green tea has high levels of cancer-fighting epicatechins.

Above: Freshly ground coffee beans contain powerful antioxidants.

is picked. White tea is made from the young leaves and bud. The leaves and bud are steamed and dried and there is minimal oxidation, producing a tea very high in catechin flavenoids. These compounds are potent antioxidants which may help in reducing the risk of cancer and heart disease. White tea has a very light and delicate flavour that is described as being slightly sweet.

Green Tea

This tea is popular with the Chinese and Japanese who prefer its light, slightly bitter but nevertheless refreshing flavour. It is produced from leaves that are steamed and dried but not fermented, a process that retains their green colour. Green tea is very high in particular flavonoid compounds called epicatechins, which have been shown to have anti-cancer activity in cell research. This property has yet to be seen definitively in humans. Avoid over-brewing green tea as it will begin to taste bitter.

Oolong Tea

Green tea leaves are bruised and allowed to partially ferment to produce a tea that falls between the green and black varieties in strength and colour. As it is partially fermented, it contains some of the epicatechins of green tea as well as the theaflavins of black tea. Fragrant oolong is brewed strong and can have quite a bitter flavour.

Honey

One of the oldest sweeteners used by man, honey was highly valued by the ancient Egyptians for its medicinal and healing properties. The colour, flavour, consistency and quality of honey depends on the source of nectar as well as the production method. In general, the darker the colour, the stronger the flavour. Nutritionally, honey offers negligible benefits, but as it contains fructose, which is much sweeter than sugar, less is needed. Honey still retains its reputation as an antiseptic, having antibacterial properties, and studies show that it is effective in healing and disinfecting wounds if applied externally. This antibacterial activity is thought to work internally also and, when mixed with lemon and hot water, it can relieve sore throats. Do not give honey to children under the age of one year, due to the risk of botulism food poisoning.

HERBAL TISANES

Although herbal tisanes are of little nutritional value, herbalists have prescribed them for centuries for a multitude of ailments and diseases. These teas (made from the leaves, seeds and flowers of herbs) are a convenient and simple way of taking medicinal herbs. They do, however, vary in strength and effectiveness. Shop-bought teas are generally mild in their medicinal properties but are good, healthy, caffeine-free drinks. Even so, some varieties are not recommended for young children and pregnant women and so it is advisable to check the packaging. Teas that are prescribed by herbalists can be incredibly powerful and should be taken with care.

Following is a selection of some of the most popular herbal teas and their properties:

Peppermint tea will release the menthol in its vapours and may help soothe a cold. It is recommended as a digestif to be drunk after a meal.

Raspberry leaf tea may help to prepare the uterus for birth. It is not, however, recommended in early pregnancy.

Rosehip tea is high in vitamin C and may help to ward off colds and flu.

Dandelion and lemon verbena teas are effective diuretics.

Rosemary tea may help stimulate the brain and improve memory and concentration.

Thyme tea freshens the breath and may help with sore throats or coughs.

Elderflower tea is a traditional remedy for colds and fever and an aid to restful sleep.

Camomile tea contains flavonoids and the essential oil bisabolol, and is

FLAVOURED TEAS

Steep your chosen herb, spice or fruit in boiling water and leave to infuse before straining. Peppermint tea is an excellent aid to digestion, and sleep-inducing camomile has a wonderfully calming effect on the nervous system.

To make camomile and peppermint tea, simply mix together 75g/3oz dried camomile flowers and 25g/1oz dried peppermint leaves. Store in an airtight container.

traditionally used to calm the nerves and help to induce sleep. It is also used as a tonic for a sore stomach. Dried camomile flowers have been used for many years to make a soothing herbal infusion. To make your own camomile infusion, use two teaspoons of dried flowers per cup, pour on boiling water and infuse for a few minutes. Camomile is traditionally drunk without milk.

Below: Honey is sweeter than table sugar so you do not require as much.

Below: Camomile tea is renowned for its calming and soothing effects.

Below: Drink elderflower tea before bedtime for a good night's sleep.

Dairy produce

Similar to meat and meat products, this valuable food group has been the subject of much bad press over the years, due to the saturated fat content of its foods. However, eaten in moderation, dairy products provide valuable nutrients such as calcium, which is in its most bioavailable form, vitamin B12 and vitamins A and D. Dairy products do provide a complete protein source for vegetarians, and if lower fat options are selected can be consumed as part of a very healthy balanced diet.

Milk

Often referred to as a complete food, milk is one of our most widely used ingredients. Cow's milk remains the most popular type, although, with the growing concern about saturated fat and cholesterol, semi-skimmed and skimmed milks now outsell the full-fat version. Skimmed milk contains half the calories of full-fat milk and only a fraction of the fat, but nutritionally it is on a par, retaining its vitamins, calcium and other minerals. Milk is an important

Below: A daily glass of milk gives you a quarter of your calcium requirement.

source of calcium and phosphorus, both of which are essential for healthy teeth and bones, and are said to prevent osteoporosis. Vitamin D is also present, which is essential for efficient calcium absorption. Milk also contains significant amounts of zinc and the B vitamins, including B12, which is one of the few non-meat products to contain it, and would be a major source for vegetarians.

Bio-yogurt

Produced by the bacterial fermentation of milk, yogurt has been praised for its health-giving qualities and has earned a reputation as one of the most valuable health foods. Yogurt is rich in calcium, phosphorus and B vitamins. Bio-yogurt contains specific bacteria strains such as bifidobacterium which work in harmony with the bacteria naturally present in the intestines to ensure that harmful bacteria do not over-populate. This is reputed to aid digestion and relieve gastrointestinal problems such as bloating. Eating bio-yogurt is thought to be

Below: Creamy, vitamin B-rich bio-yogurt is thought to aid digestion.

COOKING WITH YOGURT
Yogurt is a useful culinary ingredient, but does not respond well to heating. It is best added at the end of cooking, just before serving, to prevent it from curdling and to retain its vital bacteria. High-fat yogurts are more stable, but it is possible to stabilize and thicken low-fat yogurt by stirring in a little blended cornflour before cooking. Natural yogurt can be used in a wide range of sweet and savoury dishes, and it makes a calming addition to hot stews and curries.

particularly valuable after taking a course of antibiotics as it helps to restore the internal flora of the intestines. There is also evidence to suggest that bio-yogurt containing the acidophilus culture could prevent cancer of the colon. Bio-yogurts, which contain these extra bacteria, have a milder, creamier flavour than other yogurts, and may have far wider healing benefits. Many of these bio-yogurts are also available as yogurt drinks and are a great addition to lunchboxes or picnics.

Eggs

An inexpensive, self-contained source of almost perfect nourishment, eggs offer the cook tremendous scope, whether served simply solo or as part of a dish, whether sweet or savoury. Eggs have received much adverse publicity due to their cholesterol levels. However, attention has moved away from dietary cholesterol to saturated fats, as these have a greater influence on raising the levels of the 'bad' LDL cholesterol, and as eggs are low in saturated fat, they have been somewhat reprieved. They should, however, be eaten in moderation, and people with familial

Above: Eggs are a good source of vitamin B12, choline and iron.

hypercholesterolaemia should take particular care. Eggs provide a good source of B vitamins, especially B12, vitamins A and D, iron and phosphorus, and cooking does not significantly alter their nutritional content. Egg also contains choline, which is vitally important for healthy liver function and is critical in functions such as the metabolism of fats. Choline is also a constituent of acetylcholine, which is an important neurotransmitter in the brain, and has been shown to be deficient in those suffering from Alzheimer's disease.

Omega-3 Eggs
These eggs contain both vegetarian omega-3 and alpha-linolenic acid, and both the animal source omega-3 fats (EPA and DHA). The hens are fed on a high omega-3 diet which includes oily seeds and green vegetation. The hen is able to metabolize this source of omega-3 fats, which are then deposited in the fat of the yolk of the developing egg. This change to the feed of the hens also serves to increase the polyunsaturated fat profile, thus further reducing the level of saturates. This source of long-chain omega-3 fats is particularly useful for vegetarians and those who do not

eat fish or seafood. Eating more omega-3 fats could help our health in many ways, from heart-health benefits through to brain development and protection through to old age.

Cooking with Eggs
Eggs can be cooked in myriad ways. Simply boiled, fried or poached, they make a wonderful breakfast dish. Lightly cooked poached eggs are also filling when served as a lunch dish with high-fibre lentils or beans. Eggs are delicious baked, either on their own, with a drizzle of cream, or broken into a nest of lightly cooked peppers or leeks. They make tasty omelettes, whether cooked undisturbed until just softly set, combined with tomatoes and peppers to make an Italian frittata, or cooked with diced potato and onions to make the classic Spanish omelette. They are also often used as a filling for pies, savoury tarts and quiches.

Eggs are not, however, used only in savoury dishes. They are also an essential ingredient in many sweet dishes. They are added to cake

Below: Poaching eggs is a low-fat way to serve these nutrient-rich gems.

mixtures and batters for pancakes and popovers, are crucial to meringues, whisked sponges, mousses and hot and cold soufflés, and are used in all manner of desserts, from ice creams and custards to rice pudding.

When separated, egg yolks are used to thicken sauces and soups, giving them a rich, smooth consistency, while egg whites can be whisked into peaks to make soufflés and meringues. It is important to use eggs at room temperature, so remove them from the refrigerator about 30 minutes before cooking.

Buying and Storing Eggs
Freshness is paramount when buying eggs, so it is best to buy from a shop that has a high turnover of stock. You should reject any eggs that have a broken, dirty or damaged shell. Most eggs are date stamped, but you can easily check if an egg is fresh by placing it in a bowl of cold water: if the egg sinks and lays flat it is fresh. The older the egg, the more it will stand on its end. A really old egg will actually float and should not be consumed. It is best to store eggs in their box in the main part of the refrigerator and not in a rack in the door, as this can expose them to odours and damage. The shells are extremely porous, so eggs can be easily tainted by strong smells. Eggs should be stored large-end up for no longer than three weeks.

MISLEADING LABELS
The labels on egg boxes often have phrases such as 'farm fresh', 'natural' or 'country-fresh', which conjure up images of hens roaming around in the open, but they may well refer to eggs that are laid by birds reared in battery cages. It is therefore advisable to avoid eggs that are labelled with such claims and look for 'organic free-range' labels.

HERB OMELETTE
A simple, herb-flavoured omelette is quick to cook and, served with a salad and a chunk of crusty bread, makes a nutritious, light meal. Even if you are going to make more than one omelette, it is better to cook them individually and serve them as soon as each one is ready.

Serves 1
2 eggs
15ml/1 tbsp chopped fresh
  herbs, such as tarragon,
  parsley or chives
5ml/1 tsp butter
salt and freshly ground
  black pepper

1 Lightly beat the eggs together in a bowl, add the fresh herbs and season to taste.

2 Melt the butter in a heavy, non-stick frying pan and swirl it around to coat the base evenly.

3 Pour in the egg mixture and, as the egg sets, push the edges towards the centre using a spoon, allowing the raw egg to run on to the hot pan.

4 Cook for about 2 minutes, without stirring, until the egg is just lightly set. Quickly fold the omelette over and serve immediately on a warm plate.

Meat and poultry

Meat and poultry are often unfairly demonized because of their saturated fat content. However, it must not be overlooked that they contribute significant nutritional value to the diet when prepared and eaten in the right way, and in sensible quantities. Meat and poultry provide valuable, high-quality proteins full of essential amino acids that our bodies cannot make. It also contains the most bioavailable form of iron, as well as zinc and magnesium. Meat and poultry contain a wide array of B-vitamins, including vitamin B_{12}, which is not found in plant-based foods.

The key points to remember are to always choose lean cuts of meat, take off visible fat and skin, and do not eat too much of it. Between 100g and 150g (3¼–5oz) is a more than adequate portion per person. The same rules apply to poultry, and while it is generally lower in fat, taking the skin off can dramatically reduce this from an average of 9 per cent down to only 1 per cent for lean breast meat.

When cooking meat and poultry, try not to add any additional oil or fat, as it often has enough fat to cook in its own juices. To keep the fat content down, grill, stir-fry or bake where possible or use moist cooking methods such as steaming or pot-roasting, which also stop the meat from drying out.

Below: Iron- and vitamin-rich offal is well worth including in your diet.

Grass-fed Meat

It is a well-known phrase that 'you are what you eat' and the same is true of animals. The type of foodstuff used has a dramatic impact on the nutrient profile of animal meat and products. Most animals are either grass-fed, grain-fed or a combination of the two according to the season. When the animals are grass-fed, they are able to produce a far larger amount of a compound called Conjugated Linoleic Acid, or CLA for short, which has been shown to be beneficial to humans. CLA has antioxidant activity and has been shown to have powerful protective effects, helping to reduce atherosclerosis and stimulate the immune system. CLA also changes the way we metabolize fat, and has been shown in some human research studies to reduce body fat and increase lean muscle mass. There has been promising anti-cancer research in the laboratory, which needs more evidence to support a direct link, but most agree that CLAs appear to be beneficial to humans in many ways. The best sources are grass-fed beef and lamb or mutton, organic milk and milk products that tend to be from grass-fed cattle, and eggs.

Chicken and Turkey

Poultry meat is an easily digestible, high-quality source of protein which, with the skin removed, is also low-fat. The breast meat without skin is the lowest fat option at about 1g per 100g, compared with 9g per 100g with the skin. The leg meat is higher in fat at 12g per 100g. The high-quality protein contains essential amino acids that our bodies cannot make, particularly tryptophan. This is a precursor for serotonin, a neurotransmitter, and melatonin, a neurohormone, both of which are involved with sleep patterns and brain activity. It generally has a calming effect, which has led to it being used

Above: Remove the skin to reduce the fat content of chicken meat.

as a sleep aid as well as to help lift moods, and even as an antidepressant. It was once thought that the sleepiness experienced after the turkey-rich meals of Christmas and Thanksgiving were due to the tryptophan levels consumed. However, this is now thought to be attributable to the quantities of food and alcohol consumed.

Offal

There are many internal animal parts that are covered by this definition, however, their use in mainstream cooking is limited, so this book is restricted to the liver and kidney from pigs, sheep and cows, which are much more widely used and readily available. Liver and kidney are excellent low-fat sources of protein and iron, which is in its most available haem (heme) form. They are also an excellent source of vitamins A and B_{12}, riboflavin and selenium, and liver contains choline, which is essential for efficient fat metabolism. They are usually very good value and an excellent meat replacer if you are on a budget. Offal may have gone out of vogue in recent years, but cooked properly, it is delicious, nutritious and well worth trying.

Fish and shellfish

The vast array of fish and seafood available to us nowadays can be quite daunting. To put it simply, fish and seafood can be split into three groups: white fish, oily fish and seafood. White fish is an excellent low-fat source of protein and is easy to digest. Oily fish is slightly higher in fat, but it is a 'good' fat, called omega-3, which we all need to eat more of because of the potential benefits, such as brain and eye development and maintenance and heart health. Seafood is also rich in omega-3 fats and is a great source of protein as well.

We should all be eating two to four portions of fish per week, two of which should be oily, to ensure a good balance of nutrients. Pregnant women are advised to reduce this intake to two portions per week, due to concerns about toxins. However, the benefits of eating fish far outweigh the risks, so it should not be excluded altogether. With global fish stocks dwindling, it is important to try to select sustainable fish sources where possible. The Marine Stewardship Council runs a global certification scheme to show that products have been made in a sustainable way. Approved products can be identified by the 'Blue Tick' on the label.

WHEN BUYING FISH

• For whole fish, always look for bright eyes, a clean smell and bright red gills.

• For fillets or steaks, look for firm clean flesh with no fishy smell.

• For shellfish, look for closed shells or shells that close when touched and feel full, not light.

• Always try to purchase fish as fresh and as near to the cooking time as possible.

• Whether you buy your fish from a supermarket or fishmonger, pre-packed or loose, the same rules apply.

Salmon

Well known as a superfood because it is rich in omega-3 fats, this versatile oily fish is well worth including in your diet. As outlined previously, omega-3 fats are particularly beneficial if you suffer from heart disease, as they can help reduce your risk of further problems. There are many different forms of salmon available and all are worthy sources of omega-3. The richest type is fresh wild salmon due to the omega-3-rich diet the salmon eat in their natural habitat.

Farmed salmon has a good level of omega 3 in it but the feed used is not so rich in omega 3 as the diet of the wild salmon. Smoked salmon and tinned salmon are also good omega-3 sources and these open up a massive repertoire of dishes and meal occasions, from smoked salmon at breakfast through to fishcakes for lunch and risotto for supper.

As well as its fabulous omega-3 credentials, salmon is a good source of other vitamins and minerals, such as B vitamins for energy release, magnesium, phosphorus for calcium metabolism and selenium, which protects the body cells from oxidation. Canned salmon is also an excellent source of calcium, due to the presence of small bones that soften during the canning process, making them safe to eat.

Below: Eat fresh salmon to boost the oily fish quota in your diet.

Above: Trout is a good source of protein, omega-3 fats and B vitamins.

Trout

There are many different types of trout, which are broadly divided into inland trout such as brown trout or rainbow trout, and sea trout, which are brown trout that have migrated to the sea to feed and grow before returning to the river to spawn. Sea trout are generally much larger than inland trout and are very similar to salmon. Inland trout, especially rainbow trout, have a more delicate flavour and texture than sea trout. Both types, however, are excellent sources of protein and B-vitamins and while slightly higher in fat than white flaky fish, it is a 'good' fat containing the essential omega-3 fats. Inland trout is available whole, and can be baked in foil to retain its moisture or as fillets that can be grilled (broiled) in a matter of minutes. It is also available smoked, which makes a tasty alternative to smoked salmon. The larger sea trout is generally available as fillets and should be cooked just as you would salmon.

Tuna

This fish is very popular, primarily due to its ease of use in its canned form. However, while being an excellent protein, niacin and vitamin D and B_{12} source, canned tuna does not have all the benefits of the omega-3 fats found in the fresh fish. This is because the fish is cooked prior to canning to soften the meat, which removes some of the oil, and therefore the omega-3 fat levels are reduced. To get the full omega-3 benefit from tuna, you need to eat the widely available fresh steaks.

There has been much publicity in recent years about fishing practices, sustainability of the species and contamination. Tuna fish shoals often accompany dolphins, probably due to the risk reduction of being attacked by sharks, and this has caused problems when fishermen have used nets; now, line-caught tuna is thought to be safer for the dolphins.

The different types of tuna available have various issues with respect to sustainability and contamination; generally, the larger tuna species, like bluefin, contain the most contaminants, whereas smaller types, such as skipjack, contain the fewest. Nevertheless, all tuna is specifically mentioned as a fish to restrict intake of, especially if you are pregnant, nursing or are thinking of becoming pregnant. For the general population, the benefits of eating tuna in moderation far outweigh the risks and it is to be encouraged.

Herring
This versatile little fish comes in many forms: fresh, pickled, sweet-cured, and kippered, to name a few. It is one of the most abundant types of

Below: Fresh tuna contains far more omega 3 than tinned tuna.

oily fish and its many guises make it an extremely versatile ingredient.

All of the methods of preserving the fish mentioned above tend to retain its nutritious attributes, which include being one of the richest sources of omega-3 fats. It is also a good source of selenium and vitamins D and B_{12}. Many of the preserving methods mentioned use high levels of salt, and so the finished product is high in sodium. It is therefore sensible to eat these sparingly. Herring caught in the Baltic Seas has been known to have high levels of contamination, so try to buy Atlantic, Pacific or Mediterranean herring where possible as contaminant levels will be lower.

Mackerel
Also a very rich source of omega-3 fats, mackerel is another oily fish worthy of mention. Usually very good value for money, this fish is also a good source of selenium and vitamins D and B_{12}.

The whole fish is recognizable by its iridescent silvery-blue skin, with distinctive tiger-like stripes. This fish has been eaten for centuries and the firm, meaty flesh is ideal for grilling (broiling) or baking, the rich flavour perfectly complemented by citrus-based sauces.

Smoked mackerel is also a great source of omega-3 fats and is perhaps more versatile. The fillets can be easily turned into a sandwich filling or a tasty dip, often popular with children, providing a perfect way to include these invaluable nutrients in your family's diet.

Sardines
Who can resist the wonderful aroma of barbecued sardines, reminding us of Mediterranean holidays? The benefits of eating sardines go well beyond the relaxing memories of holidays past; they are another source of omega-3 fats, and the small, thin edible bones also contain calcium, phosphorus and vitamin D in

Above: Oysters are low in fat, yet still contain omega-3 fats and minerals.

significant amounts, all of which are essential to good bone health and the prevention of osteoporosis.

Canned sardines are a cheap alternative to fresh, and retain all of their nutrition, so they make a handy store-cupboard item. For convenience, buy butterfly fillets, which are boned and split open. These can be either marinated or grilled (broiled) with lemon. They cook quickly and need a watchful eye to prevent them from burning.

Oysters
As recently as a hundred years ago, oysters were a staple part of the diet, especially if you lived by the sea or a large river such as the Thames in London. Nowadays, even though oysters are an expensive treat, they pack a low-calorie, nutritional punch. Very rich in vitamin B_{12}, selenium, zinc and iron, oysters are also a good source of omega-3 fats. Their cholesterol content will have little relevance to our blood cholesterol levels, as this is influenced more by the amount of saturated fat that we eat. Oysters are reputed to have aphrodisiac properties and, while this remains unproven, their high levels of zinc and selenium are instrumental in testosterone and healthy sperm production. Freshness is imperative, and oysters should only be eaten or cooked live where the shell will be shut tight.

BREAKFAST

Breakfast, the most important meal of the day, is about fuelling your body to get going after the night's fast – everyone needs something, no matter how hectic a lifestyle they lead. There are plenty of alternatives to shop-bought sugary cereals and fatty fry-ups, and this chapter is packed with ideas for everyday healthy morning meals, from quick on-the-move smoothies and breakfast bars to more indulgent weekend specials, such as Lentil Kitchiri or Smoked Salmon with Scrambled Eggs.

Raspberry and oatmeal blend

This delightful combination of juicy, tangy raspberries with creamy bio-yogurt and oatmeal will see you right through to lunch with its slow-release energy. Using fresh raspberries, this drink ensures that the benefits of the antioxidants, anthocyanins and flavonoids are retained.

Serves 1

25ml/1½ tbsp medium oatmeal
150g/5oz/scant 1 cup raspberries
5–10ml/1–2 tsp clear honey
45ml/3 tbsp low-fat bio-yogurt

1 Put the oatmeal into a heatproof bowl. Pour in 120ml/4fl oz/½ cup boiling water and leave to stand for about 10 minutes or until the water has been completely absorbed.

2 Put the soaked oats in a blender or food processor and add all but two or three of the raspberries, the honey and about 30ml/2 tbsp of the yogurt. Purée until smooth, scraping the mix down from the sides if necessary.

3 Pour the smoothie into a large glass, swirl in the remaining yogurt and top with raspberries. Chill in the refrigerator – it will thicken up, so you might need to add a little juice or mineral water before serving.

SUPERFOOD TIP
The live bacteria present within bio-yogurt aid digestion.

Frozen berry and chlorella smoothie

This smoothie is packed full of berries and is a perfect pick-me-up on a hot day. This refreshing drink is positively bursting with lots of supernutrient goodness. The crushed ice makes this a revitalizing beverage that is lighter than many other smoothie drinks.

Serves 1

10 ice cubes
150g/5oz/scant 1 cup mixed
  berries (raspberries, blackberries,
  redcurrants and blackcurrants)
60ml/4 tbsp cranberry juice
10ml/2 tsp chlorella powder

1 Place all of the ice cubes in a freezer bag and use a rolling pin to crush them, then set aside.

2 Put the berries in a food processor or blender and add the cranberry juice. Pulse until the mixture breaks down into a thick purée.

3 Add the chlorella powder to the food processor or blender and pulse again until it is mixed into the purée. Finally, add the crushed ice and blend well. Pour the smoothie into a large glass and serve while it is still chilled.

Raspberry and oatmeal blend: Energy 186Kcal/793kJ; Protein 7.5g; Carbohydrate 34.6g, of which sugars 16.4g; Fat 3.1g, of which saturates 0.4g; Cholesterol 1mg; Calcium 137mg; Fibre 5.5g; Sodium 51mg.
Frozen berry and chlorella smoothie: Energy 37Kcal/161kJ; Protein 2g; Carbohydrate 8g, of which sugars 8g; Fat 0g, of which saturates 0g; Cholesterol 0mg; Calcium 70mg; Fibre 5.3g; Sodium 22mg.

Wheat bran smoothie

This high-fibre, fruity smoothie makes a great start to the day. Wheat bran and bananas provide slow-release carbohydrate to keep your energy levels stable, while fresh orange juice and sweet, fragrant mango will provide a fantastic boost to your vitamin and mineral requirements.

Serves 2

½ mango
1 banana
1 large orange
30ml/2 tbsp wheat bran
15ml/1 tbsp sesame seeds
10–15ml/2 tsp–1 tbsp honey

COOK'S TIP
Mango juice is naturally very sweet so you may wish to add less honey or leave it out altogether. Taste the drink to decide how much you need.

1 Using a small, sharp knife, skin the mango, then slice the flesh off the stone (pit). Peel the banana and break it into short lengths, then place it in a blender or food processor together with the skinned mango.

2 Squeeze the juice from the orange and add to the blender or food processor along with the bran, sesame seeds and honey. Whizz until the mixture is smooth and creamy, then pour into glasses and serve.

Wheat bran smoothie: Energy 172kcal/726kJ; Protein 4.9g; Carbohydrate 27.6g, of which sugars 23.1g; Fat 5.5g, of which saturates 0.9g; Cholesterol 0mg; Calcium 102mg; Fibre 8.5g; Sodium 11mg.

Wheatgrass tonic

Wheatgrass is grown from wheat seeds and is a concentrated source of chlorophyll and the antioxidant vitamins A, C and E. It does have a distinctive, sweet flavour so this juice is blended with mild white cabbage, but it is just as tasty combined with other vegetables or fruit juices instead.

Serves 1

50g/2oz white cabbage
90g/3½oz wheatgrass

1 Cut the core from the cabbage and roughly shred the leaves. Push through a juicer with the wheatgrass (a masticating juicer is best).

2 Pour the juice into a small glass and serve immediately.

Pineapple and ginger juice

Fresh root ginger is one of the best natural cures for stomach cramps and nausea. In this unusual fruity blend, it is simply mixed with fresh, juicy pineapple and sweet-tasting carrot, creating a quick and easy remedy that can be juiced in minutes – and which tastes delicious too.

Serves 1

½ small pineapple
25g/1oz fresh root ginger
1 carrot
ice cubes

1 Using a sharp knife, cut away the skin from the pineapple, then halve and remove the core. Roughly slice the pineapple flesh. Peel and roughly chop the ginger, then chop the carrot.

2 Push the carrot, ginger and pineapple through a juicer and pour into a glass. Add ice cubes and serve immediately.

COOK'S TIP
Before preparing the pineapple, leave it upside down for 30 minutes – this makes it juicier.

Wheatgrass tonic: Energy 36kcal/149kJ; Protein 3.2g; Carbohydrate 3.9g, of which sugars 3.8g; Fat 0.8g, of which saturates 0.1g; Cholesterol 0mg; Calcium 178mg; Fibre 2.9g; Sodium 130mg.
Pineapple and ginger juice: Energy 120Kcal/516kJ; Protein 1.1g; Carbohydrate 30.2g, of which sugars 29.9g; Fat 0.4g, of which saturates 0.1g; Cholesterol 0mg; Calcium 33mg; Fibre 1.2g; Sodium 33mg.

Dried fruit salad

Inspired by a traditional Scandinavian dessert dish, this recipe uses a wonderful array of dried fruits. Concentrated versions of their fresh counterparts, dried fruits are a rich source of vitamins, minerals and fibre, and will also count as one of the five recommended daily portions of fruit and vegetables.

Serves 6–8

50g/2oz/¼ cup currants
50g/2oz/¼ cup sultanas (golden raisins)
115g/4oz/½ cup dried apricots
115g/4oz/½ cup prunes
115g/4oz/½ cup dried apples
115g/4oz/½ cup dried peaches
115g/4oz/½ cup dried pears
15ml/1 tbsp lemon zest
7.5cm/3in cinnamon stick
5 whole cloves
40g/1½oz/¼ cup quick-cook tapioca
250ml/8fl oz/1 cup thick, creamy natural (plain) bio-yogurt

1 Chop all the dried fruit and place in a large pan together with 1 litre/ 1¾ pints/4 cups water. Cover, and leave to stand for at least 2 hours or overnight.

2 Stir the lemon zest, cinnamon stick, cloves and tapioca into the dried fruit mixture. Bring to the boil, cover and simmer for 1 hour, stirring occasionally.

3 Remove the pan from the heat. Take out the cinnamon stick and discard. Allow the fruit mixture to cool slightly before serving.

4 Serve the warm fruit salad topped with a generous dollop of thick and creamy bio-yogurt. You can refrigerate any leftover fruit for up to three days.

Dried fruit salad: Energy 305kcal/1277kJ; Protein 2.7g; Carbohydrate 37.4g, of which sugars 31.5g; Fat 17.1g, of which saturates 10.4g; Cholesterol 43mg; Calcium 51mg; Fibre 4g; Sodium 17mg.

Minted pomegranate yogurt and grapefruit

In this Moroccan-inspired dish, the ruby-red pomegranate seeds add texture, flavour and colour to the yogurt as well as a healthy-heart boost with their polyphenol content. The delicately scented grapefruit salad adds a zesty, refreshing zing to this delicious recipe.

Serves 4

300ml/½ pint/1¼ cups Greek
 (US strained plain) yogurt
2–3 ripe pomegranates
bunch of mint, finely chopped
honey or sugar, to taste (optional)

For the grapefruit salad
2 red grapefruits
2 pink grapefruits
1 white grapefruit
15–30ml/1–2 tbsp orange
 flower water
handful of pomegranate seeds
 and mint leaves, to decorate

1 Put the yogurt in a bowl and beat well. Cut open the pomegranates and scoop out the seeds, removing all the bitter pith. Fold the pomegranate seeds and chopped mint into the yogurt. Sweeten with a little honey or sugar, if using, then chill until ready to serve.

2 Peel the red, pink and white grapefruits, cutting off all the pith. Cut between the membranes to remove the segments, holding the fruit over a bowl to catch the juices.

3 Discard the membranes and mix the fruit segments with the reserved juices. Sprinkle with the orange flower water and add a little honey or sugar, if using. Stir gently.

4 Decorate the chilled yogurt with a scattering of pomegranate seeds and mint leaves, and serve with the grapefruit salad.

COOK'S TIP
Immerse pomegranates in a bowl of water when removing the seeds to help separate the bitter pith.

Minted pomegranate yogurt: Energy 188Kcal/784kJ; Protein 8.8g; Carbohydrate 18g, of which sugars 18g; Fat 10.5g of which saturates 5.2g; Cholesterol 0mg; Calcium 202mg; Fibre 3.6g; Sodium 82mg.

Raspberry cranachan

Bio-yogurt is substituted in for the double (heavy) cream in this traditional Scottish dessert recipe, making it a tempting but lighter breakfast option. Fresh antioxidant-rich raspberries and heart-healthy oats add the superfood elements that will help you to kick-start your day.

Serves 4

75g/3oz crunchy oat cereal
600ml/1 pint/2½ cups thick, creamy natural (plain) bio-yogurt
250g/9oz/1⅓ cups raspberries
heather honey, to serve

1 Preheat the grill (broiler) to high. Spread the oat cereal on a baking sheet and place under the hot grill for 3–4 minutes, stirring regularly. Set aside on a plate to cool.

2 When the cereal has cooled completely, fold it into the bio-yogurt.

3 Gently fold in 200g/7oz/generous 1 cup of the raspberries, being careful not to crush them.

4 Spoon the creamy mixture into four serving glasses or dishes, and top with the remaining raspberries.

5 Serve the crunchy raspberry cranachan immediately. Pass around a dish of heather honey to drizzle over the top, adding extra sweetness and flavour to this irresistible breakfast dish.

VARIATION
You can use almost any berries for this recipe. Stawberries and blackberries work very well. If you choose strawberries, remove the stalks and cut them into quarters beforehand.

Raspberry cranachan: Energy 276kcal/1152kJ; Protein 12.4g; Carbohydrate 17.2g, of which sugars 11.1g; Fat 19.7g, of which saturates 8.7g; Cholesterol 0mg; Calcium 255mg; Fibre 2.5g; Sodium 122mg.

Amaranth and honey porridge

The sweetness of the honey complements the slightly nutty flavour of the highly nutritious amaranth grain. The relatively heavy texture of the porridge can be lightened with the addition of your favourite fruit, dried or fresh and has the added benefit of being gluten-free.

Serves 1

100g/3¾oz amaranth grain
200ml/7fl oz milk
1 tsp honey

1 Place the milk, amaranth and honey in a pan. Heat gently, stirring occasionally for 15 minutes.

2 When the mixture becomes a porridge-like consistency, pour into a bowl and serve warm.

Popped amaranth cereal

This interesting cooking method follows a tradition of popping cereals such as rice or wheat. High in protein, B-vitamins and minerals, this grain is a nutrient-packed way to start the day. You can add some to your usual cereal or use as a delicious topping for fruit or yogurt.

Serves 1

20g/¾oz amaranth grain
2.5ml/½ tsp ground cinnamon
2.5ml/½ tsp runny honey

1 Heat a heavy-bottomed pan, with the lid on.

2 Place half the amaranth grain in the pan and shake to form a thin layer of grains. The popping should start immediately.

3 Gently shake the pan to ensure even distribution of heat so that the grains do not burn.

4 When the popping has stopped, after about 30 seconds, remove the pan from the heat and pour the popped amaranth into a bowl.

5 Repeat with the other half of the grain and add to the bowl. Add the cinnamon and honey to the popped grain and mix well.

Amaranth and honey porridge: Energy 486Kcal/2042kJ; Protein 21g; Carbohydrate 81g, of which sugars 17g; Fat 10g, of which saturates 3g; Cholesterol 12mg; Calcium 242mg; Fibre 6.7g; Sodium 91mg.
Popped amaranth cereal: Energy 86Kcal/360kJ; Protein 3g; Carbohydrate 16g, of which sugars 3g; Fat 1g, of which saturates 0g; Cholesterol 0mg; Calcium 13mg; Fibre 1.3g; Sodium 2mg.

Porridge with dates and pistachio nuts

A bowl of heart-warming porridge on a cold winter's morning is so comforting, and it is good to know that it's helping your heart stay healthy too. Oats are an excellent way to help reduce bad cholesterol in our bodies and, as they release energy slowly, should stop you snacking mid-morning.

Serves 4

250g/9oz/scant 2 cups fresh dates
225g/8oz/2 cups rolled oats
475ml/16fl oz/2 cups milk
pinch of salt (optional)
50g/2oz/½ cup shelled, unsalted
   pistachio nuts, roughly chopped

SUPERFOOD TIP
Oats have a reputation for being warming foods due to their fat and protein content, which is greater than that of most other grains. As well as providing sustained energy levels, oats are also one of the most nutritious cereals available.

---

1 First make the date purée. Halve the dates and remove the stones (pits) and stems. Cover the halved dates with boiling water and soak for 30 minutes, until softened. Strain, reserving 90ml/6 tbsp of the soaking water.

2 Remove the skin from the dates and purée them in a food processor with the reserved soaking water.

3 Place the oats in a pan with the milk, 300ml/½ pint/1¼ cups water and salt. Bring the porridge to the boil, then reduce the heat and simmer for 4–5 minutes until cooked, stirring frequently.

4 Serve the porridge in warm serving bowls, topped with a spoonful of the date purée and sprinkled with chopped pistachio nuts.

Porridge with dates: Energy 416Kcal/1754kJ; Protein 13.6g; Carbohydrate 62.5g, of which sugars 21.2g; Fat 13.8g, of which saturates 1.3g; Cholesterol 0mg; Calcium 75mg; Fibre 5.7g; Sodium 127mg.

Apricot bran muffins

These moist, fruity muffins are a nutritious option for breakfast. Apricots are packed with iron, fibre and vitamin A and their calcium content is further boosted by the yogurt and milk in the recipe. The apricots and bran mean that these are high in fibre too.

4 In a large bowl, mix together the flour, bran, bicarbonate of soda, sugar and chopped apricots.

5 Add the melted butter, yogurt and milk to the bowl of dry ingredients. Mix lightly.

6 Two-thirds fill the prepared paper cases with batter. Bake for 15–20 minutes, until a skewer inserted into the centre of one comes out clean.

7 Leave to set for 5 minutes, then turn out on to a wire rack to cool. Serve warm or eat within 2 days.

Makes 12

115g/4oz/1 cup dried apricots
225g/8oz/2 cups self-raising
   (self-rising) flour
50g/2oz/½ cup wheat or
   oat bran
2.5ml/½ tsp bicarbonate of soda
   (baking soda)
30ml/2 tbsp soft light brown sugar
30ml/2 tbsp butter, melted
150g/5oz/⅔ cup natural
   (plain) yogurt
200ml/7fl oz/scant 1 cup milk

1 Grease the cups of a muffin tin (pan) or line them with paper cases.

2 Soak the dried apricots in a small bowl of water for 15 minutes. Roughly chop the soaked apricots into small bitesize pieces.

3 Preheat the oven to 220°C/425°F/ Gas 7.

> **SUPERFOOD TIP**
> Dried apricots have an even higher concentration of beta-carotene than fresh ones. This powerful antioxidant is believed to lower the risk of cataracts, heart disease and some forms of cancer.

Apricot bran muffins: Energy 131kcal/553kJ; Protein 4g; Carbohydrate 23.6g, of which sugars 8.3g; Fat 3g, of which saturates 1.7g; Cholesterol 7mg; Calcium 83mg; Fibre 2.7g; Sodium 42mg.

Cranberry, apple and walnut muffins

Sweet, sharp and decidedly moreish, these muffins are richly spiced and packed with plenty of fruity flavours. Apples and cranberries both contain polyphenols, which may be beneficial in helping to reduce the risk of cancer and cardiovascular disease.

Makes 12

1 egg
50g/2oz/¼ cup butter, melted
100g/3¾oz/generous ½ cup caster (superfine) sugar
grated rind of 1 large orange
120ml/4fl oz/½ cup freshly squeezed orange juice
140g/5oz/1¼ cups plain (all-purpose) flour
5ml/1 tsp baking powder
2.5ml/½ tsp ground cinnamon
2.5ml/½ tsp freshly grated nutmeg
2.5ml/½ tsp ground allspice
pinch of ground ginger
pinch of salt
2 small eating apples
170g/6oz/1½ cups fresh cranberries
55g/2oz/1⅓ cups walnuts, chopped

1 Preheat the oven to 180°C/350°F/ Gas 4. Lightly grease the cups of a muffin tin (pan) or line them with paper cases.

2 In a bowl, whisk the egg with the melted butter to combine. Add the sugar, grated orange rind and juice. Whisk to blend. Set aside.

3 In a large bowl, sift together the flour, baking powder, cinnamon, nutmeg, allspice, ginger and salt.

4 Make a well in the dry ingredients and pour in the egg mixture. With a spoon, stir until just blended.

5 Peel, core and quarter the apples. Chop the apple flesh coarsely with a sharp knife.

6 Add the apples, cranberries and walnuts to the batter and stir lightly to blend.

7 Three-quarters fill the cups. Bake for 25–30 minutes, until golden. Leave to stand for 5 minutes before transferring to a wire rack and allowing to cool. Store in an airtight container for up to 3 days.

Cranberry and apple muffins: Energy 149kcal/624kJ; Protein 2.5g; Carbohydrate 20.4g, of which sugars 10.8g; Fat 6.9g, of which saturates 2.6g; Cholesterol 25mg; Calcium 30mg; Fibre 0.9g; Sodium 34mg.

Fruit and coconut breakfast bars

A perfect breakfast solution when time is short. Instead of buying cereal bars from the supermarket, try making this quick and easy version. Along with the positive effects of coconut on body fat, not skipping breakfast is a good way to get the metabolism going in the morning.

Makes 12

270g/10oz jar apple sauce
115g/4oz/½ cup ready-to-eat dried
  apricots, chopped
115g/4oz/¾ cup raisins
50g/2oz/¼ cup demerara (raw)
  sugar
50g/2oz/⅓ cup sunflower seeds
25g/1oz/2 tbsp sesame seeds
25g/1oz/¼ cup pumpkin seeds
75g/3oz/scant 1 cup rolled oats
75g/3oz/⅔ cup self-raising
  (self-rising) wholemeal (whole-
  wheat) flour
50g/2oz/⅔ cup desiccated (dry
  unsweetened shredded) coconut
2 eggs, beaten

1 Preheat the oven to 200°C/400°F/ Gas 6. Grease a 20cm/8in square shallow baking tin (pan) and line with baking parchment.

2 Pour the apple sauce into a large bowl, then add the apricots, raisins, sugar, and the sunflower, sesame and pumpkin seeds. Stir together with a wooden spoon until thoroughly mixed.

3 Add the oats, flour, coconut and eggs to the fruit mixture and gently stir together until evenly combined.

4 Turn the mixture into the tin and spread to the edges in an even layer. Bake for about 25 minutes, or until golden and just firm to the touch.

5 Leave to cool in the tin, then lift out on to a board and cut into bars.

Fruit and coconut breakfast bars: Energy 207kcal/871kJ; Protein 4.9g; Carbohydrate 29.6g, of which sugars 19.3g; Fat 8.5g, of which saturates 3g; Cholesterol 32mg; Calcium 67mg; Fibre 2.8g; Sodium 46mg.

Lentil kitchiri

This spicy lentil and rice dish is a delicious vegetarian variation of kedgeree. Served with quartered hard-boiled eggs, it is a tasty, high-protein breakfast that is rich in iron. This is a perfect recipe for vegetarians in particular, whose diets can often be low in iron.

Serves 4

50g/2oz/¼ cup dried red
  lentils, rinsed
1 bay leaf
225g/8oz/1 cup basmati rice,
  rinsed
4 cloves
30ml//2 tbsp vegetable oil
5ml/1 tsp curry powder
2.5ml/½ tsp mild chilli powder
30ml/2 tbsp chopped flat
  leaf parsley
salt and ground black pepper
4 hard-boiled eggs, quartered,
  to serve (optional)

1 Put the lentils in a pan, add the bay leaf and cover with cold water. Bring to the boil, skim off any foam, then reduce the heat. Cover and simmer for 25–30 minutes, until the lentils are tender. Drain, then discard the bay leaf.

2 Meanwhile, place the rice in a pan and cover with 475ml/16fl oz/2 cups boiling water. Add the cloves and a generous pinch of salt. Cook, covered, for 10–15 minutes, until all the water is absorbed and the rice is tender. Discard the cloves.

3 Heat the oil in a large frying pan over a gentle heat. Add the curry and chilli powders and cook for 1 minute.

4 Stir in the lentils and rice and mix well until they are coated in the spiced oil. Season and cook for 1–2 minutes, until heated through. Stir in the parsley and serve with the hard-boiled eggs, if using.

Lentil kitchiri: Energy 339kcal/1414kJ; Protein 7.6g; Carbohydrate 52.4g, of which sugars 0.7g; Fat 10.9g, of which saturates 6.5g; Cholesterol 27mg; Calcium 44mg; Fibre 1.3g; Sodium 85mg.

Egg frittata with sun-dried tomatoes

This Italian omelette, made with tangy Parmesan cheese, can be served warm or cold. The rich, intense flavour of the sun-dried tomatoes and the aromatic thyme really livens up this egg dish. The tomatoes contain lycopene, a powerful antioxidant that could help prevent prostate cancer.

Serves 4

6 sun-dried tomatoes
30ml/2 tbsp olive oil
1 small onion, finely chopped
pinch of fresh thyme leaves
6 eggs
25g/1oz/⅓ cup freshly grated
   Parmesan cheese, plus shavings
   to serve
salt and ground black pepper
thyme sprigs, to garnish

1 Place the sun-dried tomatoes in a bowl and pour over enough boiled water to just cover them. Leave the tomatoes to soak for 15 minutes.

VARIATION
For a lower-fat version, you can leave out the Parmesan cheese and instead add diced red or yellow (bell) pepper with the chopped onion.

2 Lift the tomatoes out of the hot water and pat dry on kitchen paper. Reserve the soaking water. Use a sharp knife to cut the tomatoes into thin strips.

3 Heat the olive oil in a frying pan. Cook the onion for 5–6 minutes. Add the thyme and tomatoes and cook for a further 2–3 minutes.

4 Break the eggs into a bowl and beat lightly. Stir in 45ml/3 tbsp of the tomato soaking water and the Parmesan and season to taste.

5 Raise the heat and when the oil is sizzling, add the eggs. Mix quickly into the other ingredients. Lower the heat to medium and cook for 4–5 minutes, or until the base is golden.

6 Take a large plate, invert it over the pan and, holding it firmly, turn the pan and the frittata over on to it. Slide the frittata back into the pan, and cook for 3–4 minutes until golden brown on the second side.

7 Remove the pan from the heat. Cut the frittata into wedges and garnish with Parmesan shavings and thyme.

Egg frittata: Energy 170kcal/705kJ; Protein 5.7g; Carbohydrate 3g, of which sugars 2.6g; Fat 15.2g, of which saturates 4.1g; Cholesterol 13mg; Calcium 158mg; Fibre 0.6g; Sodium 167mg.

Smoked salmon with scrambled eggs

A classic combination, this breakfast also provides a great nutritious start to the day. With omega-3 fats from the salmon and the choline from the eggs, this is brain food at its best. Serve on wholemeal toast, to ensure that the energy will be released slowly throughout your morning.

Serves 4

15ml/1 tbsp rapeseed oil
2 onions, chopped
150-200g/5–7oz smoked salmon
  trimmings
6–8 eggs, lightly beaten
ground black pepper
45ml/3 tbsp chopped fresh chives,
  plus whole chives, to garnish
wholemeal (whole-wheat) toast or
  bagels, to serve

COOK'S TIP
If you don't have any smoked salmon, you can use fresh or canned salmon, which contains just as much omega-3 oil.

1 Heat the oil in a frying pan, then add the chopped onions and fry until they are softened and just beginning to brown.

2 Add the smoked salmon trimmings to the pan and mix well to combine with the onions.

3 Pour the eggs into the pan and stir until soft curds form. Stir off the heat until creamy. Season with pepper. Spoon on to serving plates and garnish with chopped and whole chives.

4 Serve the scrambled eggs immediately with hot buttered wholemeal toast or bagels.

Scrambled eggs: Energy 316kcal/1314kJ; Protein 22.8g; Carbohydrate 6.6g, of which sugars 0.8g; Fat 22.4g, of which saturates 8.2g; Cholesterol 249mg; Calcium 68mg; Fibre 0.3g; Sodium 231mg.

Grilled kippers with marmalade toast

The delicious smokiness of these cured herrings combines wonderfully with the tangy orange marmalade for a tasty and satisfying brunch dish. Herrings are one of the richest sources of omega-3 fats, which are excellent for keeping your heart healthy.

2 Using kitchen scissors or a knife, remove the heads and tails from the kippers.

3 Lay the fish, skin-side up, on the buttered foil. Put under the hot grill and cook for 1 minute. Turn the kippers over, brush the uppermost (fleshy) side with melted butter, put back under the grill and cook for 4–5 minutes.

Serves 2

melted butter, for greasing
2 kippers
2 slices of bread
soft butter, for spreading
orange marmalade, for spreading

VARIATION
Omit the marmalade and cook the kippers sprinkled with a little cayenne pepper. Serve with a small knob (pat) of butter and plenty of lemon wedges for squeezing over.

1 Preheat the grill (broiler). Line the grill pan with foil – to help prevent fishy smells from lingering in the pan – and brush the foil with melted butter to stop the fish sticking.

4 Toast the bread and spread it first with butter and then with marmalade. Serve the sizzling hot kippers immediately with the marmalade on toast.

Grilled kippers: Energy 518kcal/2155kJ; Protein 33.9g; Carbohydrate 17.6g, of which sugars 5.9g; Fat 35.1g, of which saturates 7.6g; Cholesterol 121mg; Calcium 126mg; Fibre 0.4g; Sodium 1640mg.

Smoked haddock with spinach and egg

This rich, high-protein breakfast dish is perhaps one for a weekend treat. Gently wilting the spinach will help retain its valuable nutrients, and serving with a glass of fruit juice will improve absorption of the iron from the spinach and eggs.

Serves 4

4 undyed smoked haddock fillets
milk, for poaching
45ml/3 tbsp low-fat Greek
   (US strained plain) yogurt
   or crème fraîche
250g/9oz fresh spinach, tough
   stalks removed
white wine vinegar
4 eggs
salt and ground black pepper

1 Put the haddock in a frying pan and pour in enough milk to come half-way up the fish. Poach the fillets over a low heat, shaking the pan gently, for 5 minutes.

2 Remove the fish from the pan and keep warm. Increase the heat and simmer the milk until it reduces by about half, stirring occasionally.

3 Stir the yogurt or crème fraîche into the milk. Heat through without letting the sauce boil. Season with pepper and remove from the heat.

4 Warm a frying pan over a gentle heat, add the spinach and allow to wilt for a few minutes. Season lightly with salt and pepper to taste, then set aside, keeping the leaves warm.

5 To poach the eggs, bring 4cm/1½in water to a simmer and add a few drops of vinegar. Gently crack two eggs into the water and cook for 3 minutes. Remove the first egg using a slotted spoon and rest the spoon on some kitchen paper to remove any water.

6 Repeat with the second egg, then cook the other two in the same way.

7 Place the spinach over the fillets and a poached egg on top. Pour over the cream sauce and serve immediately.

Smoked haddock: Energy 350kcal/1455kJ; Protein 27.5g; Carbohydrate 1.5g, of which sugars 1.4g; Fat 26.3g, of which saturates 14g; Cholesterol 277mg; Calcium 170mg; Fibre 1.3g; Sodium 969mg.

Oatmeal pancakes with bacon

A healthier alternative to a fry up, these savoury, oaty pancakes are perfect topped with a poached egg or grilled tomatoes. Use good-quality back bacon and cut off the rind to lower the fat content; the oats will help to reduce your cholesterol levels.

Makes 8

115g/4oz/1 cups wholemeal
  (whole-wheat) flour
25g/1oz/¼ cup fine pinhead
  oatmeal
pinch of salt
2 eggs
about 300ml/½ pint/1¼ cups
  buttermilk
butter or oil, for greasing
8 rashers (strips) back bacon

VARIATIONS
Try alternative fillings such as grilled mushrooms, smoked mackerel or salmon, or even jam.

---

1 Mix the flour, oatmeal and salt in a bowl or food processor, beat in the eggs and add enough buttermilk to make a creamy batter of the same consistency as ordinary pancakes.

2 Thoroughly heat a cast-iron frying pan or griddle over a medium heat. When very hot, grease lightly with butter or oil.

COOK'S TIP
When whole oats are chopped into pieces they are called pinhead or coarse oatmeal. They take longer to cook than rolled oats and have a chewier texture.

3 Pour in the batter, about a ladleful at a time. Tilt the pan around to spread the batter evenly and cook for about 2 minutes on the first side, or until set and the underside is browned.

4 Turn over and cook for about 1 minute until browned. Grill the bacon and tuck inside the cooked pancakes.

Oatmeal pancakes: Energy 202kcal/845kJ; Protein 11.9g; Carbohydrate 17.8g, of which sugars 2g; Fat 11.8g, of which saturates 4.8g; Cholesterol 87mg; Calcium 59mg; Fibre 1.5g; Sodium 654mg.

Kidney and mushroom toasts

Kidneys are an excellent, cheap source of many valuable nutrients including a highly absorbable form of iron. They are very quick and easy to cook and, served with tomatoes and mushrooms on wholemeal (whole-wheat) toast, make a tasty, filling breakfast.

Serves 4

4 large, flat field (portabello)
  mushrooms, stalks trimmed
50g/2oz/¼ cup butter
10ml/2 tsp wholegrain mustard
15ml/1 tbsp chopped fresh parsley
4 lamb's kidneys, skinned, halved
  and cored
4 thick slices of wholemeal (whole-
  wheat) bread, toasted
sprig of parsley, to garnish
tomato wedges, to serve

COOK'S TIP
Before cooking kidneys, remove
the white core of membrane and
tubes found in the centre.

1 Wash the mushrooms thoroughly and gently remove the stalks.

2 Blend the butter, wholegrain mustard and chopped fresh parsley together in a bowl.

3 Rinse the prepared lamb's kidneys well under cold running water, and pat dry with kitchen paper.

4 Melt the butter mixture in a large frying pan and fry the mushrooms and kidneys for about 3 minutes on each side.

5 When the kidneys are cooked to your liking (they taste best when left a little pink in the centre). Serve with the tomato, garnished with parsley, on the hot toast.

Kidney and mushroom toasts: Energy 593Kcal/2480kJ; Protein 39.2g; Carbohydrate 26.3g, of which sugars 2.7g; Fat 37.7g, of which saturates 21.6g; Cholesterol 647mg; Calcium 145mg; Fibre 4.3g; Sodium 773mg.

SOUPS, DIPS AND APPETIZERS

Warming, nutritious and sustaining, home-made soup is the
perfect health food. Light to eat, but with substantial food value,
it is ideal as a winter warmer. Soup can be cooked ahead, made
in big batches, chilled for several days or frozen for months – it is
practical, versatile and extremely good for you. This selection of
dips and appetizers is equally tempting and packed with highly
nutritious ingredients. Choose from a varied selection including
Artichoke and Cumin Dip, Marinated Tofu and Broccoli with
Shallots, Seaweed Sushi Rolls, and Garlic Prawns in Filo Tartlets.

Chilled avocado soup with cumin

This tasty cold soup combines creamy avocados with the distinctive flavours of onions, garlic, lemon and cumin. While avocado contains fat, it is the healthy monounsaturated type that can help to lower blood cholesterol levels. Aromatic cumin contains flavonoids that help to alleviate indigestion.

Serves 4

3 ripe avocados
a bunch of spring onions
  (scallions), white parts only,
  trimmed and roughly chopped
2 garlic cloves, chopped
juice of 1 lemon
1.5ml/¼ tsp ground cumin
1.5ml/¼ tsp paprika
450ml/¾ pint/scant 2 cups fresh
  vegetable stock
300ml/½ pint/1¼ cups iced water
ground black pepper
roughly chopped fresh flat leaf
  parsley, to garnish

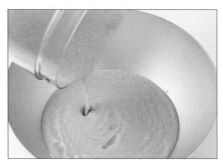

1 Starting half a day ahead, put the flesh of one avocado in a food processor or blender. Add the spring onions, garlic and lemon juice and purée until smooth. Add the second avocado and purée, then add the third, along with the spices and seasoning. Purée until smooth.

2 Gradually add the vegetable stock. Pour the soup into a metal bowl and chill for 2–3 hours.

3 To serve, stir in the iced water, then season to taste with plenty of black pepper. Garnish with chopped parsley and serve immediately.

Chilled avocado soup: Energy 220Kcal/907kJ; Protein 2.7g; Carbohydrate 2.9g, of which sugars 1.3g; Fat 21.8g, of which saturates 4.7g; Cholesterol 0mg; Calcium 22mg; Fibre 4.2g; Sodium 9mg.

Classic gazpacho

Raw tomatoes, cucumber and peppers form the basis of this classic chilled soup. Not cooking the vegetables retains all the vitamin C. Serving with a spoonful of chunky, fresh avocado salsa will add to the impressive fruit and vegetable count of this dish.

Serves 6

900g/2lb ripe tomatoes, peeled and seeded
1 cucumber, peeled and roughly chopped
2 red (bell) peppers, seeded and roughly chopped
2 garlic cloves, crushed
1 large onion, roughly chopped
30ml/2 tbsp white wine vinegar
120ml/4fl oz/½ cup olive oil
250g/9oz/4½ cups fresh white breadcrumbs
450ml/¾ pint/scant 2 cups iced water
salt and ground black pepper
12 ice cubes, to serve

For the garnish
30–45ml/2–3 tbsp olive oil
4 thick slices bread, crusts removed and cut into small cubes
2 tomatoes, peeled, seeded and finely diced
1 small green (bell) pepper, seeded and finely diced
1 small onion, very finely sliced
a small bunch of fresh flat leaf parsley, chopped

1 In a large bowl, mix the tomatoes, cucumber, peppers, garlic and onion. Stir in the vinegar, oil, breadcrumbs and water until well mixed.

3 To make the garnish, heat the oil in a frying pan and add the bread cubes. Cook over a medium heat for 5–6 minutes, stirring occasionally to brown evenly. Drain on kitchen paper and put into a small bowl.

4 Ladle the gazpacho into bowls and add two ice cubes to each, then serve immediately. Pass around the bowls of garnishing ingredients so that they can be added to suit individual taste.

2 Purée the mixture in a food processor or blender until almost smooth and pour into a large bowl. If the soup is too thick, add a little cold water. Stir in salt and pepper to taste and chill.

SUPERFOOD TIP
The powerful mix of fresh raw tomatoes, cucumbers, peppers, garlic, onion, and olive oil boosts circulation and the immune system and cleanses the body.

Classic gazpacho: Energy 244kcal/1009kJ; Protein 3g; Carbohydrate 12g, of which sugars 11g; Fat 21g, of which saturates 3g; Cholesterol 0mg; Calcium 34mg; Fibre 3.9g; Sodium 84mg.

Roasted garlic and butternut squash soup

Roasting the garlic mellows its strong flavour and enables you to eat more of this wonderful little bulb of goodness. Combined with the roasted butternut squash, a good source of vitamin A, it makes for a rich, filling soup without the need to add cream.

Serves 4

2 garlic bulbs, papery skin removed
75ml/5 tbsp olive oil
a few fresh thyme sprigs
1 large butternut squash, halved and seeded
2 onions, chopped
5ml/1 tsp ground coriander
1.2 litres/2 pints/5 cups vegetable or chicken stock
30–45ml/2–3 tbsp chopped fresh oregano or marjoram
salt and ground black pepper

For the salsa
4 large ripe tomatoes, halved and seeded
1 red (bell) pepper, halved and seeded
1 large fresh red chilli, halved and seeded
30–45ml/2–3 tbsp extra virgin olive oil
15ml/1 tbsp balsamic vinegar
pinch of caster (superfine) sugar

1 Preheat the oven to 220°C/425°F/Gas 7. Place the garlic bulbs on a piece of foil and pour over half the olive oil. Add the thyme sprigs, then fold the foil around the garlic bulbs.

2 Place the foil parcel and butternut squash on a baking sheet. Brush the squash with 15ml/1 tbsp of the rest of the olive oil. Add the tomatoes, red pepper and fresh chilli for the salsa.

3 Roast the vegetables for 25 minutes, then remove the tomatoes, pepper and chilli. Reduce the temperature to 190°C/375°F/Gas 5 and cook the squash and garlic for 20–25 minutes more, or until the squash is tender.

4 Heat the remaining oil in a large, heavy-based pan and cook the onions and ground coriander gently for about 10 minutes, or until they are softened.

5 Skin the pepper and chilli and process in a food processor or blender with the tomatoes and 30ml/2 tbsp olive oil. Stir in the vinegar and seasoning to taste, adding a pinch of caster sugar, if necessary. Add the remaining oil if you think the salsa needs it.

6 Squeeze the roasted garlic out of its papery skin into the onions and scoop the squash out of its skin, adding it to the pan. Add the stock, 5ml/1 tsp salt and plenty of black pepper. Bring to the boil and simmer for 10 minutes.

7 Stir in half the oregano or marjoram and cool the soup slightly, then process it in a blender or food processor. Alternatively, press the soup through a fine sieve (strainer).

8 Reheat the soup without allowing it to boil, then taste for seasoning before ladling it into warmed bowls. Top each with a spoonful of salsa and sprinkle over the remaining chopped oregano or marjoram. Serve immediately.

Butternut squash soup: Energy 238Kcal/986kJ; Protein 2.9g; Carbohydrate 11.9g, of which sugars 10.3g; Fat 20.2g of which saturates 3.1g; Cholesterol 0mg; Calcium 79mg; Fibre 4.1g; Sodium 11mg.

Red bean soup with avocado salsa

This aromatic, warming soup is perfect comfort food for a cold day. The cooling avocado and lime salsa make a nutritious vegetarian meal with plenty of slow-release carbohydrate. It is very high in both soluble and insoluble fibre, giving it heart-healthy credentials.

Serves 6

30ml/2 tbsp olive oil
2 onions, chopped
2 garlic cloves, chopped
10ml/2 tsp ground cumin
1.5ml/¼ tsp cayenne pepper
15ml/1 tbsp paprika
15ml/1 tbsp tomato purée (paste)
2.5ml/½ tsp dried oregano
400g/14oz can chopped tomatoes
2 x 400g/14oz cans red kidney
   beans, drained and rinsed
900ml/1½ pints/3¾ cups water
salt and ground black pepper
Tabasco sauce, to serve

For the guacamole salsa
2 avocados
1 small red onion, finely chopped
1 green chilli, seeded and finely
   chopped
15ml/1 tbsp chopped fresh
   coriander (cilantro)
juice of 1 lime

1 Heat the oil in a large, heavy-based pan and add the onions and garlic. Cook for about 4–5 minutes, until softened. Add the cumin, cayenne and paprika, and cook for 1 minute, stirring constantly.

2 Stir in the tomato purée and cook for a few seconds, then stir in the oregano. Add the chopped tomatoes, kidney beans and water.

> **COOK'S TIP**
> Make this soup in a big batch and freeze in small portions, ready to thaw in the microwave for an instant lunch or supper.

3 Bring the tomato and bean mixture to the boil and simmer for 15–20 minutes. Cool the soup slightly, then purée it in a food processor or blender until smooth. Return the mixture to the rinsed-out pan and add seasoning to taste.

4 To make the guacamole salsa, halve, stone (pit) and peel the avocados, then dice them finely. Place them in a small bowl and gently, but thoroughly, mix with the chopped red onion and chilli, and the fresh coriander and lime juice.

> **VARIATION**
> Instead of salsa, the reheated soup can be topped with a poached egg and strips of quickly sautéed red pepper.

5 Reheat the soup and serve, topped with a little guacamole salsa and a dash of Tabasco sauce as desired.

Red bean soup: Energy 254kcal/1064kJ; Protein 10.8g; Carbohydrate 29.2g, of which sugars 9.1g; Fat 11.2g, of which saturates 2.1g; Cholesterol 0mg; Calcium 111mg; Fibre 10.6g; Sodium 535mg.

Miso broth with tofu

This flavoursome broth is extremely nutritious, being high in protein and low in fat. Tofu and miso are both good sources of cholesterol-reducing soya proteins, and tofu also contains vegetarian omega 3; all of these properties are thought to be important for keeping your heart healthy.

3 Heat the mixture over a low heat until boiling, then lower the heat and simmer for about 10 minutes. Strain the broth, return it to the pan and reheat until simmering. Add the green portion of the sliced spring onions or leeks to the soup with the pak choi or Asian greens and tofu. Cook for 2 minutes.

4 In a small bowl, combine the miso with a little soup, then stir the mixture into the pan. Add soy sauce to taste.

5 Coarsely chop the coriander leaves and stir most of them into the soup with the white part of the spring onions or leeks.

6 Cook for 1 minute, then ladle the soup into warmed bowls. Sprinkle with the remaining chopped coriander and the shredded fresh red chilli, if using, and serve immediately.

COOK'S TIP
Some rice cakes make a good accompaniment for the soup, but for a more substantial snack, add noodles and simmer for the time suggested on the packet.

Serves 4

a bunch of spring onions
(scallions) or 5 baby leeks
15g/½oz fresh coriander (cilantro)
3 thin slices fresh root ginger
2 star anise
1 small dried red chilli
1.2 litres/2 pints/5 cups dashi or
vegetable stock
225g/8oz pak choi (bok choy) or
other Asian greens, thickly sliced
200g/7oz firm tofu, cut into
2.5cm/1in cubes
60ml/4 tbsp red miso
30–45ml/2–3 tbsp Japanese
soy sauce
1 fresh red chilli, seeded and
shredded (optional)

1 Cut the coarse green tops off the spring onions or baby leeks and slice the rest of the spring onions or leeks finely on the diagonal.

2 Place the spring onion or baby leek green tops in a large pan with the stalks from the coriander, ginger, star anise, dried chilli and the stock.

Miso broth with tofu: Energy 71kcal/297kJ; Protein 7.2g; Carbohydrate 4.2g, of which sugars 3.5g; Fat 2.9g, of which saturates 0.4g; Cholesterol 0mg; Calcium 372mg; Fibre 2.6g; Sodium 884mg.

Shiitake mushroom and red onion laksa

This hot-and-sour noodle soup is low in fat and calories, making it a good light lunch option. It is bursting with the flavour of the shiitake mushrooms, which are reputed to have cholesterol-reducing and anti-cancer properties. For a more hearty option use thick rice noodles instead of rice vermicelli.

Serves 6

150g/5oz/2½ cups dried shiitake
  mushrooms
1.2 litres/2 pints/5 cups boiling
  vegetable stock
30ml/2 tbsp tamarind paste
250ml/8fl oz/1 cup hot water
6 large dried red chillies, stems
  removed and seeded
2 lemon grass stalks, finely sliced
5ml/1 tsp ground turmeric
15ml/1 tbsp grated fresh galangal
1 onion, chopped
5ml/1 tsp dried shrimp paste
30ml/2 tbsp oil
10ml/2 tsp palm sugar
175g/6oz rice vermicelli
1 red onion, very finely sliced
1 small cucumber, seeded and cut
  into strips
a handful of fresh mint leaves,
  to garnish

1 Place the mushrooms in a bowl and pour in enough boiling stock to cover them, then leave to soak for about 30 minutes.

2 Put the tamarind paste in a bowl and pour in the hot water. Mash the paste with a fork to extract as much flavour as possible. Strain and reserve the liquid, discarding the pulp.

3 Soak the chillies in enough hot water to cover for 5 minutes, then drain, reserving the soaking liquid.

4 Process the lemon grass, turmeric, galangal, onion, soaked chillies and shrimp paste in a food processor or blender, adding a little soaking water from the chillies to form a paste.

5 Heat the oil in a large, heavy pan and cook the paste over a low heat for 4–5 minutes until fragrant.

6 Add the tamarind liquid and bring to the boil, then simmer for 5 minutes. Remove from the heat. Drain the mushrooms and reserve the stock.

7 Discard the stems of the mushrooms, then halve or quarter them, if large. Add the mushrooms to the pan together with their soaking liquid, the remaining stock and the palm sugar. Simmer for 25–30 minutes, or until the mushrooms are tender.

8 Put the rice vermicelli into a large bowl and cover with boiling water, then leave to soak for 4 minutes or according to the packet instructions.

9 Drain well, then divide among six bowls. Top with onion and cucumber, then ladle in the boiling shiitake soup. Add a small bunch of mint leaves to each bowl and serve immediately.

Shiitake mushroom laksa: Energy 146kcal/611kJ; Protein 4.4g; Carbohydrate 27.1g, of which sugars 3.7g; Fat 2.3g, of which saturates 0.3g; Cholesterol 4mg; Calcium 27mg; Fibre 1g; Sodium 54mg.

Chicken rice soup with lemon grass

This wholesome chicken rice soup is light and refreshing, with the fragrant aroma of lemon grass. The rice and shredded chicken are both easy to digest and this low-fat, low-calorie recipe makes a perfect pick-me-up if you have been under the weather.

Serves 4

1 small chicken or 2 meaty
  chicken legs
2 lemon grass stalks, trimmed, cut
  into 3 pieces, and lightly bruised
15ml/1 tbsp Thai fish sauce, such
  as nam pla
90g/3½oz/½ cup short grain
  rice, rinsed
1 small bunch coriander (cilantro)
  leaves, finely chopped, and
  1 green or red chilli, seeded and
  cut into thin strips, to garnish
1 lime, cut in wedges, to serve
sea salt
ground black pepper

For the stock
1 onion, quartered
2 cloves garlic, crushed
25g/1oz fresh root ginger, sliced
2 lemon grass stalks, cut in half
  lengthwise and bruised
2 dried red chillies
30ml/2 tbsp Thai dipping sauce

3 Pour the stock back into the deep pan and bring to the boil. Reduce the heat and stir in the lemon grass stalks and fish sauce. Stir in the rice and simmer, uncovered, for about 40 minutes.

4 Add the shredded chicken and season to taste. Ladle the piping hot soup into warmed individual bowls, garnish with chopped coriander and the thin strips of chilli, and serve with lime wedges to squeeze over.

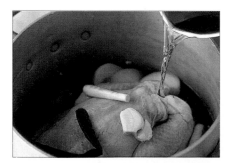

1 Put the chicken in a deep pan. Add all the stock ingredients and pour in 2 litres/3½ pints/7¾ cups water. Bring to the boil for a few minutes, then reduce the heat and simmer gently with the lid on for 2 hours.

2 Skim off any fat from the stock, strain and reserve. Remove the skin from the chicken and shred the meat. Set aside.

Chicken rice soup: Energy 147Kcal/615kJ; Protein 12.8g; Carbohydrate 19.8g, of which sugars 1.4g; Fat 1.7g, of which saturates 0.4g; Cholesterol 53mg; Calcium 37mg; Fibre 0.8g; Sodium 320mg.

Guacamole

This simple, tasty dish is popular with many, including children who love to dip. Full of heart-healthy monounsaturated fats, the avocados provide a creamy base for the dip without the need to use cream or mayonnaise. Serve with a variety of vegetable crudités to enhance its superfood credentials.

Serves 6

2 large, ripe avocados
2 red chillies, seeded
1 garlic clove
1 shallot
30ml/2 tbsp extra virgin olive oil,
 plus extra to serve
juice of 1 lemon or lime
salt and ground black pepper
flat leaf parsley leaves, to garnish
vegetable crudités, such as
 cucumber, carrot, red pepper
 and celery, to serve

1 Cut the avocados in half and carefully remove the stones.

2 Scoop out the avocado flesh into a large mixing bowl, then using a fork or potato masher, mash the avocado flesh until smooth.

3 Finely chop the seeded chillies, garlic and shallot, then stir them into the mashed avocado with the olive oil and lemon or lime juice. Season to taste.

4 Spoon the mixture into a small serving bowl. Drizzle over a little extra olive oil and sprinkle with a few flat leaf parsley leaves. Serve the dip immediately.

COOK'S TIP
In order to store the guacamole before serving, place it in a container with a lid and refrigerate. This will slow down the browning of the avocado.

SUPERFOOD TIP
Although already bursting with superfoods, you can further enhance the nutritional content of the guacamole dip, by adding finely chopped vegetables such as tomatoes or green or red (bell) peppers just before serving. Not only will it boost the vitamin content of the dish, it will also add colour and a deliciously crunchy texture.

Guacamole: Energy 172kcal/709kJ; Protein 1g; Carbohydrate 2g, of which sugars 1g; Fat 18g, of which saturates 3g; Cholesterol 0mg; Calcium 9mg; Fibre 0.1g; Sodium 70mg.

Artichoke and cumin dip

This dip is so easy to make and is extremely tasty. Artichokes are an excellent source of fibre and also contain cynarin, which helps to keep the liver healthy. Served with olives, hummus and wedges of pitta bread, this makes a healthy Mediterranean lunch plate.

Serves 4

2 x 400g/14oz cans artichoke
    hearts, drained
2 garlic cloves, peeled
2.5ml/½ tsp ground cumin
olive oil
salt and ground black pepper

COOK'S TIP
To enjoy hot, spead the dip over a flat serving dish and sprinkle with grated cheese. Grill for 5 minutes or until warmed through.

1 Put the artichoke hearts in a food processor with the garlic and ground cumin, and a generous drizzle of olive oil. Process to a smooth purée and season with plenty of salt and ground black pepper to taste.

2 Spoon the purée into a serving bowl and drizzle an extra swirl of olive oil on the top. Serve the artichoke and cumin dip with raw vegetables and slices of warm pitta bread for dipping.

Artichoke and cumin dip: Energy 42Kcal/172kJ; Protein 0.6g; Carbohydrate 1.2g, of which sugars 0.9g; Fat 3.9g, of which saturates 0.5g: Cholesterol 0mg: Calcium 41mg; Fibre 1.2g: Sodium 60mg.

Chilli bean dip

This creamy and spicy bean dip is best served warm with triangles of grilled pitta bread or a bowl of crunchy tortilla chips. The beans are high in fibre and protein and the chillies contain phytochemicals, which are stimulants and can help boost circulation.

Serves 4

2 garlic cloves
1 onion
2 green chillies
30ml/2 tbsp vegetable oil
5–10ml/1–2 tsp hot chilli powder
400g/14oz can kidney beans
75g/3oz mature Cheddar
  cheese, grated
1 red chilli, seeded
salt and pepper

1 Finely chop the garlic and onion. Seed and chop the green chillies.

2 Heat the oil in a large pan. Add the garlic, onion, green chillies and chilli powder. Cook gently for 5 minutes, stirring regularly, until the onions are softened and transparent.

COOK'S TIP
Always handle chillies peppers with care as they can irritate the skin and eyes.

3 Drain the kidney beans, reserving the liquid. Blend all but 30ml/2 tbsp of the beans to a purée with a food processor or hand blender or, for a coarser texture, simply mash them.

4 Add the puréed beans to the pan with 30–45ml/2–3 tbsp of the reserved liquor. Heat gently, stirring to mix well.

5 Stir in the whole beans and the Cheddar cheese. Cook gently for 2–3 minutes, stirring until the cheese melts. Add salt and pepper to taste.

6 Cut the red chilli into tiny strips. Spoon the dip into four individual serving bowls and sprinkle the chilli strips over the top. Serve warm with toasted pitta bread or tortilla chips.

Chilli bean dip: Energy 240Kcal/1002kJ; Protein 12.3g; Carbohydrate 20.3g, of which sugars 5.4g; Fat 12.3g, of which saturates 4.8g: Cholesterol 18mg: Calcium 219mg: Fibre 6.6g: Sodium 527mg.

Hummus

There are hundreds of recipes for hummus, but the one constant is the chickpea. Containing high-quality protein and an impressive array of vitamins and minerals, this creamy dip is an excellent addition to a healthy diet. Serve with vegetable crudités and pitta bread for a light lunch or supper.

Serves 4–6

225g/8oz dried chickpeas, soaked
    in water for at least 6 hours,
    or 2 x 400g/14oz cans chickpeas,
    drained
45–60ml/3–4 tbsp olive oil
juice of 1–2 lemons
2 garlic cloves crushed
5ml/1 tsp cumin seeds
15–30ml/1–2 tbsp natural (plain)
    bio-yogurt
salt and ground black pepper
15ml/1 tbsp olive oil and paprika,
    to garnish

1 If using dried chickpeas, drain and place them in a pan with plenty of water. Bring to the boil, reduce the heat, cover and simmer for about 1½ hours, or until they are very soft. Drain.

2 Remove any loose skins by rubbing the chickpeas in a clean kitchen towel. Put the cooked chickpeas into a food processor or blender and process to a thick purée.

3 Add the olive oil, lemon juice, garlic and cumin seeds, and blend thoroughly. Add the yogurt to lighten the mixture, and season to taste. Adjust the hummus to your taste by adding a little more lemon or olive oil.

4 Transfer the hummus to a serving bowl and drizzle a little oil over the surface to keep it moist. Sprinkle a little paprika over the top of the hummus, and serve with warm bread or carrot and celery sticks.

Hummus: Energy 190kcal/798kJ; Protein 8.4g; Carbohydrate 19.3g, of which sugars 1.4g; Fat 9.4g, of which saturates 1.3g; Cholesterol 0mg; Calcium 70mg; Fibre 4.1g; Sodium 19mg.

Tofu falafels with hemp seed oil

Traditionally made from chickpeas, this version uses vegetarian omega-3-rich tofu and hemp seed oil as its base. These protein-rich, crunchy balls are great served with wholemeal pitta bread and a sweet chilli sauce. They are also a traditional accompaniment to hummus.

Serves 4–6

30ml/2 tbsp vegetable oil
2 large onions, finely chopped
3 garlic cloves, crushed
500g/1¼lb firm tofu, drained
200g/7oz/3¾ cups fresh
  breadcrumbs
15g/½oz bunch fresh parsley,
  finely chopped
15ml/1 tbsp hemp seed oil
45ml/3 tbsp soy sauce
50g/2oz/4 tbsp sesame seeds,
  toasted
5ml/1 tsp ground cumin
15ml/1 tbsp ground turmeric
60ml/4 tbsp tahini (see Cook's Tips)
juice of 1 lemon
1.5ml/¼ tsp cayenne pepper

VARIATION
For a quick alternative dip, mix 30ml/2 tbsp of crème fraîche with 15ml/1tbsp chopped mint.

COOK'S TIPS
• Tahini, a paste made from sesame seeds, can be bought from most supermarkets or health food shops.
• If you like, process the tofu in a blender or food processor to a smooth paste before mixing with the other ingredients.

1 Heat the vegetable oil in a large frying pan and sauté the onion and garlic over a medium heat for 2–3 minutes, until softened. Set aside to cool slightly.

2 Preheat the oven to 180°C/350°F/Gas 4. In a large bowl, mix together the remaining ingredients until they are well blended, then stir in the onion mixture.

3 Form the mixture into 2.5cm/1in diameter balls and place them on an oiled baking sheet. Bake in the oven for 30 minutes, or until the balls are crusty on the outside but still moist on the inside.

4 Spear each of the hot falafels with a cocktail stick (toothpick), and serve immediately with a hummus dip and slices of warm pitta bread.

Falafels with hemp seed oil: Energy 341kcal/1422kJ; Protein 14g; Carbohydrate 22g, of which sugars 5g; Fat 23g, of which saturates 3g; Cholesterol 0mg; Calcium 611mg; Fibre 2.5g; Sodium 718mg.

Sprout salad with cashew cream dressing

This interesting salad has contrasting colours, textures and flavours and you can experiment with your own favourite sprout mix. The sprouts are very high in B-vitamins and vitamin C and the cashews and seeds are full of essential fatty acids, making this a highly nutritious salad.

2 Process the nuts with their soaking water in a food processor until you have a smooth sauce. Add more water if necessary.

3 Place the chopped pepper, sprouts, cucumber and lemon juice in a bowl and toss together. Serve with the cashew cream and sprinkle with the herbs and seeds.

COOK'S TIPS
• The cashew cream makes a smooth dressing for many different salads or can be used as a sauce. Cashews are rich in monounsaturated fatty acids, as found in the Mediterranean diet, and are favoured for their heart-protecting and anti-cancer properties.
• There are all kinds of sprouts, and beansprouts are one of the most readily commercially available. Rinse thoroughly in cold water before using in salads, juices and other recipes. Choose fresh, crisp sprouts with the seed or bean still attached. Avoid any that are slimy or appear musty. Sprouts are best eaten on the day they are bought, but, if fresh, they will keep for 2–3 days wrapped in a plastic bag in the refrigerator.

Serves 2

130g/4½oz cashew nuts
1 red (bell) pepper, seeded
  and finely chopped
90g/3½oz mung or aduki
  beansprouts or chickpea sprouts
½ small cucumber, chopped
juice of ½ lemon
small bunch fresh parsley,
  coriander (cilantro) or basil,
  finely chopped
5ml/1 tsp sesame, sunflower or
  pumpkin seeds

1 Soak the cashew nuts in 90ml/3½fl oz/6 tbsp of water for a few hours, preferably overnight, until they are plump.

Sprout salad with cashew cream: Energy 352Kcal/1459kJ; Protein 12g; Carbohydrate 18g; of which sugars 10g; Fat 26g; of which saturates 5g; Cholesterol 0mg; Calcium 78mg; Fibre 4.7g; Sodium 19mg.

Marinated tofu and broccoli with shallots

Gently steaming the tender young stems of broccoli retains their excellent nutritional content and, combined with marinated tofu, they make a very tasty and nourishing lunch. Sprinkling with shallots and sesame seeds further boosts the superfood content of this recipe.

Serves 4

500g/1¼lb block of firm
  tofu, drained
45ml/3 tbsp Indonesian soy sauce
30ml/2 tbsp sweet chilli sauce
45ml/3 tbsp soy sauce
5ml/1 tsp sesame oil
5ml/1 tsp finely grated fresh
  root ginger
400g/14oz tenderstem broccoli,
  halved lengthways
45ml/3 tbsp roughly chopped
  coriander (cilantro)
30ml/2 tbsp toasted sesame seeds
30ml/2 tbsp crispy fried shallots
steamed white rice or noodles,
  to serve

VARIATION
You could make this dish into a more substantial and satisfying meal by serving the tofu and broccoli with shallots and brown rice or buckwheat noodles.

1 Cut the tofu into four equal triangles. Place the tofu chunks in a heatproof dish.

2 In a small bowl, combine the soy sauce, chilli sauce, soy sauce, sesame oil and grated ginger. Pour over the tofu. Leave the tofu triangles to marinate for at least 30 minutes, turning them over occasionally.

3 Place the broccoli on a heatproof plate and place on a trivet or steamer rack in the wok. Cover and steam for 4–5 minutes, until just tender. Remove and keep warm.

4 Divide the broccoli among four warmed serving plates and top each one with a piece of tofu.

5 Spoon the remaining juices over the tofu and broccoli, then sprinkle over the coriander, sesame seeds and crispy shallots. Serve immediately with steamed white rice or noodles.

SUPERFOOD TIP
Firm tofu is good source of vegetarian omega-3 fats.

Marinated tofu: Energy 202Kcal/840kJ; Protein 16.5g; Carbohydrate 6.9g, of which sugars 5.6g; Fat 12.1g, of which saturates 1.7g; Cholesterol 0mg; Calcium 750mg; Fibre 3.5g; Sodium 938mg.

Red onion tart

Red onions have very high levels of flavonol antioxidants and are wonderfully mild and sweet when cooked slowly. The concentrated, caramelized onions make a juicy, sweet filling in this crumbly, buttery pastry case, and the fontina cheese is rich and creamy in contrast.

Serves 5–6

60ml/4 tbsp olive oil
1kg/2¼lb red onions, thinly sliced
2–3 garlic cloves, thinly sliced
5ml/1 tsp chopped fresh thyme,
 plus a few whole sprigs
5ml/1 tsp dark brown sugar
10ml/2 tsp sherry vinegar
225g/8oz fontina cheese,
 thinly sliced
salt and ground black pepper

For the pastry
115g/4oz/1 cup plain (all-purpose)
 flour
75g/3oz/¾ cup fine yellow
 cornmeal
5ml/1 tsp dark brown sugar
5ml/1 tsp chopped fresh thyme
90g/3½oz/7 tbsp butter
1 egg yolk
45ml/3 tbsp iced water

1 To make the pastry, sift the flour and cornmeal into a bowl with 5ml/ 1 tsp salt. Add plenty of black pepper and stir in the sugar and thyme. Rub in the butter until the mixture looks like breadcrumbs.

2 Beat the egg yolk with 30ml/ 2 tbsp iced water and use to bind the pastry, adding another 15ml/1 tbsp iced water, if necessary. Gather the dough into a ball with your fingertips, wrap and chill it for 30–40 minutes.

3 Heat 45ml/3 tbsp of the oil in a large, deep frying pan and add the onions. Cover and cook slowly, stirring occasionally, for 20–30 minutes. They should collapse but not brown.

4 Add the garlic and chopped thyme, then cook, stirring occasionally, for another 10 minutes. Increase the heat slightly, then add the sugar and sherry vinegar. Cook, uncovered, for another 5–6 minutes, until the onions start to caramelize slightly. Season to taste with salt and pepper. Cool.

5 Preheat the oven to 190°C/375°F/ Gas 5. Roll out the pastry thinly and use to line a 25cm/10in loose-based metal flan tin (quiche pan).

6 Prick the pastry all over with a fork and support the sides with foil. Bake for 12–15 minutes, or until it becomes lightly coloured.

7 Remove the foil and spread the caramelized onions evenly over the base of the pastry case (pie shell). Add the fontina and thyme and season with pepper.

8 Drizzle over the remaining oil, then bake for 15–20 minutes, until the filling is piping hot and the cheese is beginning to bubble. Garnish the tart with thyme and serve immediately. Serve with a tomato and basil salad.

Red onion tart: Energy 621kcal/2581kJ; Protein 18.1g; Carbohydrate 45.6g, of which sugars 12.5g; Fat 40.6g, of which saturates 20.7g; Cholesterol 122mg; Calcium 424mg; Fibre 3.8g; Sodium 443mg.

Roast peppers and tomatoes with sweet cicely

The aniseed flavours of sweet cicely and fennel combine beautifully with the succulent flavours of the roasted vegetables and the piquancy of capers. Rich in lycopene from red peppers and tomatoes, this dish is packed full of free-radical-neutralizing antioxidants.

Serves 4

4 red or yellow (bell) peppers,
   halved and seeded
8 small or 4 medium tomatoes
15ml/1 tbsp semi-ripe sweet
   cicely seeds
15ml/1 tbsp fennel seeds
15ml/1 tbsp capers, rinsed
4 sweet cicely flowers, newly
   opened, stems removed
60ml/4 tbsp olive oil
a few small sweet cicely leaves
   and 8 sweet cicely flowers,
      to garnish

1 Preheat the oven to 180°C/350°F/ Gas 4. Place the red pepper halves, skin side down, in a large ovenproof dish and set aside.

2 To skin the tomatoes, cut a cross at the base, then put in a bowl and pour over boiling water. Leave them to stand for 1 minute. Cut in half if they are of medium size, or leave whole if small. Place a whole small or half a medium tomato in each half of a pepper cavity.

VARIATION
If sweet cicely is not available, this dish can be made with a range of different herbs, such as chervil or lovage, although they will all impart a distinctive flavour.

3 Cover with a scattering of sweet cicely seeds, fennel seeds and capers and about half the sweet cicely flowers. Drizzle the olive oil all over. Bake in for 1 hour. Serve hot, garnished with fresh sweet cicely leaves and flowers.

Roast peppers: Energy 172Kcal/714kJ; Protein 2.5g; Carbohydrate 14.3g, of which sugars 13.8g; Fat 12g, of which saturates 1.9g; Cholesterol 0mg; Calcium 21mg; Fibre 3.8g; Sodium 16mg.

Herb and aduki bean-stuffed mushrooms

Portabello mushrooms have a rich flavour and a meaty texture that go well with this fragrant bean and herb stuffing. High in fibre and low in fat, beans add satisfying substance to this stuffing, and the garlicky pine nut accompaniment has a smooth, creamy consistency similar to that of hummus.

Serves 4–6

200g/7oz/1 cup dried or
  400g/14oz/2 cups drained,
  canned aduki beans
45ml/3 tbsp olive oil, plus extra
  for brushing
1 onion, finely chopped
2 garlic cloves, crushed
30ml/2 tbsp fresh chopped or
  5ml/1 tsp dried thyme
8 large field (portabello)
  mushrooms, stalks finely
  chopped
50g/2oz/1 cup fresh wholemeal
  (whole-wheat) breadcrumbs
juice of 1 lemon
185g/6½oz/¾ cup goat's cheese,
  crumbled
salt and freshly ground black
  pepper

For the pine nut tarator
50g/2oz/½ cup pine nuts toasted
50g/2oz/1 cup cubed white bread
2 garlic cloves, chopped
200ml/7fl oz/1 cup semi-skimmed
  (low-fat) milk
45ml/3 tbsp olive oil
15ml/1 tbsp chopped fresh parsley,
  to garnish (optional)

1 If using dried beans, soak them overnight, then drain and rinse well. Place in a pan, add enough water to cover and bring to the boil. Boil rapidly for 10 minutes, then reduce the heat, cook for 30 minutes, until tender, then drain. If using canned beans, rinse, drain well, then set aside.

2 Preheat the oven to 200°C/400°F/ Gas 6. Heat the oil in a frying pan, add the onion and garlic and sauté for 5 minutes, until softened. Add the thyme and the mushroom stalks and cook for a further 3 minutes, stirring occasionally, until tender.

3 Stir in the beans, breadcrumbs and lemon juice, season well, then cook for 2 minutes, until heated through. Mash two-thirds of the beans with a fork or potato masher, leaving the remaining beans whole.

4 Brush a baking dish and the base and sides of the mushrooms with oil, then top each one with a spoonful of the bean mixture. Put the mushrooms in the dish, cover with foil and bake for 20 minutes. Remove the foil. Top each mushroom with goat's cheese and bake for a further 15 minutes.

5 To make the pine nut tarator, blend all the ingredients until smooth and creamy. Add more milk if the mixture appears too thick. Sprinkle with parsley and serve with the mushrooms.

SUPERFOOD TIP
All beans are high in protein and fibre, and low in fat. They also contain some B vitamins and iron.

Stuffed mushrooms: Energy 406Kcal/1694kJ; Protein 17.5g; Carbohydrate 25.9g, of which sugars 5.9g; Fat 26.6g, of which saturates 8g; Cholesterol 31mg; Calcium 159mg; Fibre 6.1g; Sodium 573mg.

Leek terrine with red peppers

This attractive pressed leek and pepper terrine is a tasty summer salad dish. Both leeks and peppers are rich in antioxidants and fibre, both of which may contribute to a reduced cancer risk. The olive oil-rich dressing also contains heart-healthy monosaturated fats.

Serves 6–8

1.8kg/4lb slender leeks
4 large red (bell) peppers, halved
  and seeded
15ml/1 tbsp extra virgin olive oil
10ml/2 tsp balsamic vinegar
5ml/1 tsp ground roasted
  cumin seeds
salt and ground black pepper

For the dressing

120ml/4fl oz/½ cup extra virgin
  olive oil
1 garlic clove, bruised and peeled
5ml/1 tsp Dijon mustard
5ml/1 tsp soy sauce
15ml/1 tbsp balsamic vinegar
pinch of caster (superfine) sugar
2.5–5ml/½–1 tsp ground roasted
  cumin seeds
15–30ml/1–2 tbsp chopped mixed
  fresh basil and flat leaf parsley

1 Line a 23cm/9in-long terrine or loaf tin (pan) with clear film, leaving the ends overhanging the tin. Cut each of the leeks to the same length as the tin.

2 Cook the leeks in boiling salted water for 5–7 minutes, until just tender. Drain thoroughly and allow to cool, then squeeze out as much water as possible from the leeks and leave them to drain on a clean dish towel.

3 Grill the red peppers, skin-side uppermost, until the skin blisters and blackens. Place in a bowl, cover and leave for 10 minutes. Peel the peppers and cut the flesh into long strips, then place them in a bowl and add the oil, balsamic vinegar and ground roasted cumin. Season to taste with salt and pepper and toss well.

4 Layer the leeks and strips of red pepper in the lined tin, alternating the layers so that the white of the leeks in one row is covered by the green of the next row. Season the leeks with a little salt and pepper.

5 Cover the terrine with the overhanging clear film. Top with a plate and weigh it down with heavy food cans or scale weights. Chill for several hours or overnight.

6 To make the dressing, place the oil, garlic, mustard, soy sauce and vinegar in a jug and mix thoroughly. Season and add the caster sugar. Add the ground cumin seeds to taste and leave to stand for several hours. Discard the garlic and add the fresh herbs to the dressing.

7 Unmould the terrine and cut it into thick slices. Put 1–2 slices on each plate, drizzle with dressing and serve.

Leek terrine with red peppers: Energy 171Kcal/710kJ; Protein 4.6g; Carbohydrate 12.4g, of which sugars 10.5g; Fat 11.7g, of which saturates 1.8g; Cholesterol 0mg; Calcium 66mg; Fibre 6.4g; Sodium 161mg.

Smoked mackerel pâté

One of the most convenient sources of heart-healthy omega-3 fats, smoked mackerel is cheap and widely available, and so it makes a great way to boost your oily fish intake. Making this pâté couldn't be quicker or easier and is a sure-fire winner with children and adults alike.

Serves 4–6

225g/8oz/1 cup crème fraîche or
  Greek (US strained plain) yogurt
finely grated rind of ½ lemon
few sprigs of parsley
225g/8oz smoked mackerel fillets
5–10ml/1–2 tsp horseradish sauce
1 tbsp lemon juice, or to taste
ground black pepper
crusty bread, hot toast or crisp
  plain crackers, to serve
lemon wedges, to serve

COOK'S TIP
To turn this recipe into a dip, just add a little more crème fraîche until it is of the desired consistency.

1 Place the crème fraîche or Greek yogurt and grated lemon rind into a blender or food processor. Add a few sprigs of parsley.

2 Flake the mackerel, discarding the skin and any bones. Add the flaked fish to the blender. Blend on a medium speed until the mixture is almost smooth.

3 Add the horseradish sauce and lemon juice and blend briefly. Season with ground black pepper. Spoon the mackerel pâté into individual dishes. Cover and refrigerate.

4 Garnish with parsley and serve with warm crusty bread, hot toast or crisp plain crackers, and lemon wedges for squeezing over.

Smoked mackerel pâté: Energy 344kcal/1421kJ; Protein 10.7g; Carbohydrate 0.5g, of which sugars 0.4g; Fat 33.3g, of which saturates 14.3g; Cholesterol 88mg; Calcium 57mg; Fibre 0.1g; Sodium 518mg.

Tuna and wasabi

Unlike its canned counterpart, fresh tuna is an excellent source of omega-3 fat that is proven to keep your heart healthy as well as to improve brain function. This marinated raw dish is a classic Japanese sashimi with a tremendous warming kick from the wasabi.

Serves 4

400g/14oz very fresh tuna, skinned
1 carton mustard and cress (optional)
20ml/4 tsp wasabi paste from a tube, or the same amount of wasabi powder mixed with 10ml/2 tsp water
60ml/4 tbsp Japanese soy sauce
8 spring onions (scallions), green part only, finely chopped
4 shiso leaves, cut into thin slivers lengthways

1 Cut the tuna into 2cm/¾ in cubes. If you are using mustard and cress, tie it into pretty bunches or arrange as a bed in four small serving bowls or on plates.

2 Just 5–10 minutes before serving, blend the wasabi paste with the soy sauce in a bowl, then add the tuna and spring onions. Mix and leave to marinate for 5 minutes. Divide among the bowls and add a few slivers of shiso leaves on top. Serve immediately.

Tuna and wasabi: Energy 153Kcal/643kJ; Protein 24.5g; Carbohydrate 2.3g, of which sugars 2.1g; Fat 5.1g, of which saturates 1.3g; Cholesterol 29mg; Calcium 28mg; Fibre 0.4g; Sodium 806mg.

Seaweed sushi rolls

Nori is a type of sea vegetable that has been processed into sheets specifically for sushi making. It is packed full of essential minerals such as iodine, which is important in thyroid function. Add to the superfood count by filling the rolls with strips of salmon, tuna, avocado or pepper.

3 Place a sheet of nori, shiny-side down, on a bamboo mat. Divide the rice into 12 portions. Spread one portion over the nori, leaving a 1cm/½ in clear space at the top and bottom.

4 Spread a little wasabi paste in a horizontal line along the middle of the rice and place one or two sticks of tuna on this.

Makes 12 rolls or 72 slices

400g/14oz/2 cups sushi rice, soaked for 20 minutes in water to cover
55ml/3½ tbsp rice vinegar
15ml/1 tbsp sugar
2.5ml/½ tsp salt
6 sheets nori seaweed
200g/7oz tuna, in one piece
200g/7oz salmon, in one piece
wasabi paste
½ cucumber, quartered lengthways and seeded
pickled ginger, to garnish (optional)
Japanese soy sauce, to serve

1 Drain the rice, then put in a pan with 525ml/18fl oz/2¼ cups water. Bring to the boil, then lower the heat, cover and simmer for 20 minutes, or until all the liquid has been absorbed. Meanwhile, heat the vinegar, sugar and salt, stir well and cool. Add to the hot rice, then remove the pan from the heat and allow to stand (covered) for 20 minutes.

2 Cut the nori sheets in half lengthways. Cut each of the tuna and salmon into four long sticks, about the same length as the long side of the nori, and about 1cm/½ in square if viewed from the end.

5 Holding the mat and the edge of the yaki-nori nearest to you, roll up the seaweed and rice into a cylinder with the tuna in the middle. Use the mat as a guide – do not roll it into the food. Roll the rice tightly so that it sticks together and encloses the tuna.

6 Carefully roll the sushi off the mat. Make 11 more rolls in the same way, four for each filling ingredient, but do not use wasabi with the cucumber. Use a wet knife to cut each roll into six slices and stand them on a platter. Garnish with pickled ginger, if you wish, and serve with soy sauce.

Seaweed sushi rolls: Energy 31kcal/128kJ; Protein 1.7g; Carbohydrate 4.8g, of which sugars 0.3g; Fat 0.5g, of which saturates 0.1g; Cholesterol 2mg; Calcium 4mg; Fibre 0.1g; Sodium 3mg.

Garlic prawns in filo tartlets

These light, tasty tartlets are made with crisp golden layers of filo pastry and filled with spicy garlic and chilli prawns. Prawns are high in protein and low in fat, and when served with salad or new potatoes, make a well-balanced healthy meal.

Serves 4

For the tartlets
50g/2oz/4 tbsp butter, melted
2–3 large sheets filo pastry

For the filling
115g/4oz/½ cup butter
2–3 garlic cloves, crushed
1 red chilli, seeded and chopped
350g/12oz/3 cups cooked peeled
 prawns (shrimps)
30ml/2 tbsp chopped fresh parsley
 or chopped fresh chives
salt and freshly ground
 black pepper

1 Preheat the oven to 200°C/ 400°F/Gas 6. Brush four individual 7.5cm/3in flan tins (pans) with the melted butter.

2 Cut the filo pastry into twelve 10cm/4in squares and brush with the melted butter.

3 Place three squares of pastry inside each tin, overlapping them at slight angles and carefully frilling the edges and points, while at the same time forming a good hollow in the centre of each tartlet. Brush with a little more butter.

4 Bake in the oven for 10–15 minutes, until crisp and golden. Leave to cool slightly, then remove the pastry cases from the tins.

5 Meanwhile, make the filling. Melt the butter in a frying pan, then add the garlic, chilli and prawns and fry quickly for 1–2 minutes to warm through. Stir in the parsley or chives and season with salt and plenty of pepper. Spoon the prawn filling into the tartlets and serve at once.

COOK'S TIP
If you prefer your spicy food with a little more heat, then simply add another fresh chilli, or choose a hotter variety.

Garlic prawn tartlets: Energy 440kcal/1825kJ; Protein 17.6g; Carbohydrate 15g, of which sugars 0.7g; Fat 34.8g, of which saturates 21.6g; Cholesterol 259mg; Calcium 118mg; Fibre 1g; Sodium 419mg.

SALADS, SALSAS, SIDES AND DRESSINGS

Delicious salads, sides, salsas and dressings can be made from an endless variety of superfood ingredients, including vitamin-packed fruit and vegetables and protein-rich eggs, meat and oily fish. This chapter introduces a selection of vibrant recipes to enjoy either on their own or to complement a main dish. Choose from an enticing selection of dishes including Green Soya Bean and Rocket Salad, Watermelon and Feta Salad, Chilli Rice with Turmeric and Coriander, and Marinated Salmon with Avocado.

Tricolore salad

A classic Italian salad, the key to making this perfectly is in using the best ingredients possible. Buffalo mozzarella has the best flavour and ripe plum tomatoes are ideal. Use a ripe but not too soft avocado and your best extra virgin olive oil; both will contribute heart-healthy monounsaturated oils.

Serves 2–3

150g/5oz mozzarella, thinly sliced
4 large plum tomatoes, sliced
1 large firm and ripe avocado
about 12 basil leaves or a
    small handful of flat leaf
    parsley leaves
45–60ml/3–4 tbsp extra virgin
    olive oil
ground black pepper
ciabatta and sea salt flakes,
    to serve

1 Arrange the sliced mozzarella cheese and tomatoes randomly on two salad plates. Crush over a few good pinches of sea salt flakes. This will help to draw out some of the juices from the plum tomatoes. Set aside in a cool place and leave to marinate for about 30 minutes.

2 Just before serving, cut the avocado in half using a sharp knife and twist the halves to separate. Lift out the stone (pit) and remove the peel.

3 Carefully slice the avocado flesh crossways into half moons, or cut it into large chunks if that is easier.

4 Place the avocado on the salad, then sprinkle with the basil or parsley. Drizzle over the olive oil, add a little more salt if needed and some ground black pepper.

5 Serve immediately, with chunks of crusty Italian ciabatta for mopping up the dressing.

Tricolore salad: Energy 526kcal/2180kJ; Protein 17.5g; Carbohydrate 8.3g, of which sugars 7.2g; Fat 47.1g, of which saturates 16g; Cholesterol 44mg; Calcium 344mg; Fibre 5.8g; Sodium 327mg.

Moroccan carrot salad

Grating and slicing carrot for use in salads is a very good way of ensuring that the antioxidant carotenes are released from the cell walls where they are bound up. Choose slender carrots and slice thinly, so they only need cooking for a few minutes, which preserves optimum nutrition levels.

Serves 4–6

3–4 carrots, thinly sliced
pinch of sugar
3–4 garlic cloves, chopped
1.5ml/¼ tsp ground cumin,
   or to taste
juice of ½ lemon
30–45ml/2–3 tbsp extra virgin
   olive oil
15–30ml/1–2 tbsp red wine
   vinegar or fruit vinegar, such
   as raspberry
30ml/2 tbsp chopped fresh
   coriander (cilantro) leaves, or a
   mixture of coriander and parsley
salt and ground black pepper

1 Cook the sliced carrots by either steaming or boiling in a little water until they are just tender but not too soft. Drain the carrots and leave for a few moments to dry off, then place them in a bowl.

2 In a measuring jug (cup) mix together the sugar, garlic, cumin, lemon juice, olive oil and vinegar then pour over the carrots and toss together. Add the chopped fresh herbs and season to taste. Serve warm or chilled.

Moroccan carrot salad: Energy 53Kcal/220kJ; Protein 0.6g; Carbohydrate 4.2g, of which sugars 3.9g; Fat 3.9g, of which saturates 0.6g; Cholesterol 0mg; Calcium 29mg; Fibre 1.6g; Sodium 15mg.

Blue cheese, fig and walnut salad

A classic combination of nuts and cheese, this is a delicious fresh-tasting first course that can also be served without the figs as a cheese course. High-fibre figs are loaded with minerals. Walnuts are an excellent source of vegetarian omega 3 and antioxidants, both of which are cardioprotective.

Serves 4

Mixed salad leaves
4 fresh figs
115g/4oz Roquefort or other
    soft blue cheese, cut into
    small chunks
75g/3oz/¾ cup walnut halves

For the dressing
45ml/3 tbsp walnut oil
juice of 1 lemon
salt and ground black pepper

1 Mix all the dressing ingredients together in a bowl. Whisk briskly until thick and emulsified.

2 Wash and dry the salad leaves, then tear them gently into bitesize pieces. Place in a mixing bowl and toss with the dressing.

3 Transfer to a large serving dish or divide among four individual plates, ensuring a good balance of colour and texture on each plate.

COOK'S TIP
If you are trying to reduce your intake of saturated fats, use half the recommended amount of blue cheese. Blue cheese has a strong flavour, so a little will go a long way.

4 Cut the figs into quarters and add to the salad leaves.

5 Sprinkle the cheese over, crumbling it slightly. Then sprinkle over the walnuts, breaking them up roughly in your fingers as you go.

VARIATION
The figs may be replaced with ripe nectarines or peaches if you prefer. Wash and cut in half, discard the stone (pit), then cut each half into three or four slices. If the skin is tough, you may need to remove it.

Blue cheese and walnut salad: Energy 415kcal/1726kJ; Protein 10.6g; Carbohydrate 26.6g, of which sugars 26.4g; Fat 30.3g, of which saturates 7.3g; Cholesterol 22mg; Calcium 286mg; Fibre 4.5g; Sodium 383mg.

Watercress and pear salad with cheese dressing

A refreshing light salad, this dish combines lovely peppery watercress, soft juicy pears and a tart but creamy dressing. Watercress has high antioxidant levels and sulphur-containing phytonutrients, which together make a powerful combination.

Serves 4

25g/1oz soft blue cheese (Danish
  Blue, Roquefort or Gorganzola)
30ml/2 tbsp walnut oil
15ml/1 tbsp lemon juice
2 bunches of watercress,
  thoroughly washed
  and trimmed
2 ripe pears (see Cook's Tips)
salt and ground black pepper

1 Crumble and then mash the blue cheese into the walnut oil.

2 Whisk in the lemon juice to create a thickish mixture. If you need to thicken it further, add a little more cheese. Season to taste with salt and black pepper. Arrange a pile of watercress on the side of four plates.

SUPERFOOD TIP
Pears are a good source of both soluble and insoluble fibre, as well as vitamin C and potassium.

3 Just before serving, peel and slice the two pears, then place the pear slices to the side of the watercress, allowing half a pear per person. You can also put the pear slices on top of the watercress, if you prefer. Drizzle the dressing over the salad.

COOK'S TIPS
• Choose Comice or similar pears that are soft and juicy for this salad.
• If you want to get things ready in advance, peel and slice the pears, then rub them with some lemon juice in order to stop them from discolouring so quickly.
• If you find the flavour of the watercress is too strong on its own, you can try mixing it with baby spinach leaves or rocket (arugula) leaves to vary the taste.

Watercress and pear salad: Energy 106kcal/442kJ; Protein 2.3g; Carbohydrate 7.6g, of which sugars 7.6g; Fat 7.6g, of which saturates 1.8g; Cholesterol 5mg; Calcium 81mg; Fibre 2g; Sodium 91mg.

Green soya bean and rocket salad

This quick and simple salad is a refreshing change from mere leaves, as these young beans give a lovely texture. As well as being an excellent source of protein for vegetarians and vegans, green soya beans also contain cholesterol-reducing isoflavones.

Serves 4

250g/9oz green soya beans
70g/2¾oz rocket (arugula) leaves
10ml/2 tsp fresh basil leaves
2 tsp fresh coriander (cilantro) leaves
1 tbsp olive oil
1 tsp lemon juice
1 tsp balsamic vinegar
fresh ground black pepper

COOK'S TIP
Green soya beans are also known as edamame beans. You can buy them frozen for convenience.

1 Cook the soya beans in boiling water for 5 minutes. Drain, then set aside to cool. Chop the fresh rocket, basil and coriander leaves.

2 To make the dressing, mix together the olive oil, lemon juice and vinegar. Season with ground black pepper.

3 When the beans are cool, pour over the dressing and stir to mix both well together.

4 Toss the dressed beans together with the rocket and chopped herbs. Serve the salad immediately.

Green soya bean and rocket salad: Energy 125Kcal/520kJ; Protein 9g; Carbohydrate 4g, of which sugars 2g; Fat 8g, of which saturates 1g; Cholesterol 0mg; Calcium 59mg; Fibre 4g; Sodium 1mg.

Grated carrot, apple and alfalfa sprout salad

This refreshingly sweet and fragrant salad looks colourful and tastes good with its fat-free lemon juice and honey dressing. Grating improves the availability of all the phytonutrients, and the nutrient-rich alfalfa sprouts add a delightful nutty flavour.

Serves 1

90g/3½oz carrots, peeled and
   coarsely grated
2 desert apples, coarsely grated
2.5cm/1in piece fresh root ginger,
   peeled and finely grated
juice of ½ lemon or 15ml/
   1 tbsp cider apple vinegar
5ml/1 tsp clear honey
small handful alfalfa or
   other beansprouts of
   your choice
5ml/1 tsp sesame seeds, to
   serve (optional)

1 Place the grated carrots, apples and ginger in a large bowl. Add the lemon juice or cider apple vinegar and the clear honey, and mix all of the ingredients well together.

2 Transfer the mixed ingredients to a small bowl and press down firmly.

3 Carefully invert the bowl on to a plate to make a neat 'castle'. Top this with the alfalfa, and sprinkle liberally with sesame seeds to serve.

COOK'S TIP
Serve this dish immediately for maximum crunchiness, otherwise the grated carrots and apples will go limp.

Grated carrot and alfalfa sprout salad: Energy 194Kcal/818kJ; Protein 3g; Carbohydrate 41g, of which sugars 39g; Fat 3g; of which saturates 0g; Cholesterol 0mg; Calcium 70mg; Fibre 6.6g; Sodium 36mg.

Watermelon and feta salad

The combination of sweet juicy watermelon with salty feta cheese is refreshing and, along with the seeds and olives, makes a wonderfully nutritious Mediterranean salad. The juice of the lycopene-rich watermelon serves as a light dressing, and the seeds and olives are full of essential fatty acids.

Serves 4

4 slices watermelon, chilled
130g/4½oz feta cheese, cubed
handful of mixed seeds, such as
   pumpkin, sunflower, hemp and
   flax seed, lightly toasted
10–15 black olives
1 frisée lettuce, core removed
sprinkling of olive oil and fresh
   thyme, to garnish

COOK'S TIP
The best olives for this recipe are the plump black varieties, such as kalamata, other shiny, brined varieties or dry-cured black olives.

1 Cut the rind off the watermelon and remove as many of the seeds as you can. The sweetest and juiciest part of the fruit is at the core, and so you may want to cut off any whiter flesh just under the skin.

2 Cut the flesh into triangular chunks. Mix together the watermelon, feta cheese, mixed seeds and black olives.

3 Cover and chill for 30 minutes in the refrigerator before serving on a bed of lettuce leaves. Garnish with a drizzle of olive oil and a sprinkling of fresh thyme.

Watermelon and feta salad: Energy 256kcal/1066kJ; Protein 7.7g; Carbohydrate 12.9g, of which sugars 11.6g; Fat 19.7g, of which saturates 6.2g; Cholesterol 23mg; Calcium 165mg; Fibre 1.4g; Sodium 616mg.

Pink grapefruit and avocado salad

Peppery rocket leaves and the zesty tang of citrus fruits complement the creamy avocado beautifully in this refreshing salad. The heart-healthy monounsaturated oils of the avocado in this supernutrient-rich dish join the lycopene-rich pink grapefruit.

Serves 4

2 pink grapefruits
2 ripe avocados
30ml/2 tbsp chilli oil
90g/3½oz rocket (arugula) leaves

1 Slice the top and bottom off one of the grapefruits, then cut off all of the peel and pith from around the side – the best way to do this is to cut down in wide strips.

2 Working over a small bowl to catch the juices, cut out the segments from between the membranes and place them in a separate bowl. Squeeze any juices remaining in the membranes into the bowl, then discard them. Repeat with the remaining grapefruit.

3 Halve, stone (pit) and peel the avocados. Slice and add to the grapefruit. Whisk a pinch of salt into the grapefruit juice, followed by the chilli oil.

4 Pile the rocket leaves on to four plates and top with the grapefruit segments and avocado slices. Pour over the dressing and toss gently with your fingers. Serve immediately.

COOK'S TIP
• Coat the avocado in the grapefruit juice dressing, to stop it from browning.
• For added carbohydrate, the salad is delicious with wholemeal pasta or quinoa. Sprinkle with finely chopped walnuts and snipped fresh chives.

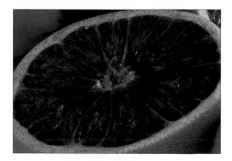

Pink grapefruit and avocado salad: Energy 151kcal/625kJ; Protein 1.1g; Carbohydrate 5.6g, of which sugars 5.2g; Fat 13.9g, of which saturates 2.4g; Cholesterol 0mg; Calcium 24mg; Fibre 1.9g; Sodium 13mg.

Grilled leek and courgette salad

This salad makes a delicious summery appetizer or main course when served on a bed of crisp, sweet lettuce. Whenever possible, choose young tender leeks and retain as much of the green part as possible, as this is where the nutrients are concentrated.

4 Heat the grill (broiler). Brush the leeks and courgettes lightly with oil. Grill (broil) the leeks for 2–3 minutes on each side and the courgettes for about 5 minutes on each side.

5 Place the grilled leeks in a shallow dish, together with the courgettes.

6 Place the remaining oil in a small bowl and whisk in the lemon rind, 15ml/1 tbsp lemon juice, the garlic, chilli and a pinch of sugar, if using. Season with salt and black pepper.

7 Pour the dressing over the leeks and courgettes. Stir in the olives and chopped mint, then set aside to marinate for a few hours, turning the vegetables once or twice.

8 If the salad has been marinating in the refrigerator, remove it 30 minutes before serving and bring back to room temperature. When ready to serve, mix in the crumbled feta cheese and garnish with several fresh mint leaves.

Serves 6

12 slender, baby leeks
6 small courgettes (zucchini)
45ml/3 tbsp extra virgin olive oil, plus extra for brushing
finely shredded rind and juice of ½ lemon
1–2 garlic cloves, finely chopped
½ fresh red chilli, seeded and diced
pinch of caster (superfine) sugar (optional)
50g/2oz/ ½ cup black olives, stoned (pitted) and roughly chopped
30ml/2 tbsp chopped fresh mint
150g/5oz feta cheese, sliced or crumbled
salt and ground black pepper
fresh mint leaves, to garnish

1 Bring a pan of water to the boil. Add the leeks and cook gently for 2–3 minutes.

2 Drain the leeks, refresh under cold water, then squeeze out any excess water and leave to drain.

3 Cut the courgettes in half lengthways. Place in a colander, adding 5ml/1 tsp salt to the layers, and leave to drain for about 45 minutes. Rinse well under running water and pat dry thoroughly on a piece of kitchen paper.

SUPERFOOD TIP
Olives are rich in vitamins A and E as well as copper and calcium.

Leek and courgette salad: Energy 197kcal/812kJ; Protein 6.2g; Carbohydrate 3.4g, of which sugars 2.9g; Fat 17.6g, of which saturates 5.3g; Cholesterol 18mg; Calcium 140mg; Fibre 2.6g; Sodium 552mg.

Quinoa salad with mango

Quinoa is a delicious gluten-free alternative to couscous or bulgur wheat, and is a wholesome vegetable protein. This nutrient-rich grain is best combined with ingredients that have a more robust flavour, such as fresh herbs, chilli, fruit and nuts, all of which feature in this fabulous salad.

Serves 4

130g/4½ oz quinoa
1 mango
60ml/4 tbsp pine nuts
large handful fresh basil,
  roughly chopped
large handful fresh flat leaf
  parsley, roughly chopped
large handful fresh mint,
  roughly chopped
1 mild long fresh red chilli,
  seeded and chopped

For the dressing
15ml/1 tbsp lemon juice
15ml/1 tbsp extra virgin olive oil
salt and ground black pepper

1 Put the quinoa in a pan and cover with cold water. Season with salt and bring to the boil. Reduce the heat, cover the pan with a lid and simmer for 12 minutes, or until the quinoa is tender. Drain well.

2 Meanwhile, prepare the mango. Cut vertically down each side of the stone (pit). Taking the two large slices, cut the flesh into a criss-cross pattern down to (but not through) the skin.

> **COOK'S TIP**
> You can enrich the flavour of quinoa by cooking in chicken or vegetable stock.

3 Press each half inside out, then cut the mango cubes away from the skin.

4 Toast the pine nuts for a few minutes in a dry frying pan until golden, then remove from the heat.

5 Mix together the ingredients for the dressing and season well.

6 Put the cooked quinoa into a bowl and add the herbs and chilli. Pour the dressing into the bowl and mix lightly until combined. Season to taste.

7 Transfer to a bowl or four shallow dishes. Arrange the mango on top of the herby quinoa and sprinkle with the pine nuts.

Quinoa salad with mango: Energy 206kcal/857kJ; Protein 4.5g; Carbohydrate 23.1g, of which sugars 6.2g; Fat 11.2g, of which saturates 1g; Cholesterol 0mg; Calcium 62mg; Fibre 2.5g; Sodium 9mg.

Lentil salad with red onion and garlic

This delicious, fragrant lentil salad is a great Moroccan-style dish, which can be served warm or chilled. As well as being high in fibre, this dish is also rich in the organosulphur compounds from the red onion and garlic, which have anti-inflammatory properties.

Serves 4

45ml/3 tbsp olive oil
2 red onions, chopped
2 tomatoes, peeled, seeded and chopped
10ml/2 tsp ground turmeric
10ml/2 tsp ground cumin
175g/6oz/¾ cup brown or green lentils, picked over and rinsed
900ml/1½ pints/3¾ cups vegetable stock or water
4 garlic cloves, crushed
small bunch of fresh coriander (cilantro), finely chopped
salt and ground black pepper
1 lemon, cut into wedges, to serve

1 Heat 30ml/2 tbsp of the oil in a large pan or flameproof casserole and fry the onions until soft.

2 Add the tomatoes, turmeric and cumin, then stir in the lentils. Pour in the stock or water and bring to the boil, then reduce the heat and simmer until the lentils are tender and almost all the liquid has been absorbed.

3 In a separate pan, fry the garlic in the remaining oil until brown and frizzled. Toss the garlic into the lentils with the fresh coriander and season to taste. Serve warm or cold, with wedges of lemon for squeezing over.

SUPERFOOD TIP
The vitamin C from the lemon juice will help to improve absorption of iron from the lentils.

Lentil salad: Energy 266Kcal/1116kJ; Protein 12.5g; Carbohydrate 35.1g, of which sugars 9.2g; Fat 9.4g, of which saturates 1.4g; Cholesterol 0mg; Calcium 73mg; Fibre 4.8g; Sodium 29mg.

Spinach and roast garlic salad

Roasting garlic sweetens its flavour and tones down its pungency, while still retaining all its goodness. Using young raw spinach leaves ensures that you are retaining all the nutrients, and the lemon juice in the dressing will help you absorb more of the iron.

Serves 4

12 garlic cloves, unpeeled
60 ml/4 tbsp extra virgin olive oil
450g/1lb baby spinach leaves
50g/2oz/½ cup pine nuts,
  lightly toasted
juice of ½ lemon
salt and freshly ground black
  pepper

COOK'S TIP
If spinach is to be served raw in a salad, the leaves need to be young and tender. Wash them well, drain and pat dry with absorbent paper.

1 Preheat the oven to 190°C/375°F/ Gas 5. Place the garlic in a small roasting dish, toss in 30ml/2 tbsp of the olive oil and bake for about 15 minutes, until the garlic cloves are slightly charred around the edges.

2 While still warm, transfer the garlic to a salad bowl. Add the spinach, pine nuts, lemon juice, remaining olive oil and a little salt. Toss well and add black pepper to taste. Serve immediately, inviting guests to squeeze the softened garlic purée out of the skin to eat.

Spinach and roast garlic salad: Energy 234Kcal/966kJ; Protein 6.1g; Carbohydrate 6g, of which sugars 3.7g; Fat 20.8g, of which saturates 2.3g; Cholesterol 0mg; Calcium 240mg; Fibre 4.6g; Sodium 23mg.

Orange, tomato and chive salsa

Both bursting with vitamin C, the orange and tomato make a cheerful combination of flavours lifted by the fragrant chopped chives and garlic. Its citrus zing makes this salsa perfect to serve with oily fish such as grilled (broiled) tuna steak or barbecued sardines.

2 Hold the orange in one hand over a bowl. Slice toward the middle of the fruit, to one side of a segment, and then gently twist the knife to ease the segment away from the membrane and out of the orange. Repeat to remove all the segments. Squeeze any juice from the remaining membrane. Prepare the second orange in the same way.

3 Roughly chop the orange segments and place them in the bowl with the collected juice.

4 Halve the tomato and use a teaspoon to scoop the seeds into the bowl. Finely dice the flesh and add to the oranges in the bowl.

5 Hold the bunch of chives neatly together and use a pair of kitchen scissors to snip them into the bowl.

Serves 4

2 large oranges
1 beefsteak tomato
a bunch of chives
1 garlic clove
30ml/2 tbsp olive oil
sea salt

VARIATION
Try adding a little diced mozzarella cheese to make a more substantial salsa.

1 Slice the top and bottom off the orange so that it will stand firmly on a chopping board. Using a large sharp knife, remove the peel by slicing from the top to the bottom of the orange.

6 Thinly slice the garlic and stir it into the orange mixture. Pour over the olive oil, season with sea salt and stir well to mix. Serve within 2 hours.

Orange, tomato and chive salsa: Energy 91Kcal/380kJ; Protein 1.3g; Carbohydrate 9.3g, of which sugars 9.3g; Fat 5.7g, of which saturates 0.8g; Cholesterol 0mg; Calcium 49mg; Fibre 2g; Sodium 7mg.

Black bean salsa

This salsa has a very striking appearance due to the black beans and bright red chillies. The beans are folate rich and this salsa is a great way to liven up any meal. Leave the salsa for a day or two after making, to allow the flavours to develop fully.

Serves 4 as an accompaniment

130g/4½oz/generous ½ cup black
  beans, soaked overnight in
  water to cover
1 dried red chilli
2 fresh red chillies
1 red onion
grated rind and juice of 1 lime
30ml/2 tbsp Mexican beer
  (optional)
15ml/1 tbsp olive oil
small bunch of fresh coriander
  (cilantro), chopped
salt

1 Drain the beans and put them in a large pan. Pour in water to cover and place the lid on the pan.

2 Bring to the boil, lower the heat slightly and simmer the beans for about 40 minutes, or until they are tender. They should still have a little bite and should not have begun to disintegrate.

3 Drain, rinse under cold water, then drain again and set the beans aside until they are cold.

4 Soak the dried red chilli in hot water for about 10 minutes, until softened. Wearing gloves if you prefer, drain, remove the stalk and then slit the chilli and scrape out the seeds with a small sharp knife. Chop the flesh finely.

5 Dry-fry the fresh red chillies in a griddle pan until the skins are scorched. Alternatively, spear them on a long-handled metal skewer and roast over the flame of a gas burner until the skins blister and darken. Don't let the flesh burn. Place the roasted chillies in a strong plastic bag and tie the top to keep the steam in. Set aside for 20 minutes.

6 Meanwhile, chop the red onion finely. Remove the chillies from the bag and peel off the skins. Slit them, remove the seeds and chop them finely.

7 Transfer the beans to a bowl and add the onion and both types of chilli. Stir in the lime rind and juice, the Mexican beer (if using), oil and coriander. Season with a little salt and mix well. Chill the salsa before serving.

> **COOK'S TIP**
> When preparing chillies, remember not to touch your eyes or face to avoid irritation.

Black bean salsa: Energy 126Kcal/533kJ; Protein 8.5g; Carbohydrate 15.8g, of which sugars 1.9g; Fat 3.5g, of which saturates 0.5g; Cholesterol 0mg; Calcium 48mg; Fibre 5.3g; Sodium 10mg.

Onion, mango and peanut chaat

Chaats are spiced relishes of vegetables and nuts served with Indian meals. This recipe combines the delightful sweet juiciness of mango with crunchy peanuts, both of which are bursting with an array of antioxidants. The fresh herbs add a fragrant aroma and flavour.

Serves 4

90g/3½oz/scant 1 cup
  unsalted peanuts
15ml/1 tbsp peanut oil
1 onion, chopped
10cm/4in piece cucumber, seeded
  and cut into 5mm/¼in dice
1 mango, peeled, stoned
  and diced
1 green chilli, seeded
  and chopped
30ml/2 tbsp chopped fresh
  coriander (cilantro)
15ml/1 tbsp chopped fresh mint
15ml/1 tbsp lime juice
pinch of light muscovado
  (brown) sugar

For the chaat masala
10ml/2 tsp ground toasted
  cumin seeds
2.5ml/½ tsp cayenne pepper
5ml/1 tsp mango powder (amchur)
2.5ml/½ tsp garam masala
pinch of ground asafoetida
salt and freshly ground
  black pepper

1 To make the chaat masala, grind all of the spices together, then season with 2.5ml/½ tsp each of salt and freshly ground black pepper.

2 Fry the peanuts in the oil until lightly browned, then drain them on kitchen paper until cool.

3 Mix the onion, cucumber, mango, chilli, fresh coriander and mint. Sprinkle in 5ml/1 tsp of the chaat masala. Stir in the peanuts and then add lime juice and/or sugar to taste. Set the mixture aside for 20–30 minutes for the flavours to mature.

4 Turn the mixture out into a serving bowl, sprinkle another 5ml/1 tsp of the chaat masala over and serve.

COOK'S TIP
Any remaining chaat masala will keep well in a sealed jar for 4–6 weeks.

VARIATION
Use other nuts such as cashews or almonds if you prefer not to use peanuts.

Onion, mango and peanut chaat: Energy 189Kcal/788kJ; Protein 6.9g; Carbohydrate 9.8g, of which sugars 6.6g; Fat 14g, of which saturates 2.4g; Cholesterol 0mg; Calcium 41mg; Fibre 2.4g; Sodium 4mg.

Brussels sprouts with chestnuts

When cooked correctly, the nutrient-packed Brussels sprout has a sweet flavour and a crunchy texture. This traditional recipe offers an inspiring way to eat this succulent vegetable. The sprouts blend wonderfully with the nutty flavour of the chestnuts and the slight saltiness of the bacon.

Serves 6

350g/12oz fresh chestnuts
300ml/½ pint/1¼ cups chicken or
   vegetable stock (optional)
   or water
5ml/1 tsp sugar
675g/1½lb Brussels sprouts
50g/2oz/4 tbsp butter
115g/4oz bacon, cut into strips

1 Cut a cross in the pointed end of each chestnut, then carefully place them in a pan of boiling water and cook for 5–10 minutes.

2 Drain the chestnuts and allow to cool before peeling off both the tough outer skin and the fine inner one of each chestnut.

3 Return the chestnuts to the pan, add the chicken or vegetable stock (if using) or water and sugar, and simmer gently for 30–35 minutes, until the chestnuts are tender, then drain thoroughly.

4 Meanwhile, cook the sprouts in lightly salted boiling water for 8–10 minutes, until just tender. Drain well and set aside.

5 Melt the butter, add the bacon, cook until it becomes crisp, then stir in the chestnuts for 2–3 minutes. Add the hot Brussels sprouts, toss together and serve.

SUPERFOOD TIP
Do not boil the Brussels sprouts for more than ten minutes, as this will destroy the sulphurous compounds which are thought to destroy pre-cancerous cells.

Brussel sprouts with chestnuts: Energy 256kcal/1070kJ; Protein 8.3g; Carbohydrate 26g, of which sugars 7.6g; Fat 13.9g, of which saturates 6.6g; Cholesterol 30mg; Calcium 59mg; Fibre 7g; Sodium 364mg.

Braised red cabbage

Red cabbage is sweeter-tasting than the green and white varieties, and combines well with fruit such as apples or raisins. The spices in this recipe enhance its sweetness, and braised red cabbage makes a wonderful accompaniment to roast pork, duck and game dishes.

Serves 4–6

1kg/2¼lb red cabbage
2 cooking apples
2 onions, chopped
5ml/1 tsp freshly grated nutmeg
1.5ml/¼ tsp ground cloves
1.5ml/¼ tsp ground cinnamon
15ml/1 tbsp soft dark brown sugar
45ml/3 tbsp red wine vinegar
25g/1oz/2 tbsp butter, diced
salt and ground black pepper
chopped flat leaf parsley,
   to garnish

1 Preheat the oven to 160°C/325°F/ Gas 3. Cut away and discard the large white ribs from the outer cabbage leaves using a large, sharp knife, then finely shred the cabbage. Peel, core and coarsely grate the apples.

2 Layer the shredded cabbage in a large ovenproof dish with the onions, apples, spices, sugar, and salt and ground black pepper. Pour over the vinegar and add the diced butter.

SUPERFOOD TIP
Cabbage is rich in vitamins A, C, B6 and K, and is high in fibre.

3 Cover the dish with a lid and bake for about 1½ hours, stirring a couple of times, until the cabbage becomes very tender. Serve immediately, garnished with the parsley.

COOK'S TIP
Baking in a little liquid ensures that valuable nutrients are retained.

Braised red cabbage: Energy 160kcal/668kJ; Protein 4.3g; Carbohydrate 23.8g, of which sugars 22.4g; Fat 5.8g, of which saturates 3.3g; Cholesterol 13mg; Calcium 140mg; Fibre 6.6g; Sodium 58mg.

Kale with mustard dressing

The antioxidant-rich kale is an attractive vegetable with its dark green, curly leaves. Lightly steaming helps to retains the valuable vitamins, and the mustard dressing complements the slightly peppery flavour of the kale perfectly.

Serves 4

250g/9oz curly kale
45ml/3 tbsp light olive oil
5ml/1 tsp wholegrain mustard
15ml/1 tbsp white wine vinegar
pinch of caster (superfine) sugar
salt and ground black pepper

1 Wash the curly kale and drain it thoroughly. Trim the leaves and cut each one in two. Steam the kale for a few minutes to wilt the leaves then drain and set aside.

2 Whisk the oil into the mustard in a bowl. When it is blended completely, whisk in the white wine vinegar. The dressing should begin to thicken.

3 Season the mustard dressing to taste with sugar, salt and ground black pepper. Toss the kale in the dressing and serve immediately.

Kale with mustard dressing: Energy 99kcal/409kJ; Protein 2.1g; Carbohydrate 1.9g, of which sugars 1.9g; Fat 9.3g, of which saturates 1.3g; Cholesterol 0mg; Calcium 82mg; Fibre 2g; Sodium 27mg.

Braised Swiss chard

Braising Swiss chard in a small amount of water retains its impressive array of antioxidants and vitamins. Swiss chard can be used to make two tasty meals: on the first day, cook the leaves only; on the second day you can use the stalks by cooking them in the same way as asparagus.

Serves 4

900g/2lb Swiss chard or spinach
15g/½oz/1 tbsp butter
a little freshly grated nutmeg
sea salt and ground black pepper

COOK'S TIP
To cook Swiss chard stalks, trim the bases, wash them well and tie in bundles. Add to a pan of boiling water with a squeeze of lemon juice, and cook for about 20 minutes, or until tender but still slightly crisp. Drain and serve with a white sauce or pour over 30ml/ 2 tbsp fresh single (light) cream. Heat gently, season and serve.

1 Remove the stalks from the Swiss chard or spinach (and reserve the chard stalks, if you like – *see* Cook's Tip).

2 Wash the leaves well and lift straight into a lightly greased heavy pan; the water clinging to the leaves will be all that is needed for cooking process.

3 Cover with a tight-fitting lid and cook over a medium heat for about 3–5 minutes, or until just tender, shaking the pan occasionally.

4 Drain well, then add the butter and nutmeg, and season to taste. When the butter has melted, toss it into the cooked Swiss chard and leaves, and serve immediately.

Braised swiss chard: Energy 84Kcal/347kJ; Protein 6.3g; Carbohydrate 3.6g, of which sugars 3.4g; Fat 4.9g, of which saturates 2.2g; Cholesterol 8mg; Calcium 383mg; Fibre 4.7g; Sodium 338mg.

Roast beetroot with horseradish cream

The sweet flavour of the vibrant pink beetroot is enhanced first by roasting and then by the nutrient-rich, cruciferous horseradish and vinegar. Opt for small and tender beets to enjoy the best of this high-fibre vitamin- and mineral-rich vegetable.

Serves 4–6

10–12 small whole beetroots (beets)
30ml/2 tbsp oil
45ml/3 tbsp grated fresh
  horseradish
15ml/1 tbsp white wine vinegar
10ml/2 tsp caster (superfine) sugar
150ml/¼ pint/⅔ cup double
  (heavy) cream
salt

COOK'S TIPS
• If you are unable to find fresh horseradish root, use preserved grated horseradish instead.
• For a lighter sauce, replace half of the cream with thick natural (plain) yogurt or crème fraîche.

1 Preheat the oven to 180°C/350°F/ Gas 4. Wash the beetroots without breaking their skins. Trim the stalks but do not remove them completely.

2 Toss the beetroot in the oil and sprinkle with salt. Spread them in a roasting pan and cover with foil. Put into the oven and cook for about 1½ hours, or until soft throughout. Leave to cool, covered, for 10 minutes.

3 Meanwhile, make the horseradish sauce. Put the horseradish, vinegar and sugar into a bowl and mix well. Whip the cream until thickened and fold in the horseradish mixture. Cover and chill until required.

4 When the beetroots are cool enough to handle, gently slip off the skins and serve them with the horseradish sauce.

Roast beetroot: Energy 254kcal/1052kJ; Protein 2.1g; Carbohydrate 10g, of which sugars 9.1g; Fat 22.2g, of which saturates 3.2g; Cholesterol 1mg; Calcium 26mg; Fibre 2.3g; Sodium 143mg.

Carrot and parsnip purée

Antioxidant and vitamin A-rich carrots are blended with creamy vitamin C- and vitamin K-rich parsnips. These two root vegetables work especially well together and are often found in a soup, or in this popular warm and comforting side dish.

Serves 6–8

350g/12oz carrots
450g/1lb parsnips
pinch of freshly grated nutmeg
　　or ground mace
15g/½oz/1 tbsp butter
15ml/1 tbsp single (light) cream,
　　or top of the milk (optional)
1 small bunch parsley leaves,
　　chopped (optional), plus extra
　　to garnish
salt and ground black pepper

1 Peel the carrots and slice thinly. Peel the parsnips and cut into bitesize chunks (they are softer and will cook more quickly than the carrots). Boil the two vegetables, separately, in salted water, until tender.

2 Drain them well and put them through a *mouli-légumes* (food mill) with the grated nutmeg or mace, a good seasoning of salt and ground black pepper, and the butter. Purée together and check for seasoning.

COOK'S TIP
Leftover purée can be thinned to taste with quality chicken stock for a quick home-made soup.

3 If you like, blend in some cream or top of the milk to taste, and add chopped parsley for extra flavour. Transfer the purée to a warmed serving bowl, sprinkle with freshly chopped parsley to garnish and serve.

Carrot purée: Energy 92Kcal/385kJ; Protein 1.8g; Carbohydrate 14.1g, of which sugars 8.7g; Fat 3.5g, of which saturates 1.8g; Cholesterol 7mg; Calcium 48mg; Fibre 4.9g; Sodium 38mg.

Roasted Jerusalem artichokes

High in iron and potassium, Jerusalem artichokes conceal a deliciously sweet, nutty white flesh inside their knobbly brown exterior. While they are most popularly used for making creamy soups, they also taste fabulous roasted or puréed and served as a side vegetable to many foods.

Serves 6

675g/1½lb Jerusalem artichokes
15ml/1 tbsp lemon juice or vinegar
salt
50g/2oz/¼ cup unsalted butter
seasoned flour, for dusting

VARIATION
Puréeing is a useful fall-back if the artichokes break up during cooking: simply blend or mash the drained boiled artichokes with salt and freshly ground black pepper to taste, and a little single (light) cream, if you like.

1 Peel the artichokes, dropping them immediately into a bowl of water acidulated with lemon juice or vinegar to prevent browning.

2 Cut up the artichokes into equal sized pieces, otherwise they will cook unevenly.

3 Preheat the oven to 180°C/350°F/Gas 4. Drain the artichokes from the acidulated water. Bring a pan of salted water to the boil.

4 Boil the drained artichokes for 5 minutes, or until just tender. Watch them carefully, as they break up easily.

5 Melt the butter in a roasting pan, coat the artichokes in the seasoned flour and roll them around in the butter in the pan.

6 Roast the butter- and flour-coated artichokes in the preheated oven for 20–30 minutes, or until golden brown. Serve immediately.

Artichokes: Energy 101Kcal/419kJ; Protein 0.7g; Carbohydrate 8.9g, of which sugars 8.4g; Fat 7.2g, of which saturates 4.5g; Cholesterol 18mg; Calcium 30mg; Fibre 2.7g; Sodium 242mg.

Split pea and shallot mash

Ring the changes with this excellent alternative to mashed potatoes. This hearty side dish is rich in nutrients and will count toward one of your five-a-day fruit and vegetables. Split peas are delicious when puréed with shallots and enlivened with cumin seeds and fresh herbs.

Serves 4–6

225g/8oz/1 cup yellow split peas
1 bay leaf
8 sage leaves, roughly chopped
15ml/1 tbsp olive oil
3 shallots, finely chopped
8ml/heaped 1 tsp cumin seeds
1 large garlic clove, chopped
50g/2oz/4 tbsp butter, softened
salt and freshly ground
    black pepper

SUPERFOOD TIPS
• Like other pulses, split peas are an excellent source of protein, fibre, minerals and B vitamins.
• Split peas are particularly good for diabetics, as they can help to control blood sugar levels.

---

1 Place the split peas in a bowl and cover with cold water. Leave to soak overnight, then rinse and drain.

2 Place the drained split peas in a pan, cover with fresh cold water and bring to the boil. Skim off any foam that rises to the surface, then reduce the heat.

3 Add the bay leaf and sage, and simmer for 30–40 minutes, until the peas are tender. Add more water during cooking, if necessary.

4 Meanwhile, heat the oil in a frying pan and cook the shallots, cumin seeds and garlic over a medium heat for 3 minutes, or until the shallots soften, stirring occasionally. Add the mixture to the split peas while they are still cooking.

5 Drain the split peas, reserving the cooking water. Remove the bay leaf, then place the split peas in a food processor or blender with the butter and season well.

6 Add 105ml/7 tbsp of the reserved cooking water and blend until the mixture forms a coarse purée. Add more water if the mash seems to be too dry. Adjust the seasoning and serve warm.

Split pea and shallot mash: Energy 201Kcal/845kJ; Protein 9.1g; Carbohydrate 22g, of which sugars 1.5g; Fat 9.2g, of which saturates 4.7g; Cholesterol 18mg; Calcium 23mg; Fibre 2g; Sodium 64mg.

Cauliflower with egg and lemon

Cauliflower is as good as broccoli on the nutritional front, and boiling it lightly retains this goodness. Serving with a sauce is very traditional, and this delicious light, zingy lemon sauce is not too rich, and is also made without wheat flour.

**Serves 4 as a main course,
6 as a starter**

75–90ml/5–6 tbsp extra virgin
   olive oil
1 medium cauliflower, divided
   into large florets
2 eggs
juice of 1 lemon
5ml/1 tsp cornflour (cornstarch),
   mixed to a cream with a little
   cold water
30ml/2 tbsp chopped fresh flat
   leaf parsley
salt

VARIATION
Replace the cauliflower with broccoli or combine both for a more colourful option.

1 Heat the olive oil in a large heavy pan, add the cauliflower florets and sauté over a medium heat until they start to brown.

2 Pour in enough hot water to almost cover the cauliflower, add salt to taste, then cover the pan and cook for 7–8 minutes, until the florets are just soft. Remove the pan from the heat and leave to stand, covered, while you make the sauce.

3 Beat the eggs in a bowl, add the lemon juice and cornflour and beat until well mixed. Now, beat in a few tablespoons of the hot liquid from the cauliflower. Pour the egg mixture over the cauliflower, then stir gently.

4 Place the pan over a very gentle heat for 2 minutes to thicken the sauce. Spoon into a warmed serving bowl, sprinkle the chopped parsley over the top and serve.

Cauliflower with egg and lemon: Energy 210Kcal/833kJ; Protein 7g; Carbohydrate 4.4g, of which sugars 2.7g; Fat 17.5g, of which saturates 3g; Cholesterol 95mg; Calcium 51mg; Fibre 2.2g; Sodium 47mg.

Chilli rice with turmeric and coriander

This is a lively rice accompaniment which is packed full of flavour, colour and heat. The chillies stimulate the body and the addition of turmeric helps to enrich its antioxidant goodness. Using brown rice adds to the nutrient content and also improves its glycaemic index.

Serves 4

15ml/1 tbsp vegetable oil or sesame oil
2–3 green or red Thai chillies, seeded and finely chopped
2 garlic cloves, finely chopped
2.5cm/1in fresh root ginger, finely chopped
5ml/1 tsp sugar
10–15ml/2 tsp–1 tbsp ground turmeric
225g/8oz/generous 1 cup long grain brown rice
30ml/2 tbsp fish sauce
600ml/1 pint/2½ cups water, or fish, vegetable or chicken stock
a bunch of fresh coriander (cilantro) leaves, finely chopped
salt and ground black pepper

1 Heat the oil in a heavy pan. Stir in the chillies, garlic and ginger with the sugar. As they begin to colour, stir in the turmeric.

2 Add the rice, coating it in the turmeric and flavourings, then pour in the fish sauce and the water or stock – the liquid should sit about 2.5cm/1in above the rice.

3 Season with salt and pepper and bring the liquid to the boil. Reduce the heat, cover and simmer for about 25 minutes, or until the water has been absorbed.

4 Remove the pan from the heat and leave the rice to steam for a further 10 minutes.

5 Pour the rice on to a serving dish. Add some of the coriander and lightly toss together using a fork. Garnish with the remaining coriander.

COOK'S TIP
Take care when chopping chillies as they can cause irritation to the skin and eyes.

Chilli rice with turmeric: Energy 252Kcal/1066kJ; Protein 5g; Carbohydrate 51g, of which sugars 1g; Fat 5g, of which saturates 1g; Cholesterol 0mg; Calcium 24mg; Fibre 0.3g; Sodium 0.5g.

Layered herring salad

This traditional Russian salad looks like a layered cake. A colourful range of nutrient-rich fruit and vegetables together with mayonnaise joins the omega 3-rich herring fillets. This dish is always topped with a layer of grated hard-boiled eggs, boosting your vitamin A, B and D intake.

**Serves 8 as an appetizer,
  4 as a main course**

250g/9oz salted herring fillets
3 carrots, total weight 250g/9oz
4 eggs
1 small red onion
200g/7oz/scant 1 cup mayonnaise
5–6 cooked beetroots (beets),
  total weight 300g/11oz
2 eating apples
45ml/3 tbsp chopped fresh dill,
  to garnish

1 Soak the herring in water overnight. The next day, rinse them under running water and then drain. Cut into small pieces and put in a bowl.

2 Put the whole carrots in a pan of cold water, bring to the boil, then reduce the heat, cover and simmer for 10–15 minutes, until just tender. Drain and put under cold running water. Set aside.

3 Meanwhile, put the eggs in a pan, cover with cold water and bring to the boil. Reduce the heat and simmer for 10 minutes. When the eggs are cooked, drain immediately and put under cold running water. Set aside.

4 Finely chop the onion and add to the herrings with 15ml/1 tbsp of the mayonnaise. Spread the mixture over a 25cm/10in serving plate.

5 Coarsely grate the carrots, beetroots and apples into small piles. Add a layer of grated beetroot over the herring mixture and spread 45–60ml/ 3–4 tbsp mayonnaise on top. Repeat with a layer of grated carrots and mayonnaise, then a layer of apple.

6 Finally spread a thin layer of mayonnaise over the top of the salad. Cover with clear film (plastic wrap) and chill in the refrigerator for at least 1 hour or overnight.

7 Just before serving, remove the shell from the eggs and grate coarsely. Sprinkle the grated egg all over the salad so that it is covered completely and creates a final layer, then garnish with chopped dill.

VARIATION
Use pickled beetroot for an added tang of vinegar.

Layered herring salad: Energy 130kcal/544kJ; Protein 12.1g; Carbohydrate 9.3g, of which sugars 8.7g; Fat 5.3g, of which saturates 0.8g; Cholesterol 95mg; Calcium 96mg; Fibre 2.2g; Sodium 1697mg.

Marinated salmon with avocado

Use only the freshest of salmon for this salad, as the marinade of lemon and dashi-konbu 'cooks' the omega 3-rich salmon. Serving with avocado, toasted almonds, salad leaves and the miso mayonnaise makes this an interesting Mediterranean and Japanese fusion of flavours.

3 Marinate for about 15 minutes, then turn once and leave for a further 15 minutes. The salmon should turn a pink 'cooked' colour.

4 Remove the salmon from the marinade and wipe with kitchen paper. Now, cut the salmon into 5mm/¼in thick slices against the grain.

5 Halve the avocado and sprinkle with a little of the salmon marinade. Remove the avocado stone (pit) and skin, then carefully slice to the same thickness as the salmon.

6 Mix the miso mayonnaise ingredients in a bowl. Spread about 5ml/1 tsp on to the back of each of the shiso leaves. Mix the remainder with 15ml/1 tbsp of the remaining marinade to loosen the mayonnaise.

Serves 4

250g/9oz very fresh salmon tail, skinned and filleted
juice of 1 lemon
10cm/4in dashi-konbu (dried kelp), wiped with a damp cloth and cut into 4 strips
1 ripe avocado
4 shiso leaves, stalks removed and cut in half lengthways
about 115g/4oz mixed leaves such as lamb's lettuce, frisée or rocket (arugula)
45ml/3 tbsp flaked (sliced) almonds, toasted in a dry frying pan until just slightly browned

For the miso mayonnaise
90ml/6 tbsp good-quality mayonnaise
15ml/1 tbsp shiromiso (white miso)
ground black pepper

1 Cut the first salmon fillet in half crossways at the tail end where the fillet is not wider than 4cm/1½in. Now, cut the wider part in half lengthways. Cut the other fillet into three pieces, in the same way.

2 Pour the lemon juice and two of the dashi-konbu pieces into a wide, shallow plastic container. Lay the salmon fillets in the base and sprinkle with the rest of the dashi-konbu.

7 Arrange the salad leaves on four plates. Top with the avocado, salmon, shiso leaves and almonds, and drizzle over the remaining miso mayonnaise.

8 Alternatively, build a tower of avocado and salmon slices by putting an eighth of the avocado slices in the centre of a plate, slightly overlapping. Add a shiso leaf, miso-side down, and top with salmon slices.

9 Repeat the process. Arrange the salad leaves and almonds, spoon over the miso mayonnaise and serve.

Salmon with avocado: Energy 432kcal/1787kJ; Protein 16.2g; Carbohydrate 2.3g, of which sugars 1.4g; Fat 39.8g, of which saturates 6.2g; Cholesterol 48mg; Calcium 54mg; Fibre 2.3g; Sodium 134mg.

Citrus chicken coleslaw

This zesty coleslaw salad makes a refreshing change from the rich mayonnaise version, its crisp shredded vegetables combining well with the protein-rich chicken and the lovely citrus dressing. Use leftover Christmas turkey for a fabulous seasonal buffet dish.

Serves 6

120ml/4fl oz/½ cup extra virgin olive oil
6 boneless chicken breasts, skinned
4 oranges
5ml/1 tsp Dijon mustard
15ml/1 tbsp clear honey
300g/11oz/2¾ cups white cabbage, finely shredded
300g/11oz carrots, peeled and finely sliced
2 spring onions (scallions), sliced
2 celery sticks, cut into matchstick strips
30ml/2 tbsp fresh tarragon, chopped
2 limes
salt and ground black pepper

2 Peel two of the oranges, cutting off all the pith, then separate the segments and set aside. Grate the rind and squeeze the juice from one of the remaining oranges and place in a large bowl.

3 Stir in the Dijon mustard, 5ml/ 1 tsp of the honey, 60ml/4 tbsp of the oil, and season to taste. Mix in the cabbage, carrots, spring onions and celery. Leave to stand for 10 minutes.

4 Meanwhile, squeeze the juice from the rest of the orange and mix it with the remaining honey and oil and the tarragon. Peel and segment the limes and lightly mix them into the dressing with the reserved orange segments. Season to taste.

5 Slice the cooked chicken breasts and stir into the dressing. Spoon the vegetable salad on to plates and add the chicken mixture. Serve at once.

1 Heat 30ml/2 tbsp of the oil in a large, heavy frying pan. Add the chicken breasts to the pan and cook for 15–20 minutes, or until the chicken is cooked through and golden brown. (If your pan is too small, cook the chicken in two or three batches.) Remove the chicken from the pan and leave to cool.

VARIATION
For a creamy result, mayonnaise, crème fraîche or sour cream can be used to dress the chicken instead of the orange, oil and honey mixture.

Citrus chicken coleslaw: Energy 293kcal/1219kJ; Protein 21g; Carbohydrate 5g, of which sugars 5g; Fat 21g, of which saturates 3g; Cholesterol 58mg; Calcium 37mg; Fibre 1.4g; Sodium 165mg.

Thai beef salad

Try to buy lean grass-fed beef if possible for this dish and cut off any excess fat. This iron-rich dish is full of flavours and textures that will liven up any lunch. Shiitake mushrooms, garlic and chillies add to the superfood count, as does serving with a crisp salad to make a delicious lunch.

Serves 4

675g/1½lb fillet or rump steak
30ml/2 tbsp olive oil
2 small mild red chillies, seeded
 and sliced
225g/8oz/3¼ cups shiitake
 mushrooms, sliced

For the dressing
3 spring onions (scallions), finely
 chopped
2 garlic cloves, finely chopped
juice of 1 lime
15–30ml/1–2 tbsp fish or oyster
 sauce, to taste
5ml/1 tsp soft light brown sugar
30ml/2 tbsp chopped fresh
 coriander (cilantro)

To serve
1 cos or romaine lettuce, torn
 into strips
175g/6oz cherry tomatoes, halved
5cm/2in piece cucumber, peeled,
 halved and thinly sliced
45ml/3 tbsp toasted sesame seeds

1 Preheat the grill until hot, then cook the steak for 2–4 minutes on each side, depending on how well done you like steak. (In Thailand, the beef is traditionally served quite rare.) Leave to cool for at least 15 minutes.

2 Use a very sharp knife to slice the meat as thinly as possible, and place the slices in a bowl.

3 Heat the olive oil in a frying pan. Add the seeded and sliced red chillies and the sliced mushrooms, and cook for 5 minutes, stirring occasionally.

4 Turn off the heat and add the grilled steak slices to the pan. Stir well to coat the beef slices in the chilli and mushroom mix.

5 Stir all the ingredients for the dressing together, then pour it over the meat mixture and toss gently.

6 Arrange the cos or romaine lettuce, tomatoes and cucumber slices on a serving plate. Spoon the warm steak mixture in the centre and sprinkle the sesame seeds over. Serve immediately.

Thai beef salad: Energy 381Kcal/1591kJ; Protein 39.8g; Carbohydrate 4.1g, of which sugars 3.8g; Fat 23g, of which saturates 6.6g; Cholesterol 103mg; Calcium 105mg; Fibre 2.5g; Sodium 352mg.

Mayonnaise

Using a combination of these omega 3-rich oils makes this a healthier mayonnaise option. Use it to make coleslaw or potato salad, or flavour it with a pesto or garlic sauce, known as aioli. It still has the same calories and fat, so remember to use it sparingly.

Makes 300ml/½ pint/1¼ cups

250ml/ 8 fl oz/1 cup rapeseed oil
50ml/2 fl oz/¼ cup flaxseed oil
1 egg
15ml/1 tbsp white wine vinegar
10ml/2 tsp smooth mustard
  (English or French)

Aioli
2 crushed garlic cloves
15ml/1 tbsp lemon juice
Salt and pepper

1 Mix the rapeseed and flaxseed oils together in a jug (pitcher).

2 Place the egg, vinegar and mustard of your choice into the liquidizer and mix well for a few seconds.

3 With the liquidizer on, pour a thin stream of oil gradually into the egg mix. The mayonnaise will start to thicken when about two-thirds of the oil has been added; a little patience may be useful at this stage!

> **WARNING**
> As this mayonnaise contains raw egg, it should be avoided by pregnant women, and the very young and old.

4 Incorporate the remaining oil into the thickened mayonnaise by stirring, if you find that the liquidizer can no longer blend the mixture fully.

5 If flavouring the mayonnaise with aioli, blend in the garlic cloves, lemon juice and seasoning.

Omega-3-rich salad dressing

Add fresh green herbs of your choice, depending on what you are serving your salad with. Add dill for fish, thyme and parsley if serving with chicken. Flaxseed oil can have a strong flavour, so combining it with the rapeseed oil tones this down a little.

Makes 120ml/4fl oz

40mls/3 tbsp sherry vinegar
40mls/3 tbsp rapeseed oil
40mls/3 tbsp flaxseed oil
30ml/2 tbsp handful of chopped
  fresh herbs such as parsley,
  chives and coriander (cilantro)
2.5ml/½ tsp coarse mustard
fresh ground black pepper

1 Place all of the ingredients in a screw-top jar or bottle, and shake up and down vigorously until well mixed. Drizzle the dressing over the salad of your choice.

Mayonnaise: Energy 2809Kcal/11588kJ; Protein 9g; Carbohydrate 3g, of which sugars 2g; Fat 308g, of which saturates 23g; Cholesterol 238mg; Calcium 48mg; Fibre 0.3g: Sodium 599mg.
Omega 3 dressing: Energy 734Kcal/3042kJ; Protein 1g; Carbohydrate 1g, of which sugars 1g; Fat 81g, of which saturates 6g; Cholesterol 0mg; Calcium 18mg; Fibre 0.6g; Sodium 117mg.

MAIN DISHES

Tempting, yet nutritionally balanced main dishes can be made from a huge variety of healthy ingredients, from lean poultry, oily fish and eggs to nuts, pulses and grains. Not only are these recipes substantial, they are also packed with fibre, vitamins and minerals. The selection of hearty dishes in this chapter offers you the freedom to choose from a quick weekday supper, such as Red Pepper Risotto or Pea and Mint Omelette, to a more relaxed weekend dinner such as Beef Stew with Oysters, or Moroccan Lamb with Honey and Prunes.

Vegetable couscous with olives and almonds

This Mediterranean-style recipe includes the cardio-protective ingredients of olives, almonds and olive oil. Couscous is a light and fluffy ingredient that is low in fat and high in starchy carbohydrate. It is actually a wheat product, so for a gluten-free version, use quinoa or brown rice.

Serves 4

275g/10oz/1⅔ cups couscous
525ml/18fl oz/2¼ cups boiling
   vegetable stock
16–20 black olives
2 small courgettes (zucchini)
25g/1oz/¼cup flaked (sliced)
   almonds, toasted
60ml/4 tbsp olive oil
15ml/1 tbsp lemon juice
15ml/1 tbsp chopped fresh
   coriander (cilantro)
15ml/1 tbsp chopped fresh parsley
good pinch of ground cumin
good pinch of paprika

1 Place the couscous in a heatproof bowl and pour over the boiling vegetable stock. Stir with a fork to combine, then set aside for 10 minutes. When the stock has been absorbed, fluff the grains with a fork.

2 Meanwhile, halve the olives and discard the stones (pits). Trim the courgettes and cut them into matchsticks.

3 Add the courgette strips, black olives and toasted almonds to the bowl of couscous and gently mix together to combine thoroughly.

4 Blend together the olive oil, lemon juice, herbs and spices. Pour the dressing over the couscous. Gently stir to combine, and serve.

> **VARIATIONS**
> • Add extra flavour to this salad by stirring in 10ml/2 tsp grated fresh root ginger.
> • Vary the flavour of this dish with alternative combinations of vegetables such as chopped tomatoes, cucumber matchsticks, diced roatsted pumpkin or diced cooked aubergine.

Vegetable couscous: Energy 319Kcal/1326kJ; Protein 6.6g; Carbohydrate 36.9g, of which sugars 1.4g; Fat 16.9g, of which saturates 2.1g; Cholesterol 0mg; Calcium 73mg; Fibre 1.9g; Sodium 287mg.

Roasted ratatouille moussaka

Roasting this colourful rainbow of vegetables in olive oil and garlic intensifies the rich flavours, contrasting with the light and mouthwatering egg-and-cheese topping. Make one large dish to share or divide the roasted vegetables and topping among individual gratin dishes.

Serves 4–6

2 red (bell) peppers, seeded and
    cut into large chunks
2 yellow (bell) peppers, seeded
    and cut into large chunks
2 aubergines (eggplant), cut into
    large chunks
3 courgettes (zucchini), sliced
45ml/3 tbsp olive oil
3 garlic cloves, crushed
400g/14oz can chopped tomatoes
30ml/2 tbsp sun-dried tomato paste
45ml/3 tbsp chopped fresh basil or
    15ml/1 tbsp dried basil
15ml/1 tbsp balsamic vinegar
1.5ml/¼ tsp soft light brown sugar
salt and fresh ground black pepper
basil leaves, to garnish

For the topping
25g/1oz/2 tbsp butter
25g/1oz/¼ cup plain
    (all-purpose) flour
300ml/½ pint/1¼ cups milk
1.5ml/¼ tsp freshly grated nutmeg
250g/9oz ricotta cheese
3 eggs, beaten
25g/1oz/⅓ cup freshly grated
    Parmesan cheese

1 Preheat the oven to 230°C/450°F/ Gas 8. Arrange the peppers, aubergines and courgettes in a large roasting tin (pan). Season well.

2 Mix together the oil and crushed garlic and pour over the vegetables.

3 Roast in the oven for 15–20 minutes, until slightly charred, lightly tossing the vegetables once during cooking time. Remove the tin (pan) from the oven and set aside. Reduce the oven temperature to 200°C/400°F/Gas 6.

4 Put the chopped tomatoes, tomato paste, basil, balsamic vinegar and brown sugar in a pan and heat to boiling point. Simmer for 10–15 minutes until thickened, stirring occasionally. Season to taste.

5 Carefully tip the roasted vegetables into the pan of tomato sauce. Mix well, and spoon the vegetables into an ovenproof dish. Level the surface.

6 For the topping, melt the butter in a large pan over a gentle heat. Stir in the flour and cook for 1 minute. Pour in the milk, stirring constantly, then whisk until blended. Add the nutmeg and whisk until thickened. Cook for 2 more minutes.

7 Remove from the heat and allow to cool slightly. Mix in the ricotta cheese and beaten eggs. Season to taste.

8 Spoon the topping over the vegetables and sprinkle with the Parmesan cheese. Bake for 30–35 minutes until the topping is golden brown. Serve immediately, garnished with basil leaves.

Moussaka: Energy 570Kcal/2367kJ; Protein 22.1g; Carbohydrate 27.5g, of which sugars 21.7g; Fat 42.1g, of which saturates 20.3g; Cholesterol 223mg; Calcium 339mg; Fibre 7.1g; Sodium 447mg.

Mediterranean vegetable hot-pot

This dish epitomizes the essence of Mediterranean cuisine, which includes vegetables, pulses, olive oil and garlic. It's a one-dish meal that is suitable for feeding large numbers of people, so it is great for family gatherings. This tastes fabulous served with crusty, fresh bread and a crisp, green salad.

Serves 4

60ml/4 tbsp extra virgin olive oil
   or sunflower oil
1 large onion, chopped
2 small or medium aubergines
   (eggplants), cut into small cubes
4 courgettes (zucchini), cut into
   small chunks
2 red, yellow or green (bell)
   peppers, seeded and chopped
115g/4oz/1 cup fresh or frozen peas
115g/4oz green beans
200g/7oz can flageolet beans,
   rinsed and drained
450g/1lb new or salad potatoes,
   peeled and cubed
2.5ml/½ tsp ground cinnamon
2.5ml/½ tsp ground cumin
5ml/1 tsp paprika
4–5 tomatoes, peeled
400g/14oz can chopped tomatoes
30ml/2 tbsp chopped fresh parsley
3–4 garlic cloves, crushed
350ml/12fl oz/1½ cups
   vegetable stock
salt and ground black pepper
black olives and fresh parsley,
   to garnish

1 Preheat the oven to 190°C/375°F/ Gas 5. Heat 45ml/3 tbsp of the oil in a heavy pan, and cook the onion until golden. Add the aubergines, sauté for 3 minutes, then add the courgettes, peppers, peas, beans and potatoes. Stir in the spices and seasoning. Cook for 3 minutes, stirring constantly.

2 Cut the tomatoes in half and scoop out the seeds. Chop the tomatoes finely and place them in a bowl. Stir in the canned tomatoes with the chopped fresh parsley, crushed garlic and the remaining olive oil. Spoon the aubergine mixture into a shallow ovenproof dish and level the surface.

3 Pour the stock over the aubergine mixture and then spoon over the prepared tomato mixture.

4 Cover the dish with foil and bake for 30–45 minutes, until the vegetables are tender. Serve hot, garnished with black olives and parsley.

Mediterranean hot-pot: Energy 365kcal/1529kJ; Protein 14.3g; Carbohydrate 48.2g, of which sugars 20.1g; Fat 14.1g, of which saturates 2.3g; Cholesterol 0mg; Calcium 141mg; Fibre 12.8g; Sodium 224mg.

Barley risotto with roasted squash

Made with nutty-flavoured, slightly chewy pearl barley, this risotto is more like a pilaff than a classic Italian risotto, which is made with rice. Using barley improves the glycaemic index of this dish, so energy is released into the body nice and slowly.

Serves 4–5

200g/7oz/1 cup pearl barley
1 butternut squash, peeled, seeded and cut into chunks
10ml/2 tsp chopped fresh thyme
60ml/4 tbsp olive oil
25g/1oz/2 tbsp butter
4 leeks, cut into fairly thick diagonal slices
2 garlic cloves, finely chopped
175g/6oz brown cap (cremini) mushrooms, sliced
2 carrots, coarsely grated
about 120ml/4fl oz/½ cup vegetable stock
30ml/2 tbsp chopped fresh flat leaf parsley
50g/2oz Pecorino cheese, grated
45ml/3 tbsp pumpkin seeds, toasted, or chopped walnuts
salt and ground black pepper

1 Rinse the barley, then cook it in simmering water, keeping the pan part-covered, for 35–45 minutes, or until tender. Drain. Preheat the oven to 200°C/400°F/Gas 6.

2 Place the squash in a roasting pan with half the thyme. Season with pepper and toss with half the oil. Roast, stirring once, for 30–35 minutes, until tender and beginning to brown.

3 Heat half the butter with the remaining oil in a large pan. Cook the leeks and garlic gently for 5 minutes.

4 Add the mushrooms and remaining thyme, then cook until the liquid from the mushrooms evaporates and they begin to fry.

5 Stir in the carrots and cook for 2 minutes, then add the barley and most of the stock. Season well and part-cover the pan. Cook for another 5 minutes. Pour in the remaining stock if the mixture seems dry.

6 Stir in the parsley, the remaining butter and half the Pecorino, then stir in the squash. Add seasoning to taste and serve immediately, sprinkled with the toasted pumpkin seeds or walnuts and the remaining Pecorino.

Barley risotto: Energy 409kcal/1713kJ; Protein 11.8g; Carbohydrate 43.4g, of which sugars 7.1g; Fat 22.1g, of which saturates 6.6g; Cholesterol 21mg; Calcium 249mg; Fibre 4.9g; Sodium 159mg.

Red pepper risotto

Rich in vitamin C and carotenoids, which are all antioxidants, red and yellow peppers are far sweeter than the green varieties. Chargrilling intensifies this sweet flavour and makes for an excellent vegetarian supper dish or even an appetizer for six people.

Serves 4

1 red (bell) pepper
1 yellow (bell) pepper
15ml/1 tbsp olive oil
25g/1oz/2 tbsp butter
1 onion, chopped
2 garlic cloves, crushed
275g/10oz/1½ cups risotto rice
1 litre/1¾ pints/4 cups simmering
  vegetable stock
50g/2oz/⅔ cup freshly grated
  Parmesan cheese
salt and freshly ground
  black pepper
freshly grated Parmesan cheese,
  to serve (optional)

1 Preheat the grill (broiler) to high. Halve the peppers, remove the seeds and pith and place, cut-side down, on a baking sheet. Place under the grill for 5 minutes, until the skin is charred. Put the peppers in a plastic bag, tie the ends and leave for 4–5 minutes.

2 Peel the peppers when they are cool enough to handle and the steam has loosened the skin. Slice into thin strips.

3 Heat the oil and butter in a pan and fry the onion and garlic for 4–5 minutes over a low heat, until the onion begins to soften. Add the peppers and cook the mixture for 3–4 minutes more, stirring occasionally.

4 Stir in the rice. Cook over a medium heat for 3–4 minutes, stirring all the time, until the rice is evenly coated in oil and the outer part of each grain has become translucent.

5 Add a ladleful of stock. Cook, stirring, until all the liquid has been absorbed. Continue to add the stock, a ladleful at a time, making sure each quantity has been absorbed before adding the next.

6 When the rice is tender but retains a bit of 'bite', stir in the Parmesan, and season to taste. Cover and leave to stand for 3–4 minutes, then serve, with extra Parmesan, if using.

> **COOK'S TIP**
> Add a few strands of saffron to the stock for vibrant yellow rice.

Red pepper risotto: Energy 555Kcal/2312kJ; Protein 16.1g; Carbohydrate 80.1g, of which sugars 10g; Fat 18g, of which saturates 8.4g; Cholesterol 34mg; Calcium 238mg; Fibre 2.6g; Sodium 241mg.

Buckwheat with pasta

This recipe takes its roots from Kasha, an Eastern European dish that is really filling and satisfying. Buckwheat is very nutritious, being packed with flavonoids and high in magnesium. Combining it with pasta and vegetables helps to lighten the porridge-like texture of pure buckwheat.

Serves 4–6

25g/1oz dried well-flavoured
  mushrooms, such as ceps
500ml/17fl oz/2¼ cups boiling
  stock or water
45ml/3 tbsp vegetable oil or
  40g/1½oz/3 tbsp butter
3–4 onions, thinly sliced
250g/9oz mushrooms, sliced
300g/11oz/1½ cups whole, coarse,
  medium or fine buckwheat
200g/7oz pasta bows
salt and ground black pepper

1 Put the dried mushrooms in a bowl, pour over half the boiling stock or water and leave to stand for 20–30 minutes, until reconstituted. Remove the mushrooms from the liquid, strain and reserve the liquid.

2 Heat the oil or butter in a frying pan, add the onions and fry for 5–10 minutes, until softened and beginning to brown. Remove the onions to a plate, then add the sliced mushrooms to the pan and fry briefly. Add the soaked mushrooms and cook for 2–3 minutes. Return the onions to the pan and set aside.

> **SUPERFOOD TIP**
> Eating buckwheat may help to reduce the risk of high cholesterol and blood pressure.

3 In a large, heavy frying pan, toast the buckwheat over a high heat for 2–3 minutes, stirring. Reduce the heat.

4 Stir the remaining boiling stock or water and the reserved mushroom soaking liquid into the buckwheat, cover the pan, and cook for about 10 minutes, until the buckwheat is just tender and the liquid has been absorbed.

5 Meanwhile, cook the pasta in a large pan of salted boiling water as directed on the packet, or until just tender, then drain.

6 When the buckwheat is cooked, toss in the onions and mushrooms, and the pasta. Season and serve hot.

Buckwheat with pasta: Energy 364kcal/1529kJ; Protein 10.3g; Carbohydrate 67g, of which sugars 4g; Fat 7.3g, of which saturates 3.6g; Cholesterol 14mg; Calcium 47mg; Fibre 2.2g; Sodium 48mg.

Pasta with roasted vegetables

This simple dish, with its fabulous array of colourful vitamin- and nutrient-rich vegetables, will spruce up any cooked pasta. Roasting the vegetables intensifies the flavours and caramelizes the natural sugars, giving a real depth to the flavour with no need to add a pasta sauce.

3 Stir the halved tomatoes and chopped garlic into the vegetable mixture, then roast for 20 minutes more, stirring once or twice. Meanwhile, cook the pasta according to the instructions on the packet.

4 Drain the pasta and tip it into a warmed bowl. Add the roasted vegetables and the remaining oil and toss well. Serve the pasta and vegetables hot, sprinkling each portion with a few herb flowers.

Serves 4–6

1 red (bell) pepper, cut into
  1cm/½ in squares
1 yellow or orange (bell) pepper,
  cut into 1cm/½ in squares
1 aubergine (eggplant), diced
2 courgettes (zucchini), diced
75ml/5 tbsp extra virgin olive oil
15ml/1 tbsp chopped fresh flat
  leaf parsley
5ml/1 tsp dried oregano or
  marjoram
250g/9oz baby Italian plum
  tomatoes, hulled and halved
  lengthways
2 garlic cloves, roughly chopped
350–400g/12–14oz/3–3½ cups
  dried conchiglie
salt and ground black pepper
4–6 fresh marjoram or oregano
  flowers, to garnish

1 Preheat the oven to 190°C/375°F/ Gas 5. Rinse the prepared peppers, aubergine and courgettes in a sieve (strainer) under cold running water, drain, then transfer the vegetables to a large roasting tin (pan).

2 Pour 45ml/3 tbsp of the olive oil over the vegetables and sprinkle with the fresh and dried herbs. Add salt and pepper to taste and stir well. Roast for about 30 minutes, stirring two or three times.

COOK'S TIP
Pasta and roasted vegetables are very good served cold, so if you have any of this dish left over, cover it tightly with clear film (plastic wrap), chill in the refrigerator overnight and serve it the next day as a salad. It would also make a particularly good salad to take on a picnic.

Pasta with roasted vegetables: Energy 319Kcal/1343kJ; Protein 8.8g; Carbohydrate 49.6g, of which sugars 8g; Fat 10.8g, of which saturates 1.6g; Cholesterol 0mg; Calcium 34mg; Fibre 4g; Sodium 9mg.

Twice-cooked tempeh

Tempeh is a heart-healthy superfood due to its phytosterol and omega-3 content. Similar to tofu, but with a nuttier, more savoury flavour and firmer texture, tempeh is cooked here with a host of superfoods – garlic, onions, peppers and spices in a delicious oriental-style tomato sauce.

Serves 4

45ml/3 tbsp vegetable oil
2 onions, finely chopped
2 garlic cloves, crushed
5ml/1 tsp fennel seeds, crushed
2.5ml/½ tsp chilli flakes
5ml/1 tsp coriander seeds, crushed
5ml/1 tsp cumin seeds, crushed
1 red (bell) pepper, seeded and
  finely chopped
450g/1lb tempeh
115g/4oz Cheddar cheese, grated

For the sauce
30ml/2 tbsp tamari soy sauce
juice of ½ lemon
45ml/3 tbsp molasses or dark
  brown sugar
30ml/2 tbsp cider (apple cider)
  vinegar
15ml/1 tbsp English (hot) mustard
90ml/6 tbsp tomato purée (paste)
150ml/¼ pint/⅔ cup water
2–3 dashes Tabasco sauce (optional)
30ml/2 tbsp chopped parsley

1 Preheat the oven to 200°C/400°F/ Gas 6. Heat 30ml/2 tbsp of the oil in a large frying pan or wok, and sauté the onions, garlic and spices for 6–7 minutes, until golden and softened. Add the pepper and cook for a further 1–2 minutes, until softened.

2 Whisk all the sauce ingredients except the parsley. Add to the pan. Simmer gently for 2–3 minutes. Finally, stir in the parsley.

3 Heat the remaining oil in a large frying pan and fry the tempeh for 2–3 minutes on each side, until golden and warmed through. Transfer to a large, shallow, heatproof serving dish.

4 Pour the finished sauce over the tempeh and sprinkle evenly with the grated cheese. Bake in the oven for approximately 10 minutes, until the cheese has melted, turned golden and is bubbling.

Twice-cooked tempeh: Energy 467Kcal/1949kJ; Protein 34g; Carbohydrate 34g, of which sugars 24g; Fat 22g, of which saturates 7g; Cholesterol 28mg; Calcium 437mg; Fibre 7.5g; Sodium 1016mg.

Mixed-bean chilli with cornbread topping

The combination of beans with grains in the yeast-free cornbread ensures that you are getting complete proteins in this one-pot, slow cooker meal. Choose your favourite superfood vegetables for the chilli and you are well on your way to five portions of vegetables in one serving.

Serves 4

115g/4oz/generous ½ cup dried
  red kidney beans
115g/4oz/generous ½ cup dried
  black-eyed beans
1 bay leaf
15ml/1 tbsp vegetable oil
1 large onion, finely chopped
1 garlic clove, crushed
5ml/1 tsp ground cumin
5ml/1 tsp chilli powder
5ml/1 tsp mild paprika
2.5ml/½ tsp dried marjoram
450g/1lb mixed vegetables such
  as potatoes, carrots, aubergines
  (eggplant), parsnips and celery
1 vegetable stock cube
400g/14oz can chopped tomatoes
15ml/1 tbsp tomato purée (paste)
salt and ground black pepper

For the cornbread topping
250g/9oz/2¼ cups fine cornmeal
30ml/2 tbsp wholemeal
  (whole-wheat) flour
7.5ml/1½ tsp baking powder
1 egg, plus 1 egg yolk,
  lightly beaten
300ml/½ pint/1¼ cups milk

1 Soak the dried beans in a large bowl of cold water for at least 6 hours, or overnight.

2 Drain the beans and rinse well. Put in a pan with 600ml/1 pint/2½ cups of cold water and the bay leaf. Bring to the boil and boil rapidly for 10 minutes. Turn off the heat, leave to cool for a few minutes, then put in the slow cooker pot and switch to high.

3 Heat the oil in a pan, add the onion and cook for 7–8 minutes. Add the garlic, cumin, chilli powder, paprika and marjoram and cook for 1 minute. Add to the cooking pot and stir.

4 Prepare the vegetables, peeling or trimming them as necessary, then cut into 2cm/¾ in chunks.

5 Add the vegetables to the mixture, making sure that those that may discolour, such as potatoes and parsnips, are submerged. It doesn't matter if the other vegetables are not completely covered. Cover with the lid and cook for 3 hours, or until the beans are tender.

6 Add the stock cube and chopped tomatoes to the cooking pot, then stir in the tomato purée and season with salt and ground black pepper. Replace the lid and cook for a further 30 minutes, until the mixture is at boiling point.

7 To make the topping, combine the cornmeal, flour, baking powder and a pinch of salt in a bowl. Make a well in the centre and add the egg, egg yolk and milk. Mix together well.

8 Spoon the cornbread topping over the bean mixture. Cover and cook for 1 hour, or until the topping is firm and cooked.

Mixed-bean chilli: Energy 613Kcal/2595kJ; Protein 29.6g; Carbohydrate 97.4g, of which sugars 15.8g; Fat 14.5g, of which saturates 3.4g; Cholesterol 112mg; Calcium 257mg; Fibre 13.4g; Sodium 413mg.

Garlic-flavoured lentils with carrots and sage

The combination of healing sage and wholesome green lentils is very traditional, and with the addition of antioxidant-rich carrots, onions and garlic is delicious. Serve this with a dollop of bio-yogurt seasoned with crushed garlic, salt and pepper, and lemon wedges for squeezing.

Serves 4–6

175g/6oz/¾ cup green lentils, rinsed and picked over
45–60ml/3–4 tbsp fruity olive oil
1 onion, cut in half lengthways, in half again crossways, and sliced along the grain
3–4 plump garlic cloves, roughly chopped and bruised with the flat side of a knife
5ml/1 tsp coriander seeds
a handful of dried sage leaves
5–10ml/1–2 tsp sugar
4 carrots, sliced
15–30ml/1–2 tbsp tomato purée (paste)
salt and ground black pepper
1 bunch of fresh sage or flat leaf parsley, to garnish

1 Bring a pan of water to the boil and add the lentils. Lower the heat, partially cover the pan and simmer for 10 minutes. Drain and rinse well under cold running water.

4 Garnish with the fresh sage or flat leaf parsley, and serve hot or at room temperature.

2 Heat the oil in a heavy pan, stir in the onion, garlic, coriander, sage and sugar, and cook until the onion begins to colour. Toss in the carrots and cook for 2–3 minutes.

3 Add the lentils and pour in 250ml/8fl oz/1 cup water, making sure the lentils and carrots are covered. Stir in the tomato purée and cover the pan, then cook the lentils and carrots gently for about 20 minutes, until most of the liquid has been absorbed. The lentils and carrots should both be tender, but still have some bite. Season with salt and pepper to taste.

> **SUPERFOOD TIP**
> Lentils are a good source of iron, folate and magnesium.

Garlic-flavoured lentils: Energy 166kcal/696kJ; Protein 7.6g; Carbohydrate 21.1g, of which sugars 6.7g; Fat 6.2g, of which saturates 0.9g; Cholesterol 0mg; Calcium 38mg; Fibre 4g; Sodium 22mg.

Stir-fried seeds and vegetables

The multitude of seeds in this recipe will provide all of the essential fatty acids the body needs, and the colourful vegetables make it very pleasing to the eye. For a more substantial meal, try this with buckwheat noodles for some useful slow-release carbohydrate.

3 Add the watercress or spinach with the fresh herbs and toss over the heat for 1 minute.

4 Stir in the black bean sauce, soy sauce and vinegar. Stir-fry for 1–2 minutes, until combined and hot. Serve immediately.

SUPERFOOD TIPS
• Crushing the hemp seeds allows the nutrient-rich omega-3 oils to be released.
• Oyster mushrooms are delicate, so it is usually better to tear them into pieces along the lines of the gills, rather than slice them with a knife.

Serves 4

30ml/2 tbsp vegetable oil
30ml/2tbsp crushed hemp seeds
30ml/2 tbsp sesame seeds
30ml/2 tbsp sunflower seeds
30ml/2 tbsp pumpkin seeds
2 garlic cloves, finely chopped
2.5cm/1in piece fresh root ginger, peeled and finely chopped
2 large carrots, cut into batons
2 large courgettes (zucchini), cut into batons
90g/3½oz/1½ cups oyster mushrooms, broken into pieces
150g/5oz watercress or spinach leaves, coarsely chopped
bunch of fresh mint or coriander (cilantro), chopped
60ml/4 tbsp black bean sauce
30ml/2 tbsp light soy sauce
15ml/1 tbsp rice vinegar

1 Heat the oil in a wok. Add the seeds. Toss over a medium heat for 1 minute, then add the garlic and ginger, and continue to stir-fry until the ginger is aromatic and the garlic is golden.

2 Add the carrot and courgette batons and mushroom pieces to the wok and stir-fry over a medium heat for a further 5 minutes, or until all the vegetables are crisp-tender and golden at the edges.

Stir-fried seeds and vegetabeles: Energy 205kcal/849kJ; Protein 6.9g; Carbohydrate 9.7g, of which sugars 7.7g; Fat 15.6g, of which saturates 2g; Cholesterol 0mg; Calcium 159mg; Fibre 3.4g; Sodium 294mg.

Thai vegetable curry with lemon grass rice

This rich, spicy recipe is jam-packed with antioxidant-rich vegetables, spices and herbs, including lemon grass. Although the ingredient list is long, it is a simple curry to make and well worth the effort. Simply change the vegetables to suit the seasons or to cater for whatever is in your refrigerator.

Serves 4

10ml/2 tsp vegetable oil
400ml/14fl oz/1⅔ cups
   coconut milk
300ml/½ pint/1¼ cups
   vegetable stock
225g/8oz new potatoes, halved
   or quartered, if large
130g/4½oz baby corn cobs
5ml/1 tsp golden caster
   (superfine) sugar
185g/6½oz broccoli florets
1 red (bell) pepper, seeded and
   sliced lengthways
115g/4oz spinach, tough stalks
   removed and shredded
30ml/2 tbsp chopped
   fresh coriander (cilantro)
salt and black pepper

For the spice paste
1 red chilli, seeded and chopped
3 green chillies, seeded
   and chopped
1 lemon grass stalk, outer leaves
   removed and lower 5cm/
   2in finely chopped
2 shallots, chopped
finely grated rind of 1 lime
2 garlic cloves, chopped
5ml/1 tsp ground coriander
2.5ml/½ tsp ground cumin
1cm/½in fresh galangal, finely
   chopped or 2.5ml/½ tsp dried
   (optional)
30ml/2 tbsp chopped fresh
   coriander (cilantro) leaves
15ml/1 tbsp chopped fresh
   coriander roots and
   stems (optional)

For the rice
225g/8oz/generous 1 cup jasmine
   rice, rinsed
1 lemon grass stalk, outer leaves
   removed, cut into 3 pieces
6 cardamom pods, bruised

1 Make the spice paste. Place all the ingredients in a food processor or blender and blend to a coarse paste.

2 Heat the oil in a large heavy pan and fry the spice paste for 1–2 minutes, stirring constantly. Add the coconut milk and stock, and bring to the boil.

3 Reduce the heat, add the potatoes and simmer for 15 minutes. Add the baby corn and seasoning, then cook for 2 minutes. Stir in the sugar, broccoli and red pepper, and cook for 2 minutes more, until the vegetables are tender. Stir in the shredded spinach and half the fresh coriander. Cook for 2 minutes.

4 Meanwhile, pour the rinsed rice into a large pan and add the lemon grass and cardamom pods. Pour over 475ml/16fl oz/2 cups water.

5 Bring to the boil, then reduce the heat, cover, and cook for 10–15 minutes, until the water is absorbed and the rice is tender and slightly sticky. Season with salt.

6 Leave the rice to stand for 10 minutes, then fluff it up with a fork.

7 Remove the spices and serve the rice with the curry, sprinkled with the remaining fresh coriander.

Thai vegetable curry: Energy 279Kcal/1161kJ; Protein 9.8g; Carbohydrate 17.4g, of which sugars 13.3g; Fat 19.4g, of which saturates 3.6g; Cholesterol 5mg; Calcium 99mg; Fibre 3.3g; Sodium 824mg.

Mixed bean and aubergine tagine

The ingredients In this satisfying vegetarian Moroccan dish are slow-cooked, producing a rich and sumptuous sauce. Full of texture, this dish is packed with cholesterol-lowering fibre from the beans and the flavour is enhanced by the chillies and herbs. It shows you can eat well without eating meat.

Serves 4

115g/4oz/generous ½ cup dried
    red kidney beans, soaked
    overnight in cold water
    and drained
115g/4oz/generous ½ cup dried
    black-eyed beans (peas) or
    cannellini beans, soaked
    overnight in cold water
    and drained
600ml/1 pint/2½ cups water
2 bay leaves
2 celery sticks, each cut into
    4 matchsticks
60ml/4 tbsp olive oil
1 aubergine (eggplant), about
    350g/12oz, cut into chunks
1 onion, thinly sliced
3 garlic cloves, crushed
1–2 fresh red chillies, seeded
    and chopped
30ml/2 tbsp tomato purée (paste)
5ml/1 tsp paprika
2 large tomatoes,
    roughly chopped
300ml/½ pint/1¼ cups
    vegetable stock
15ml/1 tbsp each chopped fresh
    mint, parsley and coriander
    (cilantro)
ground black pepper
fresh herb sprigs, to garnish

1 Place the soaked and drained kidney beans in a large pan of unsalted boiling water. Bring back to the boil and cook the beans for 10 minutes, then drain.

2 Place the soaked and drained black-eyed or cannellini beans in a separate large pan of boiling unsalted water. Boil the beans rapidly for 10 minutes, then drain.

3 Place the water in a large tagine or casserole, and add the bay leaves, celery and beans. Cover and place in the oven at 190°C/375°F/Gas 5. Cook for 1–1½ hours, or until the beans are tender, then drain.

4 Heat 45ml/3 tbsp of the oil in a frying pan or cast-iron tagine base. Add the aubergine chunks and cook, stirring for 4–5 minutes until evenly browned. Remove from the heat and set aside.

5 Add the remaining oil to the frying pan or tagine base. Add the sliced onion and cook 4–5 minutes, until softened. Add the garlic and chillies and cook for a further 5 minutes.

6 Reset the oven temperature to 160°C/325°F/Gas 3. Add the tomato purée and paprika to the onion mixture and cook for 1–2 minutes. Add the tomatoes, aubergine, cooked beans and stock to the pan, then season to taste.

7 Cover the tagine base with the lid or, if using a frying pan, transfer the contents to a clay tagine or casserole. Bake in the oven for 1 hour.

8 Just before serving, add the fresh mint, parsley and coriander and lightly stir through the vegetables. Garnish with fresh herbs.

Mixed bean tagine: Energy 209Kcal/890kJ; Protein 16.6g; Carbohydrate 33.9g, of which sugars 9.4g; Fat 1.9g, of which saturates 0.5g; Cholesterol 1mg; Calcium 173mg; Fibre 12.3g; Sodium 62mg.

Pea and mint omelette

Peas and mint have long shared a plate, and this deliciously light omelette is perfect if your appetite is reduced. The eggs provide plenty of nourishment, while the peas are rich in vitamins. Serve with a green salad for a fresh and tasty lunch. For extra carbohydrate, add halved boiled baby new potatoes.

Serves 2

4 eggs
50g/2oz/½ cup frozen peas
30ml/2 tbsp chopped fresh mint
a knob (pat) of butter
salt and ground black pepper

1 Break the eggs into a large bowl and beat with a fork. Season well with salt and pepper and set aside.

2 Cook the peas in a large pan of salted boiling water for 3–4 minutes, until tender. Drain well and add to the eggs in the bowl. Stir in the chopped fresh mint and swirl with a spoon until thoroughly combined.

3 Heat the butter in a frying pan until foamy. Pour in the egg, peas and mint, and cook over a medium heat for 3–4 minutes, until the mixture is nearly set.

4 Finish cooking the omelette under a hot grill (broiler) until set and golden on top. Fold the omelette over, transfer to a warmed plate, cut it in half and serve immediately.

VARIATIONS
• Vegetable omelettes are full of goodness: try a mixture of tiny fresh or frozen cauliflower or broccoli florets, fresh peas, skinned broad (fava) beans and sliced spring onions (scallions). Cook diced red or green (bell) peppers in a little olive oil until softened.
• Cannellini beans or chickpeas go well with the vegetables, to add carbohydrate and protein.
• Add cooked small pasta shapes.

Pea and mint omelette: Energy 205kcal/851kJ; Protein 14.3g; Carbohydrate 2.9g, of which sugars 0.6g; Fat 15.6g, of which saturates 5.8g; Cholesterol 391mg; Calcium 63mg; Fibre 1.2g; Sodium 171mg.

Sardine frittata

This recipe separates the eggs which makes for a very light omelette-style dish. Bursting with flavour, this frittata is rich in brain food as it contains omega-3 oils from the sardines and choline from the eggs. Vary the taste and boost the superfood content by adding chopped peppers or tomatoes.

2 Separate the eggs. In a bowl, whisk the yolks lightly with the parsley, chives and a little salt and pepper. Beat the whites in a separate bowl with a pinch of salt until fairly stiff. Preheat the grill (broiler) to medium-high.

3 Heat the remaining olive oil in a large frying pan, add the garlic and cook over a low heat until just golden. Gently mix together the egg yolks and whites, and ladle half the mixture into the pan.

4 Cook gently until just beginning to set on the base, then lay the sardines on the frittata and sprinkle lightly with paprika. Pour over the remaining egg mixture and cook gently until the frittata has browned underneath and is beginning to set on the top.

5 Put the pan under the grill and cook until the top of the frittata turns golden. Cut into wedges and serve immediately.

Serves 4

4 fat sardines, cleaned, filleted
   and with heads removed,
   thawed if frozen
juice of 1 lemon
45ml/3 tbsp olive oil
6 large (US extra large) eggs
30ml/2 tbsp chopped fresh parsley
30ml/2 tbsp chopped fresh chives
1 garlic clove, chopped
salt, ground black pepper
   and paprika

1 Open out the sardines and sprinkle the fish with lemon juice, a little salt and paprika. Heat 15ml/1 tbsp olive oil in a frying pan and fry the sardines for about 1–2 minutes on each side to seal them. Drain on kitchen paper, trim off the tails and set aside until required.

COOK'S TIP
It is important to use a frying pan with a handle that can be used safely under the grill (broiler). If your frying pan has a wooden handle, wrap foil around it for protection.

Sardine frittata: Energy 342kcal/1422kJ; Protein 28.9g; Carbohydrate 0.2g, of which sugars 0.2g; Fat 25.3g, of which saturates 6g; Cholesterol 285mg; Calcium 137mg; Fibre 0.4g; Sodium 220mg.

Chilli-herb seared scallops

Tender, succulent scallops taste superb when marinated in a stimulating blend of fresh chilli, fragrant mint and aromatic basil. To get the best results, sear the scallops quickly in a piping-hot wok; stir-frying the pak choi retains its excellent nutrient content.

Serves 4

20–24 king scallops, cleaned
60ml/4 tbsp olive oil
finely grated rind and juice of
   1 lemon
30ml/2 tbsp finely chopped mixed
   fresh mint and basil
1 fresh red chilli, seeded and
   finely chopped
salt and ground black pepper
500g/1¼lb pak choi (bok choy)

4 Cook the scallops for 1 minute on each side, or until cooked to your liking. Pour the marinade over the scallops.

5 When the marinade has sizzled for a moment, remove the wok from the heat. Transfer the scallops and juices to a platter and keep warm. Wipe out the wok with a piece of kitchen paper.

6 Place the wok over a high heat. When all traces of moisture have evaporated, add the remaining oil. When the oil is hot, add the pak choi and stir-fry over a high heat for 2–3 minutes, until the leaves wilt.

7 Divide the greens among four warmed serving plates, then top with the reserved scallops and their juices, and serve immediately.

1 Place the scallops in a shallow, non-metallic bowl in a single layer. In a clean bowl, mix together half the oil, the lemon rind and juice, chopped herbs and chilli, and spoon over the scallops. Season well with salt and black pepper, cover and set aside.

2 Using a sharp knife, cut each pak choi lengthways into four pieces.

3 Heat a wok over a high heat. When hot, drain the scallops (reserving the marinade) and add to the wok.

Chilli-herb seared scallops: Energy 410kcal/1714kJ; Protein 44.5g; Carbohydrate 8.3g, of which sugars 2.1g; Fat 22.3g, of which saturates 3.5g; Cholesterol 82mg; Calcium 286mg; Fibre 3.2g; Sodium 494mg.

Trout with almonds

The combination of almonds and trout is very traditional and the simplicity of this dish is the key to its success. This tasty, easy-to-prepare meal is extremely good for your heart, as the cholesterol-lowering almonds complement the omega 3 from the trout.

Serves 4

4 whole trout
45–60ml/3–4 tbsp seasoned plain (all-purpose) flour
75g/3oz/6 tbsp butter
15ml/1 tbsp olive oil
50g/2oz/½ cup flaked almonds
juice of ½ lemon
lemon wedges, to serve

3 Cook the remaining fish, then wipe the pan out with kitchen paper. Add the remaining butter and, when foaming, add the almonds. Cook gently, stirring frequently, until the almonds are golden brown. Remove from the heat and add the lemon juice.

4 Sprinkle the almonds and pan juices over the trout, and serve immediately with lemon wedges for squeezing over.

VARIATION
The trout can be grilled (broiled) if preferred. Omit the flour coating. Melt half the butter and brush over both sides of the fish. Put the fish under a medium-hot grill (broiler) and cook for 5–7 minutes on each side until golden brown and cooked all the way through. Cook the almonds in butter as in step 4 above.

1 Wash the fish, dry with kitchen paper and coat them with seasoned flour, shaking off any excess.

2 Heat half the butter with the oil in a large frying pan. When the mixture begins to foam, add one or two fish. Cook over medium heat for 3–5 minutes on each side, or until golden brown and cooked through. Lift out, drain on kitchen paper and keep warm.

COOK'S TIP
Be sure to choose a trout that will fit inside your frying pan.

Trout with almonds: Energy 475kcal/1978kJ; Protein 39.2g; Carbohydrate 7.6g, of which sugars 0.8g; Fat 32.2g, of which saturates 12.4g; Cholesterol 187mg; Calcium 101mg; Fibre 1.2g; Sodium 249mg.

Salmon and rice gratin

This all-in-one supper dish is a great way of serving salmon, especially if you are a catering for a larger number. Using wild salmon ensures that you are getting the best source of omega 3 as well as the tastiest. The eggs in this dish provide an additional omega-3 boost.

Serves 6

675g/1½lb fresh wild salmon
 fillet, skinned
1 bay leaf
a few parsley stalks
1 litre/1¾ pints/4 cups water
400g/14oz/2 cups basmati rice,
 soaked and drained
30–45ml/2–3 tbsp chopped fresh
 parsley, plus extra to garnish
175g/6oz/1½ cups grated
 Cheddar cheese
3 hard-boiled eggs, chopped
sea salt and ground black pepper

For the sauce
1 litre/1¾ pints/4 cups milk
40g/1½oz/⅓ cup plain
 (all-purpose) flour
40g/1½oz/3 tbsp butter
5ml/1 tsp mild curry paste

1 Put the salmon fillet in a wide, shallow pan. Add the bay leaf and parsley stalks, with a little salt and plenty of black pepper. Pour in the water and bring to simmering point. Poach the fish for about 12 minutes until just tender.

2 Lift the salmon fillet out of the pan using a slotted spoon, then strain the cooking liquid into a large pan. Leave the fish to cool, then remove any visible bones and flake the flesh gently into bitesize pieces with a fork.

3 Add the rice to the pan of fish-poaching liquid. Bring the liquid to the boil, then lower the heat, cover tightly with a lid and simmer gently for 10 minutes without lifting the lid.

4 Remove the pan from the heat and, without lifting the lid, allow the rice to stand, undisturbed, for 5 minutes.

5 Meanwhile, make the sauce. Mix the milk, flour and butter in a pan. Bring to the boil over a low heat, whisking constantly until the sauce is smooth and thick. Stir in the curry paste with salt and pepper to taste. Simmer for 2 minutes.

6 Preheat the grill (broiler). Remove the sauce from the heat and stir in the chopped parsley and rice, with half the cheese. Fold in the flaked fish and eggs. Spoon into a shallow gratin dish and sprinkle with the remaining cheese. Cook under the grill until the topping is golden brown. Serve garnished with chopped parsley.

Salmon an gratin: Energy 752Kcal/3137kJ; Protein 44.8g; Carbohydrate 66.5g, of which sugars 8.2g; Fat 33.5g, of which saturates 14.5g; Cholesterol 204mg; Calcium 492mg; Fibre 0.6g; Sodium 411mg.

Baked salmon with guava sauce

Guavas have a creamy flesh with a slight citrus tang, perfect for serving with salmon. Keep the cooking time of the guava sauce to a minimum to retain as much vitamin C as possible. Green guavas should be left in a warm place for a few days until they ripen.

Serves 4

6 ripe guavas
45ml/3 tbsp vegetable oil
1 small onion, finely chopped
120ml/4fl oz/½ cup well-flavoured
   chicken stock
10ml/2 tsp hot pepper sauce
4 salmon steaks
salt and ground black pepper
strips of red pepper to garnish

COOK'S TIP
Ripe guavas have yellow skin and succulent flesh that ranges in colour from white to deep-pink or salmon-red. Ripe fruit will keep in the fridge for a few days.

1 Cut each guava in half. Scoop the seeded soft flesh into a sieve (strainer) placed over a bowl. Press it through the sieve, discard the seeds and skin and set the pulp aside.

2 Heat 30ml/2 tbsp of the oil in a frying pan. Fry the chopped onion for about 4 minutes over a moderate heat until softened and turned translucent.

3 Stir in the guava pulp, with the chicken stock and hot pepper sauce. Cook, stirring constantly, until the sauce thickens. Keep it warm until needed.

4 Brush the salmon steaks on one side with a little of the remaining oil. Season them with salt and pepper. Heat a griddle pan until very hot and add the salmon steaks, oiled side down. Cook for 2–3 minutes, until the underside is golden, then brush the surface with oil, turn each salmon steak over and cook the other side until the fish is cooked and flakes easily.

5 Transfer each steak to a warmed plate. Serve, garnished with strips of red pepper on a pool of sauce. A fresh green salad is a good accompaniment.

Baked salmon: Energy 389Kcal/1621kJ; Protein 31.7g; Carbohydrate 8.7g, of which sugars 8.2g; Fat 25.5g, of which saturates 3.8g; Cholesterol 75mg; Calcium 55mg; Fibre 5.8g; Sodium 76mg.

Warm niçoise noodle salad with seared tuna

The meaty texture of fresh tuna steaks cooked on a griddle or a barbecue is a fabulous way to include more omega 3-rich fish in the diet. This recipe takes the traditional goodness of the niçoise salad ingredients and adds noodles to make a more filling dish.

Serves 4

2 fresh tuna steaks, each weighing
 about 225g/8oz
175g/6oz fine green beans,
 trimmed
3 eggs
350g/12oz medium Chinese dried
 egg noodles
225g/8oz baby plum tomatoes,
 halved
50g/2oz can anchovy fillets,
 drained and fillets separated
 (optional)
50g/2oz/½ cup small black olives
a handful of fresh basil leaves, torn
salt and ground black pepper

For the marinade
30ml/2 tbsp lemon juice
75ml/5 tbsp olive oil
2 garlic cloves, crushed

For the warm dressing
90ml/6 tbsp extra virgin olive oil
30ml/2 tbsp wine vinegar or
 lemon juice
2 garlic cloves, crushed
2.5ml/½ tsp Dijon mustard
30ml/2 tbsp capers
45ml/3 tbsp chopped herbs such as
 tarragon, chives, basil and chervil

1 To make the marinade, combine the lemon juice, olive oil and garlic in a glass or china dish. Add salt and pepper and mix well. Add the tuna and coat with the marinade. Cover and leave to marinate in a cool place for 1 hour.

2 Whisk all the ingredients for the dressing together in a small pan and leave to infuse. Meanwhile, blanch the green beans in boiling salted water for 4 minutes. Drain and refresh in cold water.

3 In a separate pan, cover the eggs with plenty of cold water. Bring to the boil, then boil for 10 minutes. Immediately, drain and cover with cold water to stop the cooking. When cool, shell and quarter the eggs.

4 Put the noodles and blanched beans into a bowl and pour boiling water over to cover. Leave for 5 minutes, then fork over the noodles. Heat the dressing and keep warm. Drain the noodles and beans, and toss with the dressing.

5 Heat a ridged griddle pan or heavy skillet until smoking. Drain the tuna steaks, pat dry and sear for 1–2 minutes on each side. Remove and immediately slice thinly. Add the tuna, tomatoes, anchovies and black olives to the noodles and beans, and toss well. Pile the salad into warmed serving bowls and scatter with the quartered eggs and basil. Season and eat while it is still warm.

Warm niçoise noodle salad: Energy 899Kcal/3761kJ; Protein 48g; Carbohydrate 67g, of which sugars 5g; Fat 5g, of which saturates 10g; Cholesterol 239mg; Calcium 154mg; Fibre 4.6g; Sodium 1099mg.

Smoked haddock with mustard cabbage

This simple, quick and easy-to-prepare smoked haddock recipe is really delicious. Steaming the cabbage ensures that all of its super vitamins and nutrients are retained, and gently poaching the haddock makes this a light, easily digestible dish.

2 Meanwhile, put the haddock in a large shallow pan with the milk, onion and bay leaves. Add the lemon slices and peppercorns. Bring to simmering point, cover and poach until the fish flakes easily. Depending on the thickness of the fish, this takes 8–10 minutes. Remove the pan from the heat. Preheat the grill (broiler).

3 Cut the tomatoes in half horizontally, season them with salt and pepper, and grill (broil) until lightly browned. Drain the cabbage, rinse in cold water and drain again.

4 Melt the butter in a shallow pan or wok, add the cabbage and toss over the heat for 2 minutes. Mix in the mustard and season to taste, then transfer to a warm serving dish.

5 Drain the haddock. Skin and cut the fish into four pieces. Place on top of the cabbage with some onion rings and grilled tomato halves. Pour on the lemon juice, then sprinkle with chopped parsley and serve.

Serves 4

1 Savoy or pointu cabbage
675g/1½lb undyed smoked
  haddock fillet
300ml/½ pint/1¼ cups milk
½ onion, sliced into rings
2 bay leaves
½ lemon, sliced
4 white peppercorns
4 ripe tomatoes
50g/2oz/¼ cup butter
30ml/2 tbsp wholegrain mustard
juice of 1 lemon
salt and ground black pepper
30ml/2 tbsp chopped fresh parsley,
  to garnish

1 Cut the cabbage in half, remove the central core and thick ribs, then shred the cabbage. Cook in a pan of lightly salted, boiling water, or steam over boiling water for about 10 minutes, until just tender. Leave in the pan or steamer until required.

Smoked haddock: Energy 319kcal/1340kJ; Protein 36.1g; Carbohydrate 14.2g, of which sugars 13.7g; Fat 13.1g, of which saturates 7.3g; Cholesterol 90mg; Calcium 146mg; Fibre 4.2g; Sodium 1512mg.

Fish pie with sweet potato topping

Combining sweet potatoes with normal potatoes is a great way to add another vegetable to a recipe. This tasty dish is full of contrasting flavours – the slightly spicy sweet potato making an interesting, brightly coloured topping for the mild-flavoured fish.

Serves 4

175g/6oz/scant 1 cup basmati
  rice, soaked
450ml/¾ pint/scant 2 cups
  well-flavoured stock
175g/6oz/1½ cups podded
  broad (fava) beans
675g/1½lb haddock or cod
  fillets, skinned
about 450ml/¾ pint/scant
  2 cups milk

For the sauce
40g/1½oz/3 tbsp butter
30–45ml/2–3 tbsp plain
  (all-purpose) flour
15ml/1 tbsp chopped fresh parsley
salt and freshly ground black
  pepper

For the topping
450g/1lb sweet potatoes, peeled
  and cut into large chunks
450g/1lb floury white potatoes,
  such as King Edwards, peeled
  and cut into large chunks
milk and butter, for mashing
10ml/2 tsp freshly chopped parsley
5ml/1 tsp freshly chopped dill

1 Preheat the oven to 190°C/375°F/ Gas 5. Drain the rice and put it in a pan. Pour in the stock, with a little salt and pepper, if needed, and bring to the boil. Cover the pan, lower the heat and simmer for 10 minutes, or until all the liquid has been absorbed.

2 Cook the broad beans in a little lightly salted water until tender. Drain thoroughly. When cool enough to handle, pop the bright green beans out of their skins.

3 To make the potato topping, boil the sweet and white potatoes separately in salted water until tender. Drain them both, then mash them with a little milk and butter. Spoon the mashed potatoes into separate bowls. Beat parsley and dill into the sweet potatoes.

4 Place the fish in a large frying pan and pour in enough of the milk (about 350ml/12fl oz/1½ cups) to just cover. Dot with 15g/½oz/1 tbsp of the butter, and season. Heat gently and simmer for 5–6 minutes, until the fish is just tender.

5 Lift out the fish and break it into large pieces. Pour the cooking liquid into a measuring jug (cup) and make up to 450ml/¾ pint/scant 2 cups with the remaining milk.

6 To make a white sauce, melt the butter in a saucepan, stir in the flour and cook for 1 minute. Gradually add the cooking liquid and milk mixture, stirring, until a fairly thin white sauce is formed. Stir in the parsley and season to taste.

7 Spread out the cooked rice on the bottom of a large oval gratin dish. Add the broad beans and fish, and pour over the white sauce. Spoon the mashed potatoes over the top, to make an attractive pattern. Dot with a little extra butter and bake for 15 minutes until lightly browned.

Fish pie: Energy 604Kcal/2545kJ; Protein 41.6g; Carbohydrate 88g, of which sugars 8.6g; Fat 10.7g, of which saturates 5.7g; Cholesterol 99mg; Calcium 94mg; Fibre 6.9g; Sodium 223mg.

Chicken with chickpeas and almonds

The chicken and chickpeas in this tasty Moroccan-style recipe are both excellent low-fat protein sources, while the heart-healthy almonds are low in saturated fats. This dish goes well with vegetable cous cous or with warmed wholemeal pitta bread.

Serves 4

75g/3oz/½ cup blanched almonds
75g/3oz/½ cup chickpeas, soaked overnight and drained
4 chicken breast portions, skinned
30ml/2 tbsp olive oil
2.5ml/½ tsp saffron threads
2 Spanish (Bermuda) onions, sliced
900ml/1½ pints/3¾ cups chicken stock
1 small cinnamon stick
60ml/4 tbsp chopped fresh flat leaf parsley, plus extra to garnish
lemon juice, to taste
salt and freshly ground black pepper

1 Place the blanched almonds and the chickpeas in a large flameproof casserole of water and bring to the boil. Boil for 10 minutes, then reduce the heat. Simmer for 1–1½ hours, until the chickpeas are soft. Drain and set aside.

COOK'S TIP
To save time, use a small can of chickpeas instead of the dried variety. This avoids having to soak the chickpeas overnight or simmer them until soft. Simply boil with the blanched almonds for 10 minutes and go to step 2.

2 Place the skinned chicken pieces in the casserole, together with the olive oil, half of the saffron, and salt and plenty of black pepper. Heat gently, stirring constantly until warmed through.

3 Add the onions and stock, bring to the boil, then add the reserved cooked almonds, chickpeas and cinnamon stick. Cover with a tightly fitting lid and cook very gently for 45–60 minutes, until the chicken is completely tender.

4 Transfer the chicken breasts to a serving plate and keep warm. Bring the sauce to the boil and cook over a high heat until it is well reduced, stirring frequently.

5 Add the chopped parsley and remaining saffron to the casserole and cook for a further 2–3 minutes. Sharpen the sauce with a little lemon juice, then pour the sauce over the chicken and serve, garnished with extra fresh parsley.

Chicken with chickpeas: Energy 431kcal/1803kJ; Protein 44.4g; Carbohydrate 11g, of which sugars 1.6g; Fat 23.6g, of which saturates 7.9g; Cholesterol 132mg; Calcium 110mg; Fibre 4g; Sodium 180mg.

Penne with chicken, broccoli and cheese

The delicious combination of broccoli, garlic and Gorgonzola is very moreish, and goes especially well with the chicken. The broccoli is cooked very quickly, which locks in vital nutrients, including vitamin C, which helps the body to absorb the iron and calcium in the chicken and cheese.

Serves 4

115g/4oz/scant 1 cup broccoli
   florets, divided into tiny sprigs
30ml/2 tbsp olive oil
2 skinless chicken breast fillets,
   cut into thin strips
2 garlic cloves, crushed
400g/14oz/3½ cups dried penne
120ml/4fl oz/½ cup dry white wine
200ml/7fl oz/scant 1 cup panna da
   cucina or double (heavy) cream
90g/3½oz Gorgonzola cheese,
   rind removed and diced small
salt and ground black pepper
freshly grated Parmesan cheese,
   to serve

1 Plunge the broccoli into a pan of boiling salted water. Bring back to the boil and cook for 2 minutes.

2 Drain in a colander and refresh under cold running water. Shake well to remove the surplus water and set aside to drain completely.

3 Heat the olive oil in a large skillet or pan, add the chicken and garlic with salt and pepper to taste, and stir well. Fry over a medium heat for 3 minutes, or until the chicken becomes white.

4 Start cooking the pasta according to the instructions on the packet.

5 Pour the wine and cream over the chicken mixture in the pan, stir to mix, then simmer, stirring occasionally, for about 5 minutes, until the sauce has reduced and thickened.

6 Add the broccoli, then increase the heat and toss gently to warm it through and mix it with the chicken. Season according to taste.

7 Drain the pasta and pour it into the sauce. Add the Gorgonzola and toss well. Top with grated Parmesan cheese to serve.

> **VARIATION**
> Try using leeks instead of broccoli if you prefer. Simply fry them with the chicken.

Penne with chicken: Energy 951Kcal/3982kJ; Protein 47.8g; Carbohydrate 80.2g, of which sugars 8.6g; Fat 48.8g, of which saturates 28.5g; Cholesterol 165mg; Calcium 324mg; Fibre 10.2g; Sodium 433mg.

Turkey and broccoli lasagne

The low-fat, protein-rich turkey in this easy meal-in-one pasta bake is healthier than the more traditional minced beef variant. Adding broccoli adds to its nutritional credentials and the intense flavour of Parmesan means that a little cheese goes a long way.

3 To make the sauce, melt the butter in a pan, stir in the flour and cook for 1 minute, still stirring. Remove from the heat and gradually stir in the milk. Return to the heat and gently bring the sauce to the boil, stirring constantly. Simmer for 1 minute, then add 50g/2oz/⅔ cup of the Parmesan together with plenty of salt and pepper.

4 Spoon a layer of the turkey mixture into a large, deep baking dish. Add a layer of broccoli and cover with sheets of lasagne. Coat with cheese sauce. Repeat these layers, finishing with a layer of cheese sauce on top. Sprinkle with the remaining Parmesan and bake for 35–40 minutes.

Serves 4

30ml/2 tbsp light olive oil
1 onion, chopped
2 garlic cloves, chopped
450g/1lb cooked turkey meat,
  finely diced
225g/8oz/1 cup mascarpone
  cheese
30ml/2 tbsp chopped
  fresh tarragon
300g/11oz broccoli, broken
  into florets
115g/4oz no pre-cook
  lasagne verde
salt and ground black pepper

For the sauce
50g/2oz/¼ cup butter
30ml/2 tbsp flour
600ml/1 pint/2½ cups milk
75g/3oz/1 cup freshly grated
  Parmesan cheese

1 Preheat the oven to 180°C/350°F/ Gas 4. Heat the oil in a heavy pan and cook the onion and garlic until softened but not coloured. Remove the pan from the heat and stir in the turkey, mascarpone and tarragon, with seasoning to taste.

2 Blanch the broccoli in a large pan of salted boiling water for 1 minute, then drain and rinse thoroughly under cold water to prevent the broccoli from overcooking. Drain well and set aside.

COOK'S TIP
This is a delicious way of using up any cooked turkey that is left over after Christmas or Thanksgiving celebrations. It is also good made with half ham and half turkey.

Turkey lasagne: Energy 732Kcal/3072kJ; Protein 61.6g; Carbohydrate 43g, of which sugars 13.1g; Fat 36.2g, of which saturates 19.4g; Cholesterol 138mg; Calcium 539mg; Fibre 3.6g; Sodium 475mg.

Beef casserole with baby onions and red wine

The fragrant, rich aromas that will fill the kitchen from this dish will make your mouth water. The slow cooking of the beef ensures that much of the fat melts away, leaving tender meat and a rich sauce, but it will not destroy the cardioprotective resveratrol in the red wine.

Serves 4

75ml/5 tbsp olive oil
1kg/2¼lb stewing or braising
  steak, cut into large cubes
3 garlic cloves, chopped
5ml/1 tsp ground cumin
5cm/2in piece of cinnamon stick
175ml/6fl oz/¾ cup red wine
30ml/2 tbsp red wine vinegar
small fresh rosemary sprig
2 bay leaves, crumbled
30ml/2 tbsp tomato purée (paste),
  diluted in 1 litre/1¾ pints/
  4 cups hot water
675g/1½lb small pickling onions,
  peeled and left whole
15ml/1 tbsp demerara (raw) sugar
salt and ground black pepper

> **COOK'S TIP**
> This dish can also be cooked in the oven. Use a flameproof casserole. Having browned the meat and added the remaining ingredients, with the exception of the onions and sugar, put the covered casserole in an oven preheated to 160°C/325°F/Gas 3. Bake for about 2 hours, or until the meat is tender. Add the onions and sugar as in steps 4 and 5 above. Return the casserole to the oven. Cook for 1 hour.

1 Heat the olive oil in a large heavy pan and brown the meat cubes, in batches if necessary, until pale golden brown all over.

2 Stir in the garlic and cumin. Add the cinnamon stick and cook for a few seconds, then pour the wine and vinegar slowly over the mixture. Let the liquid bubble and evaporate for 3–4 minutes.

3 Add the rosemary and bay leaves, with the diluted tomato purée. Stir well, season with salt and pepper, then cover and simmer gently for about 1½ hours, or until the meat is tender.

4 Dot the onions over the meat mixture and shake the pan to distribute them evenly.

5 Sprinkle the demerara sugar over the onions, cover the pan and cook gently for 30 minutes, until the onions are soft but have not begun to disintegrate. If necessary, add a little hot water at this stage.

6 Do not stir once the onions have been added, but gently shake the pan instead to coat them in the sauce. Serve immediately.

Beef casserole: Energy 672Kcal/2,798kJ; Protein 59.2g: Carbohydrate 18.4g, of which sugars 14.5g; Fat 37.4g, of which saturates 11.5g; Cholesterol 145mg; Calcium 62mg; Fibre 2.6g; Sodium 186mg.

Chilli con carne

Using lean braising steak and cutting off any visible fat keeps the saturated fat content down. Adding beans is great way of making expensive meat go further, and will make the recipe more nutritious. Serve with rice or tortillas to complete this hearty meal.

Serves 8

1.2kg/2½lb lean braising steak
30ml/2 tbsp sunflower or
 rapeseed oil
1 large onion, chopped
2 garlic cloves, finely chopped
15ml/1 tbsp plain (all-purpose) flour
300ml/½ pint/1¼ cups red wine
300ml/½ pint/1¼ cups beef stock
30ml/2 tbsp tomato purée (paste)
fresh coriander (cilantro) leaves,
 to garnish
salt and ground black pepper

For the beans
30ml/2 tbsp olive oil
1 onion, chopped
1 red chilli, seeded and chopped
2 x 400g/14oz cans red kidney
 beans, drained and rinsed
400g/14oz can chopped tomatoes

For the topping
6 tomatoes, peeled and chopped
1 green chilli, seeded and chopped
30ml/2 tbsp snipped fresh chives
30ml/2 tbsp chopped fresh
 coriander (cilantro)
150ml/¼ pint/⅔ cup sour cream

1 Cut the meat into thick strips and then into small cubes. Heat the oil in a large, flameproof casserole. Add the chopped onion and garlic, and cook until softened but not coloured. Season the flour then place it on a plate, then toss the meat in batches.

2 Use a draining spoon to remove the onion from the pan, then add a batch of floured beef and cook over a high heat until browned on all sides. Remove from the pan and set aside, then flour and brown another batch.

3 When the last batch of meat is browned, return the first batches with the onion to the pan. Stir in the wine, stock and tomato purée. Bring to the boil, reduce the heat and simmer for 45 minutes, or until the beef is tender.

4 Meanwhile, for the beans, heat the olive oil in a frying pan and cook the onion and chilli until softened. Add the kidney beans and tomatoes, and simmer gently for 20–25 minutes, or until thickened and reduced.

5 Mix the tomatoes, chilli, chives and coriander for the topping. Ladle the meat mixture on to warmed plates. Add a layer of bean mixture and tomato topping. Add a dollop of sour cream and garnish with coriander.

Chilli con carne: Energy 469Kcal/1963kJ; Protein 42g; Carbohydrate 28.3g, of which sugars 11.2g; Fat 18.8g, of which saturates 6.8g; Cholesterol 106mg; Calcium 127mg; Fibre 8.1g; Sodium 523mg.

Beef stew with oysters

At first glance, this dish may not seem too healthy, but oysters are a good source of omega-3 oils and grass-fed beef contains conjugated linoleic acid, both of which promote heart health. Serve with a sweet potato mash and mounds of green vegetables to ensure a good balance of nutrients.

Serves 4

1kg/2¼lb rump (round) steak
6 thin rashers (strips) streaky
  (fatty) bacon
12 oysters
50g/2oz/½ cup plain (all-purpose)
  flour
generous pinch of cayenne pepper
olive oil, for greasing
3 shallots, finely chopped
300ml/½ pint/1¼ cups beef stock
salt and freshly ground black
  pepper

1 Preheat the oven to 180°C/350°F/ Gas 4. You need thin strips of beef for this recipe, so place the steaks one at a time between sheets of clear film (plastic wrap) and beat them with a rolling pin until they are thin and flattened. Slice the meat into 24 thin strips, wide enough to roll around an oyster.

2 Stretch the bacon rashers lengthways by placing them on a chopping board and, holding one end down with your thumb, pulling them out using the thick side of a sharp knife. Cut each rasher into four pieces.

3 Remove the oysters from their shells, retaining the liquid from inside the shells in a separate container. Set aside.

4 Cut each oyster in half lengthways and roll each piece in a strip of bacon, ensuring that the bacon goes around at least once and preferably covers the oyster at each end. Then, roll in a strip of beef so no oyster is visible.

5 Season the flour with the cayenne pepper and salt and black pepper, then roll the meat in it.

6 Lightly grease a large flameproof casserole with olive oil. Sprinkle the shallots evenly over the base. Place the floured meat rolls on top, keeping them well spaced out.

7 Slowly pour over the beef stock, bring to the boil, then cover and cook in the oven for 1½–2 hours. The flour from around the meat will have thickened the stew sauce, producing a rich gravy.

Beef stew with oysters: Energy 528kcal/2208kJ; Protein 61.4g; Carbohydrate 12.7g, of which sugars 2.5g; Fat 24.4g, of which saturates 10.1g; Cholesterol 182mg; Calcium 52mg; Fibre 0.6g; Sodium 634mg.

Lamb and carrot casserole with barley

The sweet carrots in this recipe complement the lamb well, and their high carotenoid content is retained even after two hours of cooking. The cholesterol-lowering pot barley adds flavour and texture as well as helping to thicken the sauce.

2 Slice the onions and add to the pan. Fry gently for 5 minutes. Add the carrots and celery and cook for 3–4 minutes. Transfer to a casserole.

3 Sprinkle the pot barley over the vegetables in the casserole, then arrange the lamb pieces on top.

4 Lightly season with salt and ground black pepper, then sprinkle with the herbs. Pour the stock over the meat, so that all of the meat is covered.

5 Cover the casserole with the lid and cook in the oven for about 2 hours, or until the meat, vegetables and barley are tender.

6 Taste and adjust the seasoning before serving with spring cabbage and baked potatoes.

Serves 6

675g/1½lb boneless lamb
15ml/1 tbsp vegetable oil
2 onions
675g/1½lb carrots, thickly sliced
4–6 celery sticks, sliced
45ml/3 tbsp pot barley, rinsed
600ml/1 pint/2½ cups near-boiling lamb or vegetable stock
5ml/1 tsp fresh thyme leaves or pinch of dried mixed herbs
salt and ground black pepper
spring cabbage and baked potatoes, to serve

1 Preheat the oven to 160°C/325°F/ Gas 3. Trim the lamb. Cut the meat into 3cm/1¼in pieces. Heat the oil in a frying pan, add the lamb and fry until browned. Remove and set aside.

Lamb and carrot casserole: Energy 310kcal/1295kJ; Protein 24.2g; Carbohydrate 20.6g, of which sugars 12.2g; Fat 15.1g, of which saturates 6.2g; Cholesterol 86mg; Calcium 64mg; Fibre 3.9g; Sodium 139mg.

Moroccan lamb with honey and prunes

Even though this dish is sweet, it uses honey and prunes, which means it retains a good glycemic index. Slow roasting the lamb ensures that much of the excess fat is cooked off. A delicious accompaniment to this lamb dish would be a warm lentil salad with red onions and garlic.

Serves 6

130g/4½oz/generous ½ cup
  pitted prunes
350ml/12fl oz/1½ cups hot tea
1kg/2¼lb stewing or braising
  lamb such as shoulder, cut into
  chunky portions
1 onion, chopped
75–90ml/5–6 tbsp chopped
  fresh parsley
2.5ml/½ tsp ground ginger
2.5ml/½ tsp curry powder or
  ras el hanout
pinch of freshly grated nutmeg
10ml/2 tsp ground cinnamon
1.5ml/¼ tsp saffron threads
30ml/2 tbsp hot water
75–120ml/5–9 tbsp honey, to taste
250ml/8fl oz/1 cup beef or lamb
  stock
115g/4oz/1 cup blanched almonds,
  toasted
30ml/2 tbsp chopped fresh
  coriander (cilantro) leaves
3 hard-boiled eggs, cut into
  wedges
salt and ground black pepper

1 Preheat the oven to 180°C/350°F/ Gas 4. Put the prunes in a bowl, pour over the tea and cover. Leave to soak.

2 Meanwhile, put the lamb, chopped onion, parsley, ginger, curry powder or ras el hanout, nutmeg, cinnamon, salt and black pepper in a roasting pan. Cover and cook for about 2 hours.

3 Drain off excess fat from the lamb. Drain the prunes; add their liquid to the lamb. Combine the saffron and hot water and add to the pan with the honey and stock. Bake for 30 minutes, turning the lamb occasionally.

4 Add the prunes to the pan and stir gently to mix. Serve topped with the wedges of hard-boiled egg and sprinkled with the toasted almonds, a little curry powder or ras el hanout, and chopped coriander.

Moroccan lamb: Energy 490Kcal/2051kJ; Protein 43.6g; Carbohydrate 23.8g, of which sugars 23.4g; Fat 25.2g, of which saturates 10.3g; Cholesterol 279mg; Calcium 41mg; Fibre 1.4g; Sodium 197mg.

Pan-fried calf's liver with crisp onions

Calf's liver melts in the mouth and is a truly delicious way of eating offal. Its iron content is second to none, and serving it with any salad which includes vitamin-C-rich tomatoes will ensure that you absorb all of its goodness. Avoid cooking the liver for too long as this may cause it to toughen.

Serves 4

30ml/2 tbsp olive oil
4 onions, finely sliced
5ml/1 tsp caster (superfine) sugar
4 slices calf's liver, each weighing
   about 115g/4oz
30ml/2 tbsp plain (all-purpose) flour
30ml/2 tbsp olive oil
salt and ground black pepper
parsley, to garnish
sautéed potatoes, to serve

1 Heat the oil in a large, heavy pan with a tight-fitting lid. Add the onions and mix well to coat with the oil. Cover the pan and cook gently for 10 minutes, stirring occasionally.

2 Stir in the sugar and cover the pan. Cook the onions for a further 10 minutes, or until they are soft and golden.

3 Increase the heat, remove the lid and stir the onions over a high heat until they are deep gold and crisp. Use a draining spoon to remove the onions from the pan, draining off the fat.

4 Meanwhile, rinse the calf's liver slices in cold water and pat them dry on kitchen paper. Season the flour, put it on a plate and turn the slices of liver in it until they are lightly coated in flour.

5 Heat the oil in a large frying pan, add the liver and cook for about 2 minutes on each side, or until lightly browned and just firm. Arrange the cooked liver slices on warmed plates, with the crisp onions. Garnish with parsley, and serve with sautéed or mashed potatoes.

Pan-fried calf's liver: Energy 315Kcal/1310kJ; Protein 22.7g; Carbohydrate 11.8g, of which sugars 4.4g; Fat 19.9g, of which saturates 8.5g; Cholesterol 452mg; Calcium 39mg; Fibre 1.3g; Sodium 160mg.

Spicy Mexican tacos

This recipe uses textured vegetable protein, or TVP, instead of minced beef. TVP is a soya bean product that is low in fat and high in protein isoflavones, which are useful for reducing cholesterol. Chillies, tomatoes and peppers add to the superfood count.

Makes 8

5ml/1 tsp yeast extract
200ml/8fl oz/1 cup hot water
5ml/1 tsp soy sauce
85g/3oz unflavoured textured
 vegetable protein (TVP)
1 onion, chopped
1 red (bell) pepper, finely chopped
1 garlic clove, crushed
10ml/2 tsp chilli powder
1 x 400g/14oz can chopped
 tomatoes
8 corn taco shells
shredded lettuce, chopped fresh
 tomatoes and grated cheese,
 to serve

1 Dissolve the yeast extract in the hot water and add the soy sauce and the TVP. Mix well and leave the TVP to rehydrate.

2 Fry the chopped onion, pepper and garlic in a non-stick pan until the ingredients are softened and then add the chilli powder.

3 Add the TVP mix and the chopped tomatoes and stir well, simmering for approximately 15 minutes.

4 Prepare the lettuce, tomato and grated cheese accompaniments.

5 When the tomato and TVP mixture is cooked, fill each of the taco shells with a few tablespoonfuls of the spicy sauce. Serve the tacos topped with shredded lettuce, fresh chopped tomatoes and grated cheese.

Spicy Mexican tacos: Energy 108Kcal/376kJ; Protein 4g; Carbohydrate 13g, of which sugars 4g; Fat 1g, of which saturates 2g; Cholesterol 0mg; Calcium 15mg; Fibre 1.6g; Sodium 113mg.

DESSERTS
AND DRINKS

Being conscious of your nutritional intake does not mean that you have to exclude desserts from your diet. There are a wealth of tempting sweets that can be enjoyed that provide a great opportunity to include vitamin-packed fruit in your daily menu. All fruit is good for you, whether fresh, frozen, dried or canned (ideally in natural juice), so go ahead and tuck into fruit salads, fruit puddings, frozen yogurts, sorbets and granitas.

Ginger and kiwi sorbet

Freshly grated root ginger gives a lively, aromatic flavour to sorbets and ice creams. In this recipe, stomach-soothing ginger is combined with kiwi fruit to make a vitamin C-rich sorbet. This is certainly a light, refreshing end to a meal, and especially good after a rich main course.

Serves 6

55g/2oz fresh root ginger
115g/4oz/½ cup caster
  (superfine) sugar
300ml/½ pint/1¼ cups water
5 kiwi fruit
fresh mint sprigs or chopped
kiwi fruit, to decorate

COOK'S TIP
If you keep a ginger root in the freezer, all you have to do when you need some is to snap off the required amount. Frozen ginger is also easier to grate.

1 Peel the ginger and grate it finely. Place the sugar and water in a pan and heat gently until the sugar has completely dissolved. Add the ginger and cook for 1 minute, then leave to cool. Strain the syrup into a bowl and chill until very cold.

2 Peel the kiwi fruit and blend until smooth. Add the purée to the chilled syrup and mix well.

3 By hand: Pour the mixture into a container and freeze for 3–4 hours, beating twice as it thickens. Return to the freezer until ready to serve.

Using an ice cream maker:
Churn the mixture until it thickens. Transfer to a plastic tub or similar freezerproof container and freeze until ready to serve.

4 Spoon into glasses, decorate with mint sprigs or chopped kiwi fruit, and serve.

Ginger and kiwi sorbet: Energy 100Kcal/426kJ; Protein 0.7g; Carbohydrate 25.3g, of which sugars 25.2g; Fat 0.3g, of which saturates 0g; Cholesterol 0mg; Calcium 23mg; Fibre 1g; Sodium 3mg.

Strawberry snow

Strawberries have a delicate, fragrant taste and this dessert is best eaten soon after it is made. Only half the strawberries are cooked, retaining the vitamin C in the raw crushed strawberries. You can substitute the strawberries with any of your favourite superfruits such as blueberries or raspberries.

Serves 4

120ml/4fl oz/½ cup water
15ml/1 tbsp powdered gelatine
300g/11oz/2¾ cups strawberries,
   crushed lightly
250ml/8fl oz/1 cup double
   (heavy) cream
4 egg whites
90g/3½oz/½ cup caster
   (superfine) sugar
halved strawberries, to decorate

1 Put the water in a small bowl and sprinkle in the gelatine. Stand the bowl over a pan of hot water and heat gently until dissolved. Remove the bowl from the pan and leave to cool slightly.

2 Put half the crushed strawberries in a pan and bring to the boil. Remove from the heat, then stir in the dissolved gelatine. Chill in the refrigerator for about 2 hours until syrupy.

3 Pour the cream into a bowl and whisk until it holds its shape. Whisk the egg whites until stiff, gradually adding the sugar as they rise. Fold the egg whites into the cooled strawberry mixture, then fold in the remaining crushed strawberries, followed by the whipped cream.

4 Turn the mixture into individual serving dishes, decorate with halved strawberries, and serve immediately or chill until required.

COOK'S TIP
Strawberry Snow freezes well and can then be served as an iced strawberry parfait. All you have to do to make this is spoon the mixture into a loaf tin (pan) lined with clear film (plastic wrap), and freeze for a couple of hours, until it is firm.

Strawberry snow: Energy 443kcal/1841kJ; Protein 7.8g; Carbohydrate 29.1g, of which sugars 29.1g; Fat 33.7g, of which saturates 20.9g; Cholesterol 86mg; Calcium 56mg; Fibre 0.8g; Sodium 81mg.

Rhubarb fool

Here is a quick and simple dessert that makes the most of fibre-rich rhubarb. Although this recipe traditionally uses cream, you can substitute this with a low-fat bio-yogurt and use a low-fat custard to help to keep the fat content and calorific value to a minimum.

2 Pass the rhubarb through a fine sieve (strainer) so you have a thick purée.

3 Use equal parts of the purée, the whipped double cream and thick custard. Combine the purée and custard first then fold in the cream. Chill in the refrigerator before serving. Serve with heather honey.

Serves 4

450g/1lb rhubarb, trimmed
75g/3oz/scant ½ cup soft light
  brown sugar
whipped double (heavy) cream
  and ready-made thick custard
heather honey, to serve

COOK'S TIP
Make extra quantities of fruit purée and freeze to save time the next time you make this dessert.

1 Cut the rhubarb into pieces and wash thoroughly. Stew over a low heat with just the water clinging to it and the sugar. This takes about 10 minutes. Set aside to cool.

VARIATIONS
You can use another stewed fruit if you like for this dessert – try blackberries, apples, prunes or peaches. For something a little more exotic, you could try using mangoes.

Rhubarb fool: Energy 439kcal/1828kJ; Protein 4.6g; Carbohydrate 34.1g, of which sugars 31.8g; Fat 31.7g, of which saturates 18.9g; Cholesterol 80mg; Calcium 233mg; Fibre 1.6g; Sodium 74mg.

Raspberry fromage frais and amaretti scrunch

This pudding looks stunning but is actually very simple to make. The raspberries are not cooked in this recipe, so all of the vitamin C is retained. Honey is used as a sweetener, and along with the natural fruit sugars will give this dessert a low glycaemic index.

Serves 4–6

250g/9oz/1½ cups frozen or
  fresh raspberries
500g/1¼lb/2½ cups fromage
  frais or thick natural (plain)
  bio-yogurt
30ml/2 tbsp clear honey
finely grated rind of 1 small
  lemon
75g/3oz/1½ cups amaretti, broken
  into pieces
crystallized rose petals, for
  decoration (optional)

1 If using frozen raspberries, allow them to partly defrost. If using fresh ones, partly freeze them.

2 Place the fromage frais or yogurt in a large bowl and stir in the honey and lemon rind. Add the raspberries and fold in gently, being careful not to over-mix. Chill for 1 hour.

3 Stir in the amaretti just before serving. Decorate with crystallized rose petals, if you wish.

> **COOK'S TIP**
> Gently wash the raspberries immediately before use, otherwise they will turn soggy.

> **VARIATION**
> Instead of the raspberries, try using fresh strawberries or a mix of your favourite berries.

Raspberry fromage frais: Energy 183Kcal/771kJ; Protein 5.7g; Carbohydrate 27.2g, of which sugars 21.3g; Fat 6.4g, of which saturates 3.7g; Cholesterol 17mg; Calcium 99mg; Fibre 1.2g; Sodium 72mg.

Summer berry frozen yogurt

This dessert is a fabulous, healthier and lower-fat alternative to ice cream. Any combination of sweet, juicy summer fruits can be used, and they will all contribute a wonderful array of antioxidants and vitamin C, which also helps the body to absorb the calcium from the yogurt.

Serves 6

350g/12oz/3 cups frozen summer
  fruits, plus whole fresh or frozen
  berries, to decorate
200g/7oz/scant 1 cup low-fat
  bio-yogurt
25g/1oz icing (confectioners')
  sugar

COOK'S TIP
To make a more creamy frozen yogurt, use Greek (US strained plain) yogurt. This will still be healthy, just slightly higher in fat.

1 Place all the ingredients into a food processor and process until the mixture is well combined but still quite chunky in texture. Spoon the mixture into six 150ml/¼ pint/ ⅔ cup ramekin dishes.

2 Cover each dish with clear film (plastic wrap) and place in the freezer for about 2 hours, or until firm.

3 To turn out the frozen yogurts, dip the ramekin dishes briefly in hot water, taking care not to allow water to get on to the dessert itself. Invert the ramekins on to small serving plates. Tap the base of the dishes and the yogurts should come out.

4 Serve the frozen yogurt immediately, decorated with fresh or frozen berries of your choice, such as blueberries, blackberries or raspberries.

Summer berry frozen yogurt: Energy 51Kcal/215kJ; Protein 2.2g; Carbohydrate 10.4g, of which sugars 10.4g; Fat 0.4g, of which saturates 0.2g; Cholesterol 0mg; Calcium 75mg; Fibre 0.7g; Sodium 32mg.

Watermelon granita

The pastel pink flakes of ice, subtly blended with the citrus freshness of lime and the delicate flavour of watermelon, make this refreshing granita a delight for the eyes as well as the tastebuds. The watermelon is rich in the antioxidant lycopene, so this is a treat for the body, too.

Serves 6

150g/5oz/⅔ cup caster
    (superfine) sugar
150ml/¼ pint/¾ cup water
1 whole watermelon, about
    1.75kg/4–4½ lb
finely grated rind and juice
    of 2 limes, plus lime wedges,
    to serve

1 Bring the sugar and water to the boil in a pan, stirring until the sugar has dissolved. Pour into a bowl. Cool, then chill. Cut the watermelon into quarters.

2 Discard most of the seeds, scoop the flesh into a food processor and process briefly until smooth. Alternatively, use a blender, and process the watermelon quarters in small batches.

5 Freeze for 2 hours more, mashing the mixture every 30 minutes, until the granita turns slushy. Scoop it into dishes and serve with lime wedges.

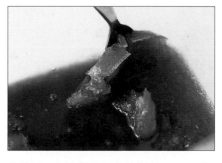

3 Strain the purée into a large plastic container. Discard the seeds. Pour in the chilled syrup, lime rind and juice and mix well.

4 Cover and freeze for 2 hours, until the mixture around the sides of the container is mushy. Mash the ice finely with a fork and return the granita to the freezer.

VARIATION
For an indulgent cocktail-style granita, dip the rim of each glass serving dish in a little water or beaten egg white, then dip it into sugar. Spoon in the granita, pour in a little tequila or white rum and decorate with lime wedges.

Watermelon granita: Energy 153Kcal/653kJ; Protein 1g; Carbohydrate 38g, of which sugars 38g; Fat 1g, of which saturates 0g; Cholesterol 0mg; Calcium 20mg; Fibre 0.3g; Sodium 5mg.

Peach and cardamom yogurt ice

Low-fat frozen desserts that rely on natural fruit sugar for their sweetness are perfect for diabetics. Cardamom contains volatile oils that freshen the breath, and make this dessert particularly refreshing and cleansing. Mangoes or strawberries can also be used in place of the peaches.

Serves 4

8 cardamom pods
6 peaches, total weight about 500g/1¼lb, halved and stoned (pitted)
30ml/2 tbsp water
200ml/7fl oz/scant 1 cup natural (plain) bio-yogurt

COOK'S TIP
Use natural (plain) bio-yogurt for its extra mild taste. Greek (US strained plain) yogurt or ordinary natural yogurt are both much sharper, and tend to overwhelm the delicate taste of peach.

1 Put the cardamom pods on a board and crush them with the base of a ramekin, or use a mortar and pestle.

2 Chop the peaches and put them in a pan. Add the crushed cardamom pods, with their black seeds, and the measured water. Cover and simmer gently for about 10 minutes, or until the fruit is tender. Remove the pan from the heat and leave to cool.

3 Pour the peach mixture into a food processor or blender, process until smooth, then press through a sieve (strainer) placed over a bowl.

4 Add the yogurt to the purée and mix. Pour into a freezerproof tub and freeze for about 6 hours, beating once or twice with a whisk or in a food processor. To serve, scoop the ice cream on to a platter or into bowls.

Peach and cardamom yogurt ice: Energy 69kcal/296kJ; Protein 3.8g; Carbohydrate 13.3g, of which sugars 13.3g; Fat 0.6g, of which saturates 0.3g; Cholesterol 1mg; Calcium 104mg; Fibre 1.9g; Sodium 43mg.

Date and tofu ice

Low in saturated fat and high in soya protein, this unusual dairy-free ice cream is truly heart healthy. While it also contains no added sugar, the dates and cinnamon ensure there is no compromise on flavour, and make a delicious dessert.

Serves 4

250g/9oz/1½ cups stoned (pitted) dates
600ml/1 pint/2½ cups apple juice
5ml/1 tsp ground cinnamon
285g/10oz pack chilled tofu, drained and cubed
150ml/¼ pint/⅔ cup unsweetened soya milk

1 Put the dates in a pan. Pour in 300ml/½ pint/1¼ cups of the apple juice and leave to soak for 2 hours. Simmer for 10 minutes, then leave to cool. Using a slotted spoon, lift out one-quarter of the dates, chop roughly and set aside.

2 Purée the remaining dates in a food processor or blender. Add the cinnamon and process with enough of the remaining apple juice to make a smooth paste.

3 Add the cubes of tofu to the food processor, a few at a time, processing after each addition. Finally, add the remaining apple juice and the soya milk and mix well to combine.

VARIATIONS
Make this ice cream with any soft dried fruits, such as figs, apricots or peaches, or use a mix of your favourite fruits.

4 Churn the mixture in an ice cream maker until very thick, but not thick enough to scoop. Scrape into a plastic tub.

5 Stir in most of the chopped dates, retaining a few pieces for garnishing, and freeze for 2–3 hours, until firm.

6 Scoop the ice cream into dessert glasses and decorate with the remaining chopped dates.

SUPERFOOD TIP
Remember that dried fruits are naturally high in sugar and can cause fluctuations in blood sugar levels. This tofu and date ice does not have added sugar, and it can be served with fresh fruit or have fresh fruit mixed in at the last minute. Try fresh strawberries, raspberries or cherries to bulk out the ice and boost its vitamin and fibre content.

Date and tofu ice: Energy 290kcal/1232kJ; Protein 9.1g; Carbohydrate 58.2g, of which sugars 57.9g; Fat 3.9g, of which saturates 0.5g; Cholesterol 0mg; Calcium 407mg; Fibre 2.5g; Sodium 24mg.

Crispy mango stacks with raspberry coulis

The mango and raspberries supercharge this stunning dessert with antioxidants. Filo pastry is a far healthier alternative to short crust or puff pastry because it is so much lower in fat. There is no added sugar, but if the raspberries are a little sharp, you may prefer to add a pinch of sugar to the purée.

Serves 4

3 filo pastry sheets, thawed
   if frozen
50g/2oz/¼ cup butter, melted
2 small ripe mangoes
115g/4oz/⅔ raspberries, thawed
   if frozen

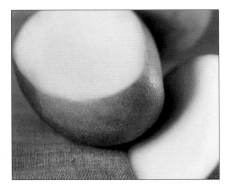

1 Preheat the oven to 200°C/400°F/ Gas 6. Lay the filo sheets on a clean work surface and cut out four 10cm/4in rounds from each.

2 Brush each round with the melted butter and lay the rounds on two baking sheets. Bake for 5 minutes, or until crisp and golden. Place on wire racks to cool.

3 Peel the mangoes, remove the stones (pits) and cut the flesh into thin slices. Blend the raspberries in a food processor with 45ml/3 tbsp water to make a purée. Place a pastry round on each of four plates. Top with a quarter of the mango and drizzle with raspberry purée. Repeat until all the ingredients are used, finishing with a layer of mango and a dash of purée.

Crispy mango stacks: Energy 186Kcal/779kJ; Protein 2.2g; Carbohydrate 21.7g, of which sugars 11.9g; Fat 10.7g, of which saturates 6.7g; Cholesterol 27mg; Calcium 36mg; Fibre 3.1g; Sodium 79mg.

Pomegranate jewelled cheesecake

This whisked cheesecake is lighter in texture than most, and subtly flavoured with orange juice and coconut cream. The polyphenol-rich pomegranate topping offers a spectacular colour as well as providing cardioprotective benefits.

Serves 8

225g/8oz oat biscuits (cookies)
75g/3oz/⅓ cup unsalted butter, melted

For the filling
45ml/3 tbsp orange juice
15ml/1 tbsp powdered gelatine
250g/9oz/generous 1 cup mascarpone cheese
200g/7oz/scant 1 cup full-fat soft cheese
75g/3oz/¾ cup icing (confectioner's) sugar, sifted
200ml/7fl oz/scant 1 cup coconut cream
2 egg whites

For the topping
2 pomegranates, peeled and seeds separated
grated rind and juice of 1 orange
30ml/2 tbsp caster (superfine) sugar
15ml/1 tbsp arrowroot, mixed to a paste with 30ml/2 tbsp Kirsch
a few drops of red food colouring (optional)

1 Grease a 23cm/9in springform cake tin (pan). Crumb the biscuits in a food processor or blender, or by placing in a strong plastic bag and crushing them with a rolling pin. Add the melted butter and process briefly to combine. Spoon the mixture into the prepared tin and press it down firmly, then chill.

2 For the filling, pour the orange juice into a heatproof bowl, sprinkle the gelatine on top and set aside for 5 minutes until spongy. Place the bowl in a pan of hot water and stir until the gelatine has dissolved.

3 In a bowl, beat together both cheeses and the icing sugar, then gradually beat in the coconut cream. Whisk the egg whites in a grease-free bowl to soft peaks. Quickly stir the melted gelatine into the coconut mixture and fold in the egg whites. Pour over the biscuit base, level and chill until set.

COOK'S TIP
Cut the pomegranates in half and immerse in a bowl of water. Break the halves into quarters and remove the seeds with your fingers. The seeds will sink and the pith will float.

4 Make the cheesecake topping. Place the pomegranate seeds in a pan and add the orange rind and juice and caster sugar. Bring to the boil, then lower the heat, cover and simmer for 5 minutes. Add the arrowroot paste and heat, stirring constantly, until thickened. Stir in the food colouring, if using. Allow to cool, stirring occasionally.

5 Pour the glaze over the top of the set cheesecake, then chill. To serve, run a knife between the edge of the tin and the cheesecake, then remove the side of the tin.

Pomegranate cheesecake: Energy 407Kcal/1702kJ; Protein 8.2g; Carbohydrate 37.3g, of which sugars 26.1g; Fat 26.1g, of which saturates 15.2g; Cholesterol 56mg; Calcium 57mg; Fibre 1.1g; Sodium 336mg.

Red grape and cheese tartlets

Fruit and cheese is a natural combination in this delicious, low-sugar recipe. Choose the darkest red grapes available, as these contain the highest concentration of the cholesterol-reducing phytochemicals. To further reduce the fat content, you could use a low-fat cottage cheese.

Makes 6

350g/12oz shortcrust pastry,
  thawed if frozen
225g/8oz/1 cup curd cheese or
  cottage cheese
150ml/¼ pint/⅔ cup natural
  (plain) bio-yogurt
2.5ml/½ tsp pure vanilla extract
15ml/1 tbsp caster (superfine) sugar
200g/7oz/2 cups red grapes,
  halved, seeded if necessary
5ml/1 tsp arrowroot
90ml/6 tbsp unsweetened
  apple juice

1 Preheat the oven to 200°C/400°F/ Gas 6. Roll out the pastry and line six deep 9cm/3½in tartlet tins (muffin pans). Prick the bases and line with baking parchment and baking beans.

2 Bake the tartlets for 10 minutes, remove the paper and beans, then return the cases to the oven for 5 minutes until golden and fully cooked. Remove the pastry cases from the tins and cool on a wire rack.

3 Meanwhile, beat the curd cheese, yogurt, vanilla extract and caster sugar in a bowl.

4 Divide the curd cheese mixture among the pastry cases. Smooth the surfaces flat and arrange the halved grapes on top.

5 To make the glaze, mix the arrowroot in a small pan with the apple juice. Bring to the boil, then remove from the heat. Cool, stirring occasionally.

6 Spoon the arrowroot over the grapes. Cool, then chill until set in the refrigerator before serving.

VARIATIONS
You can try using cranberry jelly or redcurrant jelly for the glaze. There will be no need to strain either of these. You can also vary the fruit topping, if you like. Try blackberries, blueberries, raspberries, sliced strawberries, kiwi fruit slices, banana slices or well-drained pineapple slices.

Red grape tartlets: Energy 559kcal/2330kJ; Protein 10.4g; Carbohydrate 45.1g, of which sugars 19.7g; Fat 39.3g, of which saturates 23.9g; Cholesterol 164mg; Calcium 123mg; Fibre 1.3g; Sodium 331mg.

Blackcurrant tart

Blackcurrants grow in the wild and are cultivated throughout Europe and North America. This vitamin C-rich tart makes the most of these exquisite summer fruits, and is quick and easy to prepare. Serve with a generous dollop of low-fat crème fraîche.

Serves 4

115g/4oz plain (all-purpose) flour,
  plus 55g/2oz for the fruit mixture
55g/2oz butter, cut into chunks
30ml/2 tbsp cold water
500g/1¼lb blackcurrants
115g/4oz sugar
30ml/2 tbsp lemon juice

1 Pre-heat the oven to 200°C/400°F/ Gas 6. Lightly grease the base and edges of a 18cm/7in tart tin (pan).

2 In a large mixing bowl, rub the chunks of butter into the flour until the mix resembles breadcrumbs. Add the water, mix gently to form a dough, and place in a refrigerator for a few hours to rest.

3 In another bowl, gently mix together the fruit, sugar, lemon juice and flour.

4 Roll out the pastry to the correct size and line the tart tin (pan).

5 Spoon the fruit mixture into the tart tin and spread out evenly.

6 Bake in the centre of the oven for about 25 minutes.

7 Remove from the oven and cool. Serve with ice cream or low-fat crème fraîche.

VARIATION
Anthocyanin-rich elderberries are a great superfruit alternative to blackcurrants, but are harder to come by. In the UK, when in season, they grow in hedgerows. Collect as many as you can, then freeze them in batches so that you can use them all year round.

Blackcurrant tart: Energy 395Kcal/1669kJ; Protein 5g; Carbohydrate 71g, of which sugars 39g; Fat 12g, of which saturates 7g; Cholesterol 29mg; Calcium 140mg; Fibre 5.8g; Sodium 90mg.

Raspberry and almond tart

The antioxidant-rich, juicy, ripe raspberries and the LDL cholesterol-reducing almonds in this delicious recipe are a classic pairing for their taste as well as for their benefits to health. This stunning tart is ideal for serving at the end of a special lunch or at a dinner party.

Serves 4

200g/7oz shortcrust pastry
2 large (US extra large) eggs
75ml/2½fl oz/⅓ cup double
  (heavy) cream
50g/2oz/¼ cup caster
  (superfine) sugar
50g/2oz/½ cup ground almonds
20g/¾oz/4 tsp butter
350g/12oz/2 cups raspberries

1 Line a 20cm/8in flan tin (pan) with the pastry. Prick the base all over and leave to rest for at least 30 minutes. Preheat the oven to 200°C/400°F/Gas 6.

2 Put the eggs, cream, sugar and ground almonds in a bowl and whisk together briskly. Melt the butter and pour into the mixture, stirring to combine thoroughly.

3 Sprinkle the raspberries evenly over the pastry case. The ones at the top will appear through the surface, so keep them evenly spaced. You can also create a pattern with them.

4 Pour the egg and almond mixture over the top. Once again, ensure that it is spread evenly throughout the tart.

5 Bake in the preheated oven for 25 minutes. Serve warm or cold.

VARIATION
Peaches make a very attractive and tasty tart. Use 6 large, ripe peaches and remove the skin and stone (pit). Cut into slices and use in the same way as the raspberries above.

Raspberry and almond tart: Energy 548kcal/2284kJ; Protein 10.9g; Carbohydrate 41.7g, of which sugars 18.4g; Fat 38.8g, of which saturates 14.8g; Cholesterol 158mg; Calcium 128mg; Fibre 4.1g; Sodium 282mg.

Vanilla, honey and saffron pears

These sweet, juicy pears poached in a vanilla-, saffron- and lime-infused honey syrup make a truly elegant dessert. This low-fat dessert is good enough to eat on its own, but if you prefer, a serving of fresh-tasting bio-yogurt, crème fraîche or ice cream goes well.

Serves 4

150g/5oz/¾ cup caster (superfine) sugar
105ml/7 tbsp clear honey
5ml/1 tsp finely grated lime rind
a large pinch of saffron
2 vanilla pods (beans)
4 large, firm, ripe dessert pears
bio-yogurt, half-fat crème fraîche or ice cream, to serve

1 Place the caster sugar and honey in a medium, non-stick wok, then add the lime rind and the saffron. Using a small, sharp knife, split the vanilla pods in half and scrape the seeds into the wok, then add the vanilla pods as well.

2 Pour 500ml/17fl oz/scant 2¼ cups water into the wok and bring the mixture to the boil. Reduce the heat to low and simmer, stirring occasionally, as you prepare the pears.

3 Peel the pears, then add to the wok and gently turn in the syrup to coat evenly. Cover the wok and simmer gently for 12–15 minutes, turning the pears halfway through cooking, until they are just tender.

4 Lift the pears from the syrup using a slotted spoon and transfer to four serving bowls. Set aside.

5 Bring the syrup back to the boil and cook gently for about 10 minutes, or until reduced and thickened. Spoon the syrup over the pears and serve either warm or chilled with bio-yogurt, crème fraîche or ice cream.

VARIATIONS
For different syrup flavourings, try 10ml/2 tsp chopped fresh root ginger and 1–2 whole star anise in place of the saffron and vanilla, or 1 cinnamon stick, 3 cloves and 105ml/7 tbsp maple syrup instead of the spices and honey.

Vanilla and honey pears: Energy 283Kcal/1207kJ; Protein 0.8g; Carbohydrate 74.3g, of which sugars 74.3g; Fat 0.2g, of which saturates 0g; Cholesterol 0mg; Calcium 38mg; Fibre 3.3g; Sodium 10mg.

Winter fruit poached in mulled wine

A fabulous winter warmer, this dish combines fresh apples and pears with dried apricots and figs. These are then cooked in a fragrant, spicy mulled wine until tender and intensely flavoured. Boiling the wine will drive off some of the alcohol, but the healthy phytochemicals will remain.

3 Add the pears, figs and apricots to the pan and cook, covered, for 25 minutes, occasionally turning the fruit in the wine mixture. Add the sliced apples and cook for a further 12–15 minutes, until the fruit is tender.

4 Remove the fruit from the pan and discard the spices. Cook the wine mixture over a high heat until reduced and syrupy, then pour it over the fruit. Serve, decorated with the reserved orange rind, if wished.

Serves 4

300ml/½ pint/1¼ cups red wine
300ml/½ pint/1¼ cups fresh
  orange juice
finely grated rind and juice of
  1 orange
45ml/3 tbsp clear honey or barley
  malt syrup
1 cinnamon stick, broken in half
4 cloves
4 cardamom pods, split
2 pears, such as Comice or
  Williams (Bartlett), peeled, cored
  and halved
8 ready-to-eat dried figs
12 ready-to-eat dried unsulphured
  apricots
2 eating apples, peeled, cored and
  thickly sliced

1 Put the wine, the fresh and squeezed orange juice and half the orange rind in a pan with the honey or syrup and spices.

2 Bring to the boil, then reduce the heat and simmer for 2 minutes, stirring occasionally.

SUPERFOOD TIPS

• The combination of fresh and dried fruit ensures a healthy amount of vitamins and minerals, particularly vitamin C, beta-carotene, potassium and iron. The fruit is also rich in fibre.
• Cardamom and cinnamon soothe indigestion and, along with cloves, can offer relief from colds and coughs.

Poached winter fruit: Energy 494Kcal/2100kJ; Protein 7.3g; Carbohydrate 105.5g, of which sugars 105.5g; Fat 2.2g, of which saturates 0g; Cholesterol 0mg; Calcium 309mg; Fibre 14.6g; Sodium 85mg.

Apple and banana crumble

An old favourite, this crumble is sure to be popular with children and adults alike. While low in sugar and fat, this dessert remains rich in nutrients. The predominance of oats in the topping means that it will have a low glycaemic index and release energy slowly.

Serves 6

2 large cooking apples
2 large bananas
60ml/4 tbsp water
50g/2oz/¼ cup low-fat spread
30–45ml/2–3 tbsp pear and
   apple spread
25g/1oz/¼ cup wholemeal
   (whole-wheat) flour
115g/4oz/1 cup rolled oats
30ml/2 tbsp sunflower seeds
low-fat yogurt, to serve (optional)

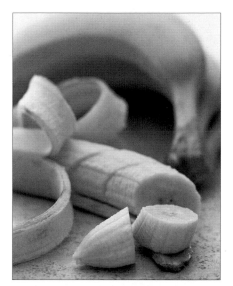

3 Transfer the apple and banana mixture to a 18cm/7in baking dish and spread the oat crumble over the top. Bake for about 20 minutes or until the topping is golden brown. Serve warm or at room temperature, as it is or with low-fat yogurt.

1 Preheat the oven to 180°C/350°F/ Gas 4. Cut the apples into quarters, remove the cores, and then chop them into small pieces, leaving the skin on. Peel and slice the bananas. Mix the apples, bananas and water in a pan and cook until they become soft and pulpy.

2 Melt the low-fat spread with the pear and apple spread in a separate pan. Stir in the flour, oats and sunflower seeds and mix well.

Apple and banana crumble: Energy 207kcal/870kJ; Protein 5g; Carbohydrate 31g, of which sugars 14g; Fat 8g, of which saturates 2g; Cholesterol 1mg; Calcium 25mg; Fibre 3.8g; Sodium 58mg.

Grilled pineapple with papaya sauce

Warming fruit such as pineapple releases all the wonderful flavours and aromas, and chargrilling it gives them depth too. The fragrant papaya sauce complements the pineapple with its carotenoid rich orange-pink colour. Serve this dessert warm for a fragrant, fruity treat.

Serves 6

1 sweet pineapple
7.5ml/1½ tsp rapeseed oil,
   for greasing
2 pieces drained stem ginger in
   syrup, cut into fine matchsticks,
   plus 30ml/2 tbsp of the syrup
   from the jar
30ml/2 tbsp demerara
   (raw) sugar
pinch of ground cinnamon

For the sauce
1 ripe papaya, peeled and seeded
175ml/6fl oz/¾ cup apple juice

1 Peel the pineapple and cut spiral slices off the outside to remove the eyes. Cut the pineapple crossways into six 2.5cm/1in thick slices.

2 Line a baking sheet with foil, rolling up the sides to make a rim. Grease the foil with the oil.

3 Preheat the grill (broiler). Arrange the pineapple slices on the lined baking sheet. Top with the ginger matchsticks, sugar and cinnamon. Drizzle over the stem ginger syrup.

4 Grill (broil) for 5–7 minutes, or until the slices are golden and lightly charred on top.

5 Meanwhile, make the sauce. Cut a few slices from the papaya and set aside, then purée the rest with the apple juice in a food processor or blender.

6 Sieve (strain) the purée, then stir in any cooking juices from the pineapple. Serve the pineapple drizzled with the sauce and decorated with the papaya slices.

COOK'S TIPS
• You can use the papaya sauce made in this recipe as an accompaniment to savoury dishes, too. It tastes great with grilled chicken and game birds, as well as pork and lamb.
• Make the sauce in advance and freeze in an ice-cube tray. Defrost as needed.

Grilled pineapple with papaya sauce: Energy 92kcal/393kJ; Protein 1g; Carbohydrate 20g, of which sugars 20g; Fat 2g, of which saturates 0g; Cholesterol 0mg; Calcium 27mg; Fibre 1.8g; Sodium 4mg.

Summer berry crêpes

The delicate flavour of these crêpes contrasts beautifully with the nutrient-rich array of tangy berry fruits. This recipe very gently warms the summer fruits but retains their excellent vitamin content. Unsweetened apple juice makes a flavoursome alternative to sugar-water syrups.

Serves 4

115g/4oz/1 cup self-raising
   (self-rising) flour
1 large egg
300ml/½ pint/1¼ cups milk
a few drops of vanilla extract
15g/½oz/1 tbsp butter
15ml/1 tbsp sunflower oil
5ml/1 tsp icing (confectioners')
   sugar, for dusting

For the fruit
300ml/½ pint/1¼ cups
   unsweetened apple juice
juice of 2 oranges
thinly pared rind of ½ orange
350g/12oz/3 cups mixed
   summer berries

1 Preheat the oven to 150°C/300°F/ Gas 2.

2 To make the crêpes, sift the flour into a large bowl and make a well in the centre. Break in the egg and gradually whisk in the milk to make a smooth batter. Stir in the vanilla extract. Set the batter aside in a cool place for up to half an hour.

3 Heat the butter and oil together in an 18cm/7in non-stick frying pan. Swirl to grease the pan, then pour off the excess fat into a small bowl.

4 If the batter has been left to stand, whisk it until smooth. Pour a little of the batter into the hot pan, swirling to coat the pan evenly.

5 Cook until the crêpe comes away from the sides and is golden underneath. Flip over the crêpe with a palette knife or metal spatula and cook the other side briefly until golden.

6 Slide the crêpe on to a plate, cover it with foil and keep warm in the oven. Make seven more crêpes.

7 To prepare the fruit, bring the apple juice to the boil in a pan. Boil until reduced by half. Add the orange juice and rind, and cook until slightly syrupy. Add the fruit and warm through.

8 Fold the pancakes into quarters and arrange two on each plate. Spoon some of the fruit over and dust lightly with icing sugar.

COOK'S TIP
Boiling unsweetened apple juice until it is reduced makes a good alternative to sugar-water syrups.

Summer berry crepes: Energy 260kcal/1099kJ; Protein 8g; Carbohydrate 45.9g, of which sugars 24.6g; Fat 3.5g, of which saturates 0.9g; Cholesterol 51mg; Calcium 235mg; Fibre 2.4g; Sodium 184mg.

Apple pudding

The understated vitamin C- and antioxidant-rich apple is at the heart of this very light soufflé-style pudding. This comforting, warm apple pudding is a perfect way to use up an autumnal glut, as the recipe works just as well with stewed or frozen apples.

2 Put the milk, butter and flour in a pan. Stirring constantly with a whisk, cook over a medium heat until the sauce thickens and comes to the boil. Let it bubble gently for 1–2 minutes, stirring well to make sure it does not stick and burn on the bottom of the pan. Pour into a bowl, add the sugar and vanilla extract, and then stir in the egg yolks.

3 In a separate bowl, whisk the egg whites until stiff peaks form. With a large metal spoon, fold the egg whites into the custard. Pour the custard mixture over the apples in the dish.

4 Put into the hot oven and cook for about 40 minutes until puffed up, deep golden brown and firm to the touch.

5 Serve immediately from the oven, before the soufflé-like topping begins to fall.

Serves 4

4 crisp eating apples
a little lemon juice
300ml/½ pint/1¼ cups milk
40g/1½oz/3 tbsp butter
40g/1½oz/⅓ cup plain
  (all-purpose) flour
25g/1oz/2 tbsp caster
  (superfine) sugar
2.5ml/½ tsp vanilla extract
2 eggs, separated

1 Preheat the oven to 200°C/400°F/ Gas 6. Butter a dish measuring 20–23cm/8–9in diameter and 5cm/2in deep. Peel, core and slice the apples and put in the dish.

VARIATIONS
Stewed fruit, such as cooking apples, plums, rhubarb or gooseberries sweetened with honey or sugar, would also make a good base for this pudding, as would fresh summer berries (blackberries, raspberries, redcurrants and blackcurrants).

Apple pudding: Energy 240kcal/1006kJ; Protein 7g; Carbohydrate 26.8g, of which sugars 19.2g; Fat 12.5g, of which saturates 6.8g; Cholesterol 121mg; Calcium 127mg; Fibre 1.9g; Sodium 131mg.

Caramel rice pudding with fruity compote

The fresh, fruity compote balances the sweetness of the caramel rice pudding and is quite wonderful. Dried apricots contain all of the concentrated goodness of their fresh counterparts and count as one of your five-a-day fruit portions, as well as being rich in calcium and iron.

Serves 4

1 vanilla pod (bean), split
300ml/½ pint/1¼ cups milk
300ml/½ pint/1¼ cups evaporated
    milk
50g/2oz/¼ cup short grain
    pudding rice

For the caramel
115g/4oz/½ cup granulated
    (white) sugar
90ml/6 tbsp water

For the compote
75g/3oz/6 tbsp caster (superfine)
    sugar
225g/8oz/1 cup ready-to-eat
    dried apricots
50g/2oz/½ cup whole blanched
    almonds
a few drops bitter almond extract,
    optional

1 Preheat the oven to 150°C/300°F/ Gas 2. To make the caramel, put the sugar and half the water in a heavy pan. Leave over a low heat, without stirring, until the sugar has dissolved and the liquid is clear. Increase the heat and gently boil until the liquid turns a caramel colour. Remove the pan from the heat, stand back and add the remaining water – take care as it will hiss and splutter.

2 Return the pan to a low heat and stir to dissolve the hardened pieces of caramel. Take the caramel off the heat and leave to cool for 2 minutes.

COOK'S TIP
If you don't like the skin, you can simmer the rice pudding on top of the hob for about an hour rather than baking it in the oven.

3 To make the rice pudding, put the split vanilla pod, milk and evaporated milk into a pan and bring slowly to the boil. Stir in the rice and cooled caramel, bring back to the boil, then pour into a shallow 900ml/1½ pint/ 3¾ cup ovenproof dish.

4 Bake the pudding for about 3 hours, or until a brown skin forms on top and the rice beneath is cooked and creamy.

5 Meanwhile, make the compote. Put the caster sugar and 300ml/½ pint/1¼ cups water in a pan and heat until the sugar has dissolved. Add the apricots, then cover and simmer for 20 minutes, until very soft. Stir in the almonds and extract, if using. Leave to cool, then chill.

6 Serve the rice pudding warm, with the cooled apricot and almond compote spooned on top.

Caramel rice pudding: Energy 545Kcal/2304kJ; Protein 15g; Carbohydrate 92g, of which sugars 81g; Fat 16g, of which saturates 6g; Cholesterol 30mg; Calcium 384mg; Fibre 4.5g; Sodium 180mg.

Berry and semolina pudding

Bursting with vitamins, antioxidants and a host of other supernutrients, berries are a fabulous addition to traditional desserts such as semolina. This whisked version is light and frothy and, with the amazing colour of the berries, will look stunning too.

Serves 4

1 litre/1¾ pints/4 cups water
300g/11oz lingonberries,
   bilberries or cranberries
150g/5oz/scant 1 cup semolina
about 90g/3½oz/½ cup caster
   (superfine) sugar
fresh berries, to decorate

1 Put the water and berries in a pan and bring to the boil. Strain the liquid into a clean pan. Discard the berries or sieve (strain) them into the liquid.

2 Put the semolina in the pan and, stirring all the time, return to the boil. Reduce the heat and simmer gently for 5 minutes, until the semolina is cooked.

3 Add the sugar according to taste and the type of fruit used.

4 Turn the mixture into a bowl and, using an electric whisk, whisk for at least 5 minutes until light and frothy.

5 Divide the mixture among individual serving dishes and sprinkle over a few berries to decorate.

COOK'S TIP
For added texture and flavour, you can add extra fresh berries at the end of step 2.

Berry and semolina pudding: Energy 246kcal/1050kJ; Protein 4.4g; Carbohydrate 59.3g, of which sugars 30.2g; Fat 0.8g, of which saturates 0g; Cholesterol 0mg; Calcium 22mg; Fibre 2g; Sodium 7mg.

Cherry clafoutis

Rich in anthocyanins, the dark red cherry is an integral part of this classic French dessert. You can also use canned, bottled or frozen cherries as fresh are not always available. Make sure you choose cherries in juice rather than syrup so as to keep your sugar intake to a minimum.

Serves 4

50g/2oz/½ cup plain
  (all-purpose) flour
50g/2oz/4 tbsp caster (superfine)
  sugar, plus extra to serve
2 eggs, separated
300ml/½ pint/1¼ cups milk
75g/3oz/5 tbsp butter, melted
450g/1lb dark cherries, pitted,
  fresh or canned/bottled in juice

VARIATIONS
Replace the cherries with plums, blackberries or blueberries.

1 Stir the flour and sugar together in a mixing bowl, then slowly stir in the egg yolks and milk to make a smooth batter. Stir half the melted butter into the mixture and leave it to rest for 30 minutes.

2 Preheat the oven to 220°C/425°F/Gas 7. Pour the remaining melted butter over the bottom of a 600ml/1 pint/2½ cup ovenproof dish and put it in the oven to heat up.

3 Stiffly whisk the egg whites and fold into the batter with the cherries. Pour into the dish, and bake for 15 minutes. Reduce the heat to 180°C/350°F/Gas 4 and cook for 20 minutes, until golden and set. Serve sprinkled with sugar.

Cherry clafoutis: Energy 357kcal/1493kJ; Protein 8.1g; Carbohydrate 39.4g, of which sugars 29.8g; Fat 19.7g, of which saturates 11.4g; Cholesterol 140mg; Calcium 147mg; Fibre 1.4g; Sodium 183mg.

Tofu and strawberry whizz

This energizing blend is bursting with goodness. Not only is tofu a perfect source of protein, it is also rich in minerals. With seeds and strawberries, this creamy blend makes a delicious alternative to an after-meal dessert. You can make it in advance and store in the refrigerator for later in the day.

Serves 2

250g/9oz firm tofu
200g/7oz/1¾ cups strawberries
45ml/3 tbsp pumpkin or sunflower
    seeds, plus a few extra for
    sprinkling
juice of 2 large oranges

1 Roughly chop the tofu, then hull and roughly chop the strawberries. Reserve a few strawberry chunks.

VARIATIONS
Almost any fruit can be used instead of strawberries. Mangoes, bananas and peaches blend well.

2 Put all the ingredients in a blender or food processor and blend until completely smooth, scraping the mixture down from the side of the bowl, if necessary.

3 Pour the smoothie into tumblers and sprinkle the top with extra seeds and a few strawberry chunks.

Creamy acai berry smoothie

The banana and bio-yogurt ingredients in this thick and creamy smoothie help to calm down the somewhat acidic flavour of the nutrient-rich acai berry juice. This recipe makes one glass of rich purple-coloured, detoxifying smoothie. Serve with blueberries for an extra nutrient punch.

Serves 1

100ml/3 fl oz acai berry juice
1 large ripe banana
150ml/5 fl oz bio-yogurt
a handful of blueberries, to serve

1 Place the acai berry juice, the banana and the bio-yogurt into a blender together.

2 Pulse all of the ingredients gently together until they reach a smooth consistency and serve immediately.

SUPERFOOD TIP
Acai berries are rich in potassium, anthocyanins, B vitamins and fibre, as well as omega-3 fatty acids.

Tofu and strawberry whizz: Energy 267kcal/1112kJ; Protein 15.7g; Carbohydrate 15.5g, of which sugars 11.2g; Fat 16.1g, of which saturates 1.7g; Cholesterol 0mg; Calcium 684mg; Fibre 2.5g; Sodium 17mg.
Creamy acai berry smoothie: Energy 307Kcal/1248kJ; Protein 9g; Carbohydrate 33g, of which sugars 31g; Fat 16g, of which saturates 10g; Cholesterol 25mg; Calcium 194mg; Fibre 0.7g; Sodium 100mg.

Green tea latte

This Asian twist on an Italian classic is a delightful, sweet beverage. The flavonoids in the green tea are thought to be responsible for its health benefits, and serving it with hot milk calms its flavour a little. You can use water instead of milk if you wish to enhance the green tea flavour.

Serves 4

1 litre/1¾ pints/4 cups milk
60ml/4 tbsp green tea powder
  or maacha
30ml/2 tbsp sugar
120ml/4fl oz/½ cup whipping
  cream (optional)
10ml/2 tsp caster (superfine) sugar
  or honey (optional)

1 Heat the milk in a pan over a low heat until it simmers gently. Add the green tea powder and sugar, and stir well.

2 Remove from the heat and pour the tea into a bowl or jug (pitcher). Leave to cool before chilling.

3 When ready to serve the tea, whisk the cream until it begins to thicken. Then add the caster sugar or honey and continue to whisk until the cream is light and fluffy.

4 Pour the chilled green tea into tall glasses and top with whipped cream. and a dusting of green tea powder.

Cardamom hot chocolate

Using dark chocolate instead of a chocolate powder is better as you get the goodness of the cocoa without the sugar. Cardamom is traditionally used to flavour milky drinks in the Middle East and is a wonderful partner for chocolate in this indulgent, soothing treat.

Serves 4

900ml/1½ pints/3¾ cups milk
2 cardamom pods, bruised
200g/7oz plain (semisweet)
  chocolate, broken into pieces

1 Put the milk in a pan with the cardamom pods and bring to the boil. Add the chocolate and whisk until melted.

2 Using a slotted spoon, remove the cardamom pods and discard. Pour the hot chocolate into heat-proof glasses, mugs or cups, and serve immediately.

Green tea latte: Energy 269kcal/1126kJ; Protein 9.2g; Carbohydrate 23g, of which sugars 23g; Fat 16.4g, of which saturates 10.3g; Cholesterol 46mg; Calcium 323mg; Fibre 0g; Sodium 116mg.
Cardamom hot chocolate: Energy 359Kcal/1567kJ: Protein 10g: Carbohydrate 42g of which sugars 42g: Fat 18g of which saturates 11g: Cholesterol 6mg: Calcium 127mg: Fibre 0g: Sodium 100mg.

CAKES, BAKES AND BREADS

You may be surprised to learn that you don't have to overload on sugars and fats just because you're partial to home-baking. Plenty of delicious bakes fit well into a healthy diet for balancing blood-sugar levels, with naturally sweet foods used instead of huge amounts of sugar. High-fibre and low GI-value foods can make tempting alternatives to commercial sugar-laden goods. Make a special treat, such as Apple and Cinnamon Cake or Green Tea Fruit Loaf, to share with family and friends.

Courgette and ginger cake

Both fresh and preserved ginger is used to flavour this unusual tea bread, which complements the very subtle flavour of courgette. It is delicious served warm, cut into thick slices and spread with a little butter or margarine. Try a slice about twenty minutes before travelling to help alleviate nausea.

Serves 8–10

3 eggs
225g/8oz/generous 1 cup
  caster (superfine) sugar
250ml/8fl oz/1 cup sunflower oil
5ml/1 tsp vanilla extract
15ml/1 tbsp syrup from a jar of
  stem ginger
225g/8oz courgettes (zucchini),
  grated
2.5cm/1in piece fresh root
  ginger, grated
350g/12oz/3 cups unbleached
  plain (all-purpose) wholemeal
  (whole-wheat) flour
5ml/1 tsp baking powder
pinch of salt
5ml/1 tsp ground cinnamon
6 pieces stem ginger, chopped
15ml/1 tbsp demerara (raw) sugar

1 Preheat the oven to 190°C/375°F/ Gas 5. Beat together the eggs and sugar until light and fluffy. Slowly beat in the oil until the mixture forms a batter.

2 Mix in the vanilla essence and ginger syrup, then stir in the courgettes and grated fresh ginger.

3 Sift together the flour, baking powder and salt into a large bowl. Add the cinnamon and mix well, then stir the dried ingredients into the courgette mixture.

4 Lightly grease a 900g/2lb loaf tin (pan) and pour in the courgette mixture. Smooth and level the top, then sprinkle the chopped ginger and demerara sugar over the surface.

5 Bake for 1 hour, until a skewer inserted into the centre comes out clean. Leave the cake in the tin to cool for about 20 minutes, then turn out on to a wire rack.

SUPERFOOD TIPS
• Courgettes are a good source of vitamin C, beta-carotene and folate.
• Ginger has many attributes, not least its ability to help alleviate stomach cramps, vertigo and travel sickness.

Courgette cake: Energy 252Kcal/1060kJ; Protein 5.6g; Carbohydrate 35.6g, of which sugars 8.8g; Fat 10.7g, of which saturates 1.6g; Cholesterol 57mg; Calcium 73mg; Fibre 1.3g; Sodium 82mg.

Poppy seed pineapple carrot cake

The pineapple in this classic carrot cake recipe gives it extra moistness as well as a fabulous, fruity boost. The mascarpone cheese topping is lighter in texture than a more traditional cream cheese topping and the walnuts add an omega-3 boost, too.

Makes 1 large loaf

250g/9oz/2¼ cups plain
 (all-purpose) flour
10ml/2 tsp baking powder
5ml/1 tsp bicarbonate of soda
 (baking soda)
2.5ml/½ tsp salt
5ml/1 tsp ground cinnamon
45ml/3 tbsp poppy seeds
225g/8oz/1⅓ cups soft light
 brown sugar
3 eggs, beaten
finely grated rind of 1 orange
225g/8oz raw carrots, grated
 75g/3oz/½ cup fresh or canned
 pineapple, drained and
 finely chopped
75g/3oz/¾ cup walnut pieces
115g/4oz/½ cup butter, melted
 and cooled

For the mascarpone icing
150g/5oz/scant 1 cup mascarpone
30ml/2 tbsp icing (confectioners')
 sugar, sifted
finely grated rind of 1 orange

1 Preheat the oven to 180°C/350°F/ Gas 4.

2 Line the base of a 1.5 litre/2½ pint/ 6¼ cup loaf tin (pan) with baking parchment. Grease the sides of the tin and dust with flour.

3 Sift together the flour, baking powder, bicarbonate of soda, salt and cinnamon in a bowl. Stir in the poppy seeds.

4 Mix together the sugar, eggs and orange rind in a separate bowl. Lightly squeeze the excess moisture from the grated carrots and stir the carrots into the egg mixture with the pineapple and walnut pieces. Gradually stir the sifted flour mixture into the egg mixture until well combined, then gently fold in the butter.

5 Spoon the mixture into the prepared tin, level the top and bake for about 1–1¼ hours, until risen and golden brown. (To check if the cake is cooked in the centre, push a thin metal skewer into the middle and pull it out immediately. If the skewer comes out clean the cake is done, if not, cook for another 10 minutes.)

6 Remove the cake from the loaf tin and allow to cool on a wire rack. Remove the baking parchment when completely cold.

7 To make the icing, beat the mascarpone with the icing sugar and orange rind. Cover and chill until needed. When ready to serve, beat well, then spread thickly over the top of the cake. Cut into slices and eat.

> **COOK'S TIP**
> Substitute half of the plain flour with wholemeal (whole-wheat) flour to increase the fibre content of the cake.

> **SUPERFOOD TIP**
> For an essential fatty-acid boost, try using a mix of sunflower seeds, pumpkin seeds and flax seed instead of poppy seeds.

Poppy seed cake: Energy 4051Kcal/16950kJ; Protein 72g; Carbohydrate 465g, of which sugars 271g; Fat 249g, of which saturates 103g; Cholesterol 941mg; Calcium 1378mg; Fibre 10.8g; Sodium 4069mg.

Dark chocolate and prune cake

This dark, cocoa rich cake is high in soluble fibre, which is good for gut health. It is also quite high in sugar, but this comes from the prunes and not from added sugar, so its energy will be released slowly, contributing to a lower glycaemic index. It is also gluten-free.

2 Mix the low-fat spread and prunes in a food processor. Process until light and fluffy, then scrape into a bowl.

3 Gradually fold in the melted chocolate and the eggs, alternately with the flour mixture. Beat in the soya milk.

4 Spoon the mixture into the cake tin, level the surface with a spoon, then bake for 20–30 minutes, or until the cake is firm to the touch. Leave to cool on a wire rack.

Makes a 20cm/8in cake

300g/11oz dark (bittersweet) chocolate
150g/5oz/⅔ cup low-fat spread
200g/7oz/generous 1 cup ready-to-eat stoned (pitted) prunes, quartered
3 eggs, beaten
150g/5oz/1¼ cups gram flour, sifted with 10ml/2 tsp baking powder
120ml/4fl oz/¼ cup soya milk

1 Preheat the oven to 180°C/350°F/Gas 4. Grease and base-line a deep 20cm/8in round cake tin (pan). Melt the chocolate in a heatproof bowl over a pan of hot water.

> **COOK'S TIP**
> For best results, use dark (bittersweet) chocolate with a high proportion of cocoa solids (70 per cent).

> **VARIATION**
> Try using ready-to-eat apricots in place of the prunes.

Dark chocolate and prune cake: Energy 3173kcal/13294kJ; Protein 65g; Carbohydrate 376.8g, of which sugars 259.8g; Fat 166.1g, of which saturates 72.6g; Cholesterol 598mg; Calcium 537mg; Fibre 23.6g; Sodium 1268mg.

Apple and cinnamon cake

This cake is firm and moist, with pieces of apple peeking through the top. Keeping the apple skins on helps to increase the fibre content of the cake. The skins also retain the highest concentration of nutrients. This classic combination of apple with cinnamon is simply scrumptious.

Serves 6–8

375g/13oz/3¼ cups self-raising (self-rising) flour
3–4 large cooking apples, or cooking and eating apples
10ml/2 tsp ground cinnamon
500g/1¼lb/2½ cups caster (superfine) sugar
4 eggs, lightly beaten
250ml/8fl oz/1 cup vegetable oil
120ml/4fl oz/½ cup orange juice
10ml/2 tsp vanilla extract
2.5ml/½ tsp salt

3 In a separate bowl, beat the eggs together with the remaining sugar, the vegetable oil, orange juice and vanilla extract until all the ingredients are well combined. Sift in the remaining flour and salt, then stir into the mixture.

4 Pour two-thirds of the mixture into the tin and top with one-third of the apples. Pour over the rest of the cake mixture and top with the rest of the apples. Bake for 1 hour, or until golden brown. Cool in the tin to allow the juices to soak in. Cut into squares.

1 Preheat the oven to 180°C/350°F/ Gas 4. Grease a 30 × 38cm/12 × 15in square cake tin (pan) and dust with a little of the flour. Core and thinly slice the apples, but do not peel.

2 Put the sliced apples in a bowl, and mix with the cinnamon and 75ml/ 5 tbsp of the sugar.

SUPERFOOD TIP
Cinnamon can help to lower 'bad' LDL cholesterol.

COOK'S TIP
This recipe uses orange juice instead of milk, which makes it ideal for those that suffer from lactose intolerance.

Apple cake: Energy 653Kcal/2751kJ; Protein 7.8g; Carbohydrate 105.4g, of which sugars 70.6g; Fat 25.2g, of which saturates 3.4g; Cholesterol 95mg; Calcium 215mg; Fibre 2.1g; Sodium 210mg.

Green tea fruit loaf

This is a fabulous all-in-one, low-fat loaf cake. Use your favourite dried-fruit mix in this and make sure it is all well chopped to keep the cake light and moist. Soaking the fruit in the green tea adds to the antioxidant power of this delicious recipe.

Makes 1 loaf

300ml/10fl oz green tea (made up
    with 3 green tea bags)
250g/9oz dried fruit – any or a
    combination of raisins, sultanas
    (golden raisins), mixed peel,
    apricots and dates
225g/8oz self-raising
    (self-rising) flour
1 egg beaten
115g/4oz soft dark brown sugar
1 tbsp water (optional)

1 Make up the green tea using boiling water and soak the dried fruit in it for at least 4 hours.

2 Pre-heat oven 160°C/325°F/ Gas 3. Grease your loaf tin (pan) and line with baking parchment.

3 Add the flour, beaten egg and sugar into the soaked fruit and stir thoroughly. Add the water if it is too dry.

4 Pour into the loaf tin and bake in the centre of the oven for 1 hour. Check that the centre of the cake is cooked by inserting a skewer into the middle of the cake. The loaf is cooked when the skewer comes out clean.

5 Remove the cooked loaf from oven and let cool for 5 minutes. Turn out of the tin and leave to cool completely.

SUPERFOOD TIP
Add your favourite chopped nuts and seeds to the batter to boost the nutrient content.

Green tea fruit loaf: Energy 1918Kcal/8183kJ; Protein 34g; Carbohydrate 457g, of which sugars 290g; Fat 10g, of which saturates 2g; Cholesterol 232mg; Calcium 1070mg; Fibre 12.5g: Sodium 1051mg.

Goji berry and cinnamon muffins

These lovely muffins are high in fibre that keeps the glycaemic index down, and this helps you to feel fuller for longer. The soaking of the nutrient-packed goji berries and raisins keeps them succulent, and makes them a delight to eat. They are a tasty treat for any time of the day.

Makes 12

55g/2oz goji berries
55g/2oz raisins
100ml/3fl oz apple juice
115g/4oz melted butter
115g/4oz golden caster
  (superfine) sugar
150ml/4fl oz milk
2 eggs, beaten
125g/4¼oz self-raising
  (self-rising) flour
125g/4¼oz wholemeal
  (whole-wheat) self-raising
  (self-rising) flour
10ml/2 tsp baking powder
10ml/2 tsp ground cinnamon
5ml/1 tsp vanilla extract
25g/1oz porridge oats

1 Pre-heat the oven to 190°C/375°F/ Gas 5. Grease a muffin tin (pan) and line with muffin cases.

2 Soak the goji berries and raisins in the apple juice.

3 In a jug (pitcher), mix the melted butter, sugar, milk and beaten eggs.

4 In a large bowl, sift together the two flours, baking powder and cinnamon, add the oats.

5 Make a well in the centre and pour in the jug of liquid. Mix together and fold in the fruit.

6 Spoon into the muffin cases, sprinkle over the oats and place in the centre of the oven for 20 minutes.

7 Ensure that that a skewer comes out clean before removing from the oven to cool.

Goji berry muffins: Energy 233Kcal/979kJ; Protein 5g; Carbohydrate 37g, of which sugars 20g; Fat 10g, of which saturates 6g; Cholesterol 63mg; Calcium 97mg; Fibre 2g; Sodium 200mg.

Beetroot and bitter chocolate muffins

Unusual in baking, freshly cooked beetroot contrasts well with the intense cocoa flavour of bitter chocolate. Both beetroot and cocoa are heart-healthy, as they keep the blood vessels strong and 'bad' cholesterol levels in check, and are rich in antioxidants.

3 Whisk the beetroot into the melted chocolate and butter with the eggs.

4 Fold in the sifted flour, baking powder and sugar. Do not overmix. Spoon the batter into the prepared tin. Dust with the rye flour.

5 Bake for 25 minutes until risen and springy to the touch. Leave to cool for 5 minutes, then transfer to a wire rack to go completely cold.

6 To make the ganache topping, bring the cream to the boil. Remove from the heat and leave for 1 minute. Break the chocolate into the hot cream. Stir until the chocolate melts and the mixture is smooth.

7 Add the butter and continue to stir until the mixture looks glossy. Use it immediately for a topping.

8 Spread the top of each muffin with the chocolate ganache and eat fresh.

Makes 10

115g/4oz dark (bittersweet) chocolate (70% cocoa solids)
115g/4oz/½ cup butter
250g/9oz beetroot (beets), cooked, peeled and grated
3 eggs, lightly beaten
225g/8oz/2 cups self-raising (self-rising) flour
2.5ml/½ tsp baking powder
200g/7oz/1 cup caster (superfine) sugar
20–30ml/1½–2 tbsp rye flour

For the ganache topping
75ml/2½ fl oz/⅓ cup double (heavy) cream
175g/6oz dark (bittersweet) chocolate (70% cocoa solids)
25g/1oz/2 tbsp butter

1 Preheat the oven to 180°C/350°F/Gas 4. Lightly grease the cups of a muffin tin (pan) or line them with paper cases.

2 Melt the chocolate and butter in a large heatproof bowl set over a pan of barely simmering water. Stir occasionally. Remove from the heat once the mixture is fully melted.

COOK'S TIP
To cook beetroot, trim the stems 2.5cm/1in above the bulbs, taking care not to tear the skin. Put the beetroot in a pan of boiling water and boil for 1½ hours, until tender. Drain and cool, then nip off the stems and roots.

Beetroot and chocolate muffins: Energy 342kcal/1437kJ; Protein 5.4g; Carbohydrate 50g, of which sugars 30.2g; Fat 14.8g, of which saturates 8.7g; Cholesterol 85mg; Calcium 112mg; Fibre 1.5g; Sodium 218mg.

Raisin and bran muffins

Low in fat and in sugar, these delicious muffins are made with a combination of wholemeal flour, bran and juicy raisins, and are flavoured with cinnamon. Their low glycaemic index makes them a perfect option for an on-the-go breakfast or a tasty mid-afternoon snack.

Makes 5

40g/1½oz/⅓ cup plain
　(all-purpose) flour
50g/2oz/½ cup wholemeal
　(whole-wheat) flour
7.5ml/1½ tsp bicarbonate of soda
　(baking soda)
5ml/1 tsp ground cinnamon
30g/1oz/⅓ cup bran
85g/3oz raisins
65g/2½oz/⅓ cup soft dark
　brown sugar
50g/2oz/¼ cup caster
　(superfine) sugar
1 egg, beaten
250ml/8fl oz/1 cup buttermilk
juice of ½ lemon
50g/2oz/4 tbsp butter, melted

1 Preheat the oven to 200°C/400°F/Gas 6.

2 Grease the cups of a muffin tin (pan) or line them with paper cases.

3 In a mixing bowl, sift together the flours, bicarbonate of soda and cinnamon.

4 Add the bran, raisins and sugars and stir until blended.

5 In another bowl, mix together the egg, buttermilk, lemon juice and melted butter. Add the buttermilk mixture to the dry ingredients, and whisk lightly and quickly until just moistened.

6 Spoon the mixture into the prepared paper cases, filling the cups almost to the top. Half-fill any empty cups with water so that the muffins bake evenly.

7 Bake for 15–20 minutes. Leave to stand for 5 minutes, before turning out on to a wire rack to cool. Serve warm or at room temperature. Store in an airtight container for up to 3 days.

COOK'S TIP
If buttermilk is not available, add 10ml/2 tsp lemon juice or vinegar to milk. Let the mixture stand and curdle, about 30 minutes.

Raisin and bran muffins: Energy 89kcal/374kJ; Protein 2g; Carbohydrate 13.4g, of which sugars 8.9g; Fat 3.4g, of which saturates 1.9g; Cholesterol 20mg; Calcium 34mg; Fibre 1.1g; Sodium 36mg.

Date and muesli slice

Full of oats, seeds, dates, raisins and bio-yogurt, this is a supernutrient-packed treat. The light lemon-flavoured icing tops these scrumptious, low-fat muesli bars, making them the perfect mid-morning pick-me-up, or a welcome addition to a lunchbox or picnic.

Makes 12–16

175g/6oz/¾ cup light muscovado (brown) sugar
175g/6oz/1 cup ready-to-eat dried dates, chopped
115g/4oz/1 cup self-raising (self-rising) flour
50g/2oz/½ cup muesli (granola)
30ml/2 tbsp sunflower seeds
15ml/1 tbsp poppy seeds
30ml/2 tbsp sultanas (golden raisins)
150ml/¼ pint/⅔ cup natural (plain) low-fat bio-yogurt
1 egg, beaten
200g/7oz/1¾ cups icing (confectioners') sugar, sifted
lemon juice
15–30ml/1–2 tbsp pumpkin seeds

1 Preheat the oven to 180°C/350°F/Gas 4. Line a 28 x 18cm/11 x 7in shallow baking tin (pan) with baking parchment. Mix together all the ingredients except the icing sugar, lemon juice and pumpkin seeds.

2 Spread the mixture evenly in the tin and bake for about 25 minutes, until golden brown. Allow to cool.

3 To make the topping, put the icing sugar in a bowl and stir in just enough lemon juice to give a thick, spreading consistency.

4 Spread the lemon topping over the baked mixture and sprinkle generously with pumpkin seeds. Leave to set before cutting into squares or bars.

Date and muesli slice: Energy 176kcal/749kJ; Protein 3g; Carbohydrate 38.7g, of which sugars 31.3g; Fat 2.1g, of which saturates 0.3g; Cholesterol 12mg; Calcium 72mg; Fibre 1.1g; Sodium 45mg.

Almond, orange and carrot bars

Carrot cake becomes a cookie bar in this more portable version, and is a great way to add to the fruit and vegetable count of lunchboxes. The almonds and walnuts also add some essential fatty acids into the mix, as well as B vitamins and a host of minerals.

Makes 16

75g/3oz/6 tbsp unsalted
  butter, softened
50g/2oz/¼ cup caster (superfine)
  sugar
150g/5oz/1¼ cups wholemeal
  (whole-wheat) flour
finely grated rind of 1 orange

For the filling
90g/3½oz/7 tbsp unsalted
  butter, diced
75g/3oz/scant ½ cup caster
  (superfine) sugar
2 eggs
2.5ml/½ tsp almond extract
175g/6oz/1½ cups ground almonds
1 large cooked carrot, finely
  chopped

For the topping
175g/6oz/¾ cup cream cheese
30–45ml/2–3 tbsp chopped
  walnuts

1 Preheat the oven to 190°C/375°F/ Gas 5. Lightly grease a 28 x 18cm/ 11 x 7in shallow baking tin (pan).

2 Put the butter, caster sugar, flour and orange rind into a bowl and rub together until the mixture resembles coarse breadcrumbs. Add water, a teaspoon at a time, to mix to a firm but not sticky dough. Roll out on a lightly floured surface and use to line the base of the tin.

3 To make the filling, cream the butter and sugar together. Beat in the eggs and almond essence. Stir in the ground almonds and the finely chopped carrot. Spread the mixture over the dough base and bake for about 25 minutes until firm in the centre and golden brown. Leave to cool in the tin.

4 To make the topping, beat the cream cheese until smooth and spread it over the cooled, cooked filling. Swirl with a small palette knife or metal spatula, and sprinkle with the chopped walnuts. Cut into bars with a sharp knife.

Almond, orange and carrot bars: Energy 85Kcal/355kJ; Protein 1.4g; Carbohydrate 5.3g, of which sugars 2.9g; Fat 6.6g, of which saturates 3g; Cholesterol 18mg; Calcium 20mg; Fibre 0.4g; Sodium 34mg.

Fruit and millet treacle cookies

Brimming with dried fruit, these tasty little cookies are very quick and simple to make. The highly nutritious millet flakes give them a lovely crumbly texture and they are sure to be popular with the whole family, as a quick on-the-go snack or served with tea.

Makes 25–30

90g/3½oz/7 tbsp margarine
150g/5oz/⅔ cup light muscovado (brown) sugar
30ml/2 tbsp black treacle (molasses)
1 egg
150g/5oz/1¼ cups self-raising (self-rising) flour
50g/2oz/½ cup millet flakes
50g/2oz/½ cup almonds, chopped
200g/7oz/generous 1 cup luxury mixed dried fruit

COOK'S TIP
Millet flakes can be replaced with rolled oats, wheat flakes or barley flakes.

1 Preheat the oven to 190°C/375°F/Gas 5. Line two large baking sheets with baking parchment.

2 Put the margarine, muscovado sugar, treacle and egg in a large bowl and beat together until well combined. (The mixture should be soft and fluffy.)

3 Stir in the flour, millet flakes, almonds and dried fruit. Put tablespoonfuls of the mixture well apart on to the prepared baking sheet.

4 Bake for about 15 minutes until brown. Leave on the baking sheets for a few minutes, then transfer to a wire rack to cool completely.

Fruit and millet treacle cookies: Energy 99kcal/416kJ; Protein 1.4g; Carbohydrate 15.7g, of which sugars 10.6g; Fat 3.8g, of which saturates 1.2g; Cholesterol 7mg; Calcium 26mg; Fibre 0.5g; Sodium 33mg.

Psyllium, ginger and chocolate chip cookies

You wouldn't believe that these cookies were stacked full of fibre from the cardioprotective, cholesterol-reducing psyllium seed husk. The ginger pieces and dark chocolate are a tasty combination that makes these cookies a real tea-time treat.

Makes 8

rapeseed oil, for greasing
50g/2oz olive oil-based spread
85g/3oz golden caster
  (superfine) sugar
115g/4oz plain (all-purpose) flour
1 egg, beaten
25g/1oz psyllium fibre
2.5ml/½ tsp baking powder
2.5ml/½ tsp vanilla extract
50g/2oz plain chocolate chips
50g/2oz crystallized ginger,
  chopped
2–3 tbsp milk

1 Preheat the oven to 180°C/350°F/ Gas 4. Lightly grease a large 20cm/8in baking sheet.

2 Using a wooden spoon, soften the olive oil spread and sugar together in a bowl until creamy and pale. Sift the flour into the mixing bowl and add the beaten egg. Mix well.

3 Stir in the psyllium fibre, baking powder and vanilla extract, followed by the chocolate chips and ginger.

4 Gradually add the milk until the mixture is soft and spoonable. Spoon eight balls on to the baking sheet, leaving enough space between each to allow them to spread. Gently flatten each into a round.

5 Bake in the centre of the oven for 15 minutes. Leave on the baking sheet to cool for a few minutes, then lift off the sheet and transfer to a wire rack. Leave the cookies to cool completely before eating.

Psylliium and chocolate chip cookies: Energy 193Kcal/811kJ; Protein 3g; Carbohydrate 31g, of which sugars 17g; Fat 7g, of which saturates 2g; Cholesterol 30mg; Calcium 45mg; Fibre 3.0g; Sodium 90mg.

Apricot and coconut kisses

The apricots and orange juice will retain all their vitamin C in this no-bake recipe. Coconut adds an interesting texture to these tangy, fruity treats and, with its unusual form of saturated fat, may even help to metabolize our unwanted body-fat stores.

Makes 12

130g/4½oz/generous ½ cup
   ready-to-eat dried apricots
100ml/3½fl oz/scant ½ cup
   orange juice
40g/1½oz/3 tbsp unsalted butter,
   at room temperature, diced
75g/3oz/¾ cup icing
   (confectioners') sugar, plus extra
   for dusting (optional)
90g/3½oz/generous 1 cup
   desiccated (dry unsweetened
   shredded) coconut,
   lightly toasted
2 glacé (candied) cherries, each
   cut into 6 wedges

COOK'S TIP
Ensure the orange juice has been completely absorbed by the apricots before adding them to the butter and sugar mixture.

---

1 Finely chop the dried apricots, then transfer them to a bowl. Pour in the orange juice and leave to soak for about 1 hour until all the juice has been absorbed.

2 In a large bowl, beat together the butter and sugar with a wooden spoon until pale and creamy.

3 Gradually add the soaked apricots to the creamed butter and sugar mixture. Beat well after each addition, then stir in the lightly toasted coconut.

4 Line a small baking tray with baking parchment.

5 Place teaspoonfuls of the coconut mixture on to the paper, piling them up into little pyramid shapes. Gently press the mixture together with your fingers to form neat shapes.

6 Top each kiss with a tiny wedge of cherry, gently pressing it into the mixture. Chill the kisses for about 1 hour until firm, then serve, lightly dusted with a little icing sugar.

Apricot and coconut kisses: Energy 115Kcal/480kJ; Protein 1g; Carbohydrate 11.7g, of which sugars 11.7g; Fat 7.5g, of which saturates 5.7g; Cholesterol 7mg; Calcium 14mg; Fibre 1.7g; Sodium 25mg.

Oatmeal biscuits

Oats are great for reducing blood cholesterol levels as well as the glycaemic index of foods. These high-fibre savoury home-made biscuits are an ideal quick snack. Simply spread with hummus, cottage cheese or a little light cream cheese, and serve with grapes.

Makes 18

75g/3oz/⅔ cup plain
  (all-purpose) flour
2.5ml/½ tsp salt
1.5ml/¼ tsp baking powder
115g/4oz/1 cup fine pinhead
  oatmeal
65g/2½ oz/generous ¼ cup white
  vegetable fat (shortening)

1 Preheat the oven to 200°C/400°F/ Gas 6 and grease a baking sheet.

2 Sift the flour, salt and baking powder into a mixing bowl. Add the oatmeal and mix well. Rub in the fat to make a crumbly mixture.

3 Gradually add water to the dry ingredients, mixing in just enough to make a stiff dough.

SUPERFOOD TIP
The soluble fibre in oatmeal makes you feel fuller for longer.

4 Turn out the dough on to a worktop sprinkled with fine oatmeal, and knead until smooth and manageable. Roll out to about 3mm/⅛in thick and cut into rounds, squares or triangles. Place on the baking sheets.

5 Bake in the preheated oven for about 15 minutes, until crisp. Cool the biscuits (cookies) on a wire rack.

6 Store in an airtight container lined with baking parchment. Check for crispness before serving: reheat for 4–5 minutes in a preheated oven at 200°C/400°F/Gas 6 if necessary.

COOK'S TIP
Chunks of hard mature cheese are delicious with these oatmeal biscuit (cookies). Slices of pear or apple add the finishing touch.

Oatmeal biscuits: Energy 67kcal/279kJ; Protein 1.2g; Carbohydrate 7.9g, of which sugars 0.1g; Fat 3.6g, of which saturates 1.3g; Cholesterol 1mg; Calcium 10mg; Fibre 0.6g; Sodium 31mg.

Herby seeded oatcakes

The thyme and sunflower seeds in this traditional recipe add to the heart-healthy credentials of the oats by reducing cholesterol levels. Their triangular shape and sunflower-seed topping gives them an interesting rustic appearance, perfect for a cheese board or simply to snack on.

Makes 32

175g/6oz/1½ cups plain
  wholemeal (whole-wheat) flour
175g/6oz/1½ cups fine oatmeal
5ml/1 tsp salt
1.5ml/¼ tsp bicarbonate of soda
  (baking soda)
75g/3oz/6 tbsp white vegetable
  fat (shortening)
15ml/1 tbsp fresh thyme leaves,
  chopped
30ml/2 tbsp sunflower seeds
rolled oats, for sprinkling

1 Preheat the oven to 150°C/300°F/ Gas 2. Sprinkle two ungreased, non-stick baking sheets with rolled oats and set aside.

2 Put the flour, oats, salt and soda in a bowl and rub in the fat until the mixture resembles fine breadcrumbs. Stir in the thyme.

3 Add just enough cold water (about 90–105ml/6–7 tbsp) to the dry ingredients to mix to a stiff, but not sticky, dough.

4 Gently knead the dough on a lightly floured surface until smooth, then cut roughly in half and roll out one piece on a lightly floured surface to make a 23–25cm/9–10in round.

5 Sprinkle sunflower seeds over the dough and press them in with the rolling pin. Cut into triangles and arrange on one of the baking sheets. Repeat with the remaining dough. Bake for 45–60 minutes, until crisp but not brown. Cool on wire racks.

Herby seeded oatcakes: Energy 62Kcal/259kJ; Protein 1.6g; Carbohydrate 7.7g, of which sugars 0.2g; Fat 3g, of which saturates 0.9g; Cholesterol 0mg; Calcium 6mg; Fibre 0.9g; Sodium 21mg.

Sultana and walnut bread

Featuring the cardioprotective might of the walnut, this bread is versatile and delicious with sweet or savoury foods. Serve with soups or salads or with a little jam for afternoon tea. Try substituting the walnuts with chopped brazil nuts for a selenium boost.

Makes 1 loaf

300g/11oz/2¾ cups strong
  white bread flour
2.5ml/½ tsp salt
15ml/1 tbsp butter
7.5ml/1½ tsp easy-blend
  dried yeast
115g/4oz/scant 1 cup sultanas
  (golden raisins)
75g/3oz/½ cup walnuts or brazil
  nuts, roughly chopped
melted butter, for brushing

4 Knead the sultanas and walnuts or brazil nuts into the dough until they are evenly distributed. Shape into a rough oval, place on a lightly oiled baking sheet and cover with oiled clear film (plastic wrap). Leave to rise in a warm place for 1–2 hours, until doubled in bulk. Preheat the oven to 220°C/425°F/Gas 7.

5 Uncover the loaf and bake for 10 minutes, then reduce the oven temperature to 190°C/375°F/Gas 5 and bake for a further 20–25 minutes.

6 Transfer to a wire rack, brush with melted butter and cover with a dish towel. Cool before slicing.

1 Sift the flour and salt into a bowl, cut in the butter with a knife, then stir in the yeast.

2 Gradually add 175ml/6 fl oz/¾ cup tepid water to the flour mixture, stirring with a spoon at first, then gathering the dough together with your hands.

3 Turn the dough out on to a floured surface and knead for about 10 minutes until smooth and elastic.

Sultana bread: Energy 1971kcal/8303kJ; Protein 50g; Carbohydrate 308g, of which sugars 86g; Fat 68g, of which saturates 13g; Cholesterol 32mg; Calcium 569mg; Fibre 23.2g; Sodium 1111mg.

Wholemeal sunflower bread

Adding seeds to bread is a wonderful way of making it more nutritious and interesting. Sunflower seeds give a nutty crunchiness to this high-fibre wholemeal loaf, which tastes delicious served simply with a chunk of cheese and lycopene-rich tomato chutney.

Makes 1 loaf

450g/1lb/4 cups wholemeal
   (whole-wheat) flour
2.5ml/½ tsp easy-blend dried yeast
2.5ml/½ tsp salt
50g/2oz/½ cup sunflower seeds,
   plus extra for sprinkling

SUPERFOOD TIP
You can try adding 10ml/2 tbsp of honey to give a sweet note to this scrumptious bread.

1 Grease and lightly flour a 450g/1lb loaf tin (pan). Mix together the flour, yeast, salt and sunflower seeds in a large bowl. Make a well in the centre and gradually stir in 300ml/½ pint/1¼ cups warm water. Mix vigorously with a wooden spoon to form a soft, sticky dough.

2 Cover the bowl with a damp dish towel and leave the dough to rise in a warm place for 45–50 minutes, or until doubled in bulk.

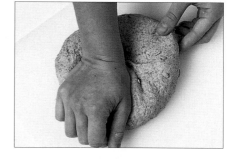

3 Preheat the oven to 200°C/400°F/ Gas 6. Turn out the dough on to a floured work surface and knead for 10 minutes – it will still be quite sticky.

4 Form the dough into a rectangle and put in the tin. Sprinkle sunflower seeds. Cover with a damp dish towel and leave to rise for 15 minutes.

5 Bake for 40–45 minutes, until golden. Leave for 5 minutes, then turn out of the tin and leave to cool.

Wholemeal bread: Energy 1686Kcal/7136kJ; Protein 67g; Carbohydrate 296.9g, of which sugars 10.3g; Fat 33.6g, of which saturates 3.6g; Cholesterol 0mg; Calcium 226mg; Fibre 43.5g; Sodium 998mg.

Rosemary and rock salt focaccia

Enriched with monounsaturate-rich black olives and olive oil and flavoured with rosemary and garlic, this popular Italian bread makes it a truly Mediterranean treat and a perfect accompaniment to a salad. Rosemary is supposed to be good for the memory, so remember not to overdo the salt.

Makes 1 loaf

225g/8oz/2 cups unbleached plain (all-purpose) flour, sifted
2.5ml/½ tsp salt
7g/¼oz sachet easy-blend dried yeast
4 garlic cloves, finely chopped
2 sprigs of rosemary, leaves removed and chopped
10 black olives, stoned (pitted) and roughly chopped (optional)
15ml/1 tbsp olive oil

For the topping
90ml/6 tbsp olive oil
sprinkling of rock salt
1 sprig of rosemary, leaves removed

1 Mix together the flour, salt, yeast, garlic, rosemary and olives, if using, in a large bowl. Make a well in the centre and add the olive oil and 150ml/¼ pint/⅔ cup warm water. Mix well until a soft dough is formed.

2 Turn out the dough on to a floured work surface and knead for 10–15 minutes. Put the dough in an oiled bowl and cover with oiled clear film or a dish towel. Leave to rise in a warm place for 45 minutes, until the dough has doubled in bulk.

3 Turn out the dough and knead lightly again. Roll out to an oval shape, about 1cm/½in thick. Put the dough on a greased baking sheet, cover loosely with oiled clear film (plastic wrap) or a dish towel and leave in a warm place for 25–30 minutes to rise again.

4 Preheat the oven to 200°C/400°F/Gas 6. Make indentations with your fingertips all over the top of the bread. Drizzle two-thirds of the olive oil over the top, then sprinkle with the rock salt and rosemary. Bake for 25 minutes until golden.

5 When ready, the bread will sound hollow when tapped underneath. Transfer to a wire rack, and spoon the remaining olive oil over the top.

SUPERFOOD TIP
Olives are a good source of iron and the antioxidant vitamin E.

Rosemary focaccia: Energy 1699Kcal/7177kJ; Protein 37.8g; Carbohydrate 311g, of which sugars 9.7g; Fat 42.3g, of which saturates 6.1g; Cholesterol 0mg; Calcium 568mg; Fibre 13.1g; Sodium 14mg.

Glossary

A

Alpha-linolenic acid – an omega-3 fatty acid found in some vegetables.

Acetylcholine – an important neurotransmitter in the brain, deficient in those suffering from Alzheimer's. Formed from choline, found in eggs, liver and wheatgerm.

Acidophilus (culture) – a specific strain of bacteria which helps with digestion.

Alginic acid – found in seaweed and is capable of binding heavy metals and removing them from our body.

Allicin – the active compound found in onions and garlic, which reduces heart disease and cancer risk.

Amino acid – the basic building blocks used to make proteins.

Anthocyanin – water-soluble pigments found in fruits and vegetables that reduce cancer and heart disease risk.

Anthraquinone – a type of polyphenol found in rhubarb that has laxative effects in the body.

Antioxidant – compounds that inhibit the oxidation and potential damage to body cells by free radicals.

Ascorbic acid – also known as vitamin C, found in most fruit and vegetables and essential for healthy skin and blood vessels, and a strong immune system.

Atherosclerosis – a condition where the arteries become clogged with fatty deposits such as cholesterol.

B

Beta-carophyllene – an essential oil found in cloves, rosemary and basil. It has anti-inflammatory properties.

Beta-carotene (b-carotene) – an orange pigment found in carrots, mangoes, papayas and pumpkins that can be converted by the body into vitamin A, which is essential for good eyesight.

Beta-cryptoxanthin – a red pigment found in egg yolks, papayas and orange rind, that can be converted in the body to vitamin A, which is essential for maintaining good eyesight.

Beta-glucan – a type of fibre found in oats, barley and mushrooms that helps reduce cholesterol levels.

Betalain – a red/orange pigment found in beetroot (beet) that has strong antioxidant activity so could reduce cancer risk.

Bifidobacterium – bacteria found in bio-dairy products that contribute to a healthy gastrointestinal tract.

Bioavailability – a measure of how available a nutrient is for absorption and use by the body.

Bromelain – an enzyme found in pineapples that can break down protein and can have anti-inflammatory effects.

C

Calciferol – another name for vitamin D, found in dairy products, canned fish with bones and vegetable oils, it is essential for healthy bones and the absorption of calcium and phosphorus.

Capsaicin – the active compound found in chillies that can stimulate the release of endorphins in the body and may relieve pain.

Carnosic acid – found in rosemary, this powerful antioxidant may have benefits for brain health.

Carotenoid – a large family of pigments found in plants and algae. Carotenes are a type of carotenoid.

Catechin – a compound found in tea that has potent antioxidant activity.

Chlorophyll – a green pigment found in plant cells that enables them to convert sunlight into energy.

Cholesterol – a substance made by the liver which circulates in the blood, is used to make hormones and is part of all cell tissues. A raised blood concentration of cholesterol is a risk factor in heart disease and stroke.

Cineole – a volatile oil found in cardamom and eucalyptus, which is thought to help alleviate congestion.

Citral – a volatile compound found in lemongrass, lemon, lime and lemon balm that has high antioxidant activity.

Conjugated Linoleic Acid (CLA) – forms of the fatty acid linoleic acid found in dairy products and the meat of ruminant animals; may be able to reduce body fat percentage.

Coumaric acid – found in peanuts, this compound has a very high level of antioxidant activity.

Cruciferous – vegetables from the brassica family such as cabbage, sprouts, spinach, broccoli and kale. Eating cruciferous vegetables three or four times a week may reduce cancer risk.

Cyanocobalamin (or vitamin B$_{12}$) – found in dairy foods, eggs and yeast, it is essential for a healthy nervous system and maintaining energy levels.

Cynarin – found in artichokes, this compound is thought to help in liver health and cholesterol metabolism.

D

Deoxyribonucleic acid (DNA) – found in the cells of all living things, DNA forms the chromosomes and genes.

Docosahexanoic acid (DHA) – a type of omega-3 fatty acid found in fish. Particularly significant in the structure of the brain and of the retina in the eye.

E

Epicatechin – a very similar compound to catechin, found in cocoa and tea.

EPA (Eicosapentanoic acid) – a type of omega-3 fatty acid found in fish. Significant in the production of anti-inflammatory compounds that can reduce the severity of conditions such as rheumatoid arthritis and atherosclerosis.

Essential amino acid – a constituent of protein foods that cannot be made by the body and so has to be supplied by the diet.

Essential fatty acid – a constituent of fat

that cannot be made by the body and so has to be supplied by the diet.

Eugenol – an oily liquid compound with antibacterial and antiviral properties, found in clove oil, nutmeg, cinnamon and basil.

F

FDA (Food and Drug Administration) – the American agency responsible for protecting and promoting public health.

Fisetin – a compound found in strawberries that may help improve brain function.

Flavonoids (or bioflavonoids) – are a large family of compounds found in plants that include many plant pigments. They have potent antioxidant properties and are associated with the health benefits of tea, red wine and of fruit and vegetables.

Folate (or folic acid) – is a B-vitamin found in wholegrains and green leafy vegetables, it is essential for healthy cell division especially in the foetus.

Free radicals – the potentially damaging agents found both naturally in the body and externally in cigarette smoke. Can cause cell damage and may lead to cancer, heart disease, stroke and diabetes.

G

Glycemic Index (GI) – a measure of how quickly energy is released in the body by food. One hundred is the highest and represents the fastest energy release from pure glucose. The lower the number the slower the energy release.

Gingerol – the active compound found in ginger that is responsible for its anti-nausea and anti-inflammatory properties.

Glucosinolate – sulphur-containing compounds found in brassica vegetables that are thought to be responsible for their potential anti-cancer properties.

H

HDL (High Density Lipoprotein) – a compound sometimes known as 'good cholesterol' found in the blood that carries cholesterol back to the liver and removes it from the blood.

Hesperidin – a type of flavonoid found in citrus fruits that can help strengthen blood vessels and may reduce heart disease risk.

Hypercholesterolaemia – a genetic condition whereby the blood cholesterol levels are very high.

I

Insoluble fibre – the type of fibre that is able to absorb water but not dissolve in it, helping bulk and good intestinal health.

Inulin – a type of soluble fibre found in Jerusalem artichokes that has probiotic properties and thus helps to maintain the population of good bacteria in the gut.

Isoflavones – are compounds found in soya and alfalfa that have phytoestrogen properties and the potential to reduce circulating blood cholesterol levels.

L

LDL (Low density Lipoprotein) – the form of cholesterol that stays in the blood and is sometimes known as 'bad cholesterol'. High LDL levels increase the risk of heart disease.

Lectins – a toxic substance found in red kidney beans that is removed by boiling the dried beans vigorously for 15 minutes.

Lentinan – the specific beta-glucan found in mushrooms that is responsible for its anti-tumour properties.

Lignin – a substance found in plant cell walls that acts as a type of dietary fibre.

Lipid – an alternative word for fat or oil.

Lutein – a yellow-pigmented compound found in mangoes and pumpkins that contributes to good vision and may reduce risk of age-related macular degeneration.

Lycopene – a red-pigmented carotene that does not have vitamin A properties like other carotenes. It is found in tomatoes, pink grapefruit and watermelon and can help reduce prostate cancer risk.

M

Mono-unsaturated fat – a type of fat found in olive oil, avocado and nuts that can reduce heart disease risk.

N

Nutrient – a chemical that the body needs in order to live and grow and maintain itself. Food is our main source of nutrients.

O

ORAC (oxygen radical absorption capacity) – a way of measuring how

powerful the antioxidant capacity of a food or substance is. The higher the ORAC score the more potent the activity.

Omega-3 fat – a type of fat found in oily fish, walnuts, rapeseed and soya, that has many health benefits, including benefits for the heart and brain and anti-flammatory effects in the body.

Omega 6 – a type of essential polyunsaturated fat found in sunflower and corn oil. Eating more polyunsaturates is beneficial to health as they help to lower cholesterol and reduce heart disease risk.

Omega 9 – a type of monounsaturated fat found in olive oil and avocado; eating more monosaturates helps to reduce cholesterol and heart disease risk.

Organosulphur – pungent sulphur-containing compounds found in garlic, onions and leeks that have antioxidant and anti-carcinogenic activity in the body.

Oil – a fat that is liquid at room temperature.

Oxalate – compounds found in foods such as rhubarb and spinach that bind to micronutrients such as magnesium and calcium, reducing the bioavailability of these minerals to the body.

P

Papain – found in papaya, this enzyme is able to break down meat fibre and may have digestive benefits in the body.

Phytochemical (or Phytonutrient) – a general name given to a plant-derived compound that is beneficial to health.

Phytate – a compound found in high-fibre foods such as bran and dried pulses that can reduce the absorption of certain nutrients, such as calcium, iron and zinc.

Phytonutrient (or Phytochemical) – a general name given to a plant-derived compound that is beneficial to health.

Phytosestrogen – the plant hormone equivalent to animal hormones found in soya products, which have been found to reduce circulating blood cholesterol levels.

Phytosterol – a chemical similar to cholesterol that is able to reduce blood cholesterol levels by interfering with absorption in the intestines.

Polyphenol – a compound with antioxidant properties found in foods such as red wine, cocoa and peanuts, thought to reduce heart disease risk.

Polyunsaturate – a type of fat found in sunflower oil, nuts, fish oil and rapeseed oil. A diet high in polyunsaturated fats is known to be beneficial to health.

Proanthocyanidin – a type of flavonoid, found in cocoa, apples, grapes and red wine, which is a powerful antioxidant and has benefits in heart health, weight management and in preventing cancer.

Probiotics – bacterias such as bifidobacterium and lactobacillus found in bio-yogurts, thought to improve gastrointestinal health by boosting levels of good bacteria.

Protein – made up of amino acids, proteins are essential for healthy growth and maintenance of the body. Good sources of protein are meat, fish and eggs.

Proteolytic enzyme – an enzyme that can break down proteins such as papain or bromelain.

Pyridoxine (or vitamin B6) – found in eggs, wholegrains and cruciferous vegetables, and essential for making red blood cells and maintaining a healthy immune system.

Q

Quercetin – a flavonoid found in tea, red grapes and apples, that has antioxidant and anti-inflammatory activity and may reduce cancer and heart disease risk.

Quinone – yellow pigment found in spices such as turmeric. Also found in vitamin K, which is essential for blood clotting.

R

RDA (Recommended Dietary Allowance) – the US standard for the amount of a nutrient the average person requires each day to remain healthy.

Resveratrol – a polyphenol found in grapes, red wine and blueberries that has anti-cancer and anti-inflammatory effects.

Retinol – a nutrient that has vitamin A properties and is found in animal foods such as liver, cod liver oil and eggs .

Riboflavin (or vitamin B2) – found in dairy products, pulses and pumpkin seeds. It is essential for energy production and tissue repair.

RNI (Reference Nutrient Intake) – the UK standard for the amount of a nutrient that will meet the needs of most healthy people within a group.

Rosmarinic acid – a compound found in rosemary that is high in antioxidants.

S

Shogaol – formed when gingerol in ginger is broken down and is useful for its anti-diarrhoea properties.

Sinigrin – a type of glucosinolate found in Brussels sprouts and broccoli that may have anti-cancer effects.

Solanine – a toxic compound produced by potatoes when exposed to light.

Soluble fibre – a type of fibre found in oats and pulses that dissolves in water and is partially digested by the body. It has benefits for lower intestinal health.

Stanol – compound found in grains such as amaranth that has blood-cholesterol-reducing activity.

T

Tannin – a polyphenol compound found in red wine, pomegranates and berries thought to have antibacterial affects.

Theaflavin – a polyphenol flavonoid found in black tea which acts as a powerful antioxidant to protect the body cells from damage by free radicals.

Thearubin – a polyphenol flavonoid found in black tea which is a powerful antioxidant and helps protect the body cells from damage by free radicals.

Thiamin (or vitamin B1) – found in wholegrain foods, yeast, pulses and milk and is essential for efficient energy maintenance and muscle growth.

Tocopherol – another name for vitamin E, found in seed oils, eggs, wholegrains and green vegetables; this antioxidant is essential for healthy circulation and skin.

Triglycerides – part of the chemical structure of fats and oils and is made up of three fatty acids. The type of fatty acid found characterizes the type of fat and how it is used by the body.

Tryptophan – an essential amino acid found in poultry, eggs and spirulina, needed for production of the feel-good hormone serotonin and the B-vitamin niacin.

V

Vitamin – a compound needed by the body in very small amounts, for growth and development, and to support metabolism.

W

World Health Organization (WHO) – the co-ordinating body within the United Nations that is responsible for health. The WHO produces policies and standards in the quest to improve public health.

Wholegrain – a food that contains all three parts of the grain, the bran, the germ and endosperm, thus retaining all its vitamins, minerals and nutrients.

Z

Zeaxanthin – a type of carotenoid yellow pigment found in kale and pumpkins. It is essential for protection of the human eye from damage by free radicals and the development of age-related macular degeneration (ARMD).

Zingerone – formed when gingerone is heated, zingerone is useful in the treatment of diarrhoea.

Index

Figures in italics refer to illustrations.

ACKNOWLEDGEMENTS

Recipes: Catherine Atkinson, Alex Barker, Ghillie Basan, Georgina Campbell, Judith H Dern, Joanna Farrow, Jenni Fleetwood, Brian Glover, Nicola Graimes, Anja Hill, Christine Ingram, Becky Johnson, Bridget Jones, Emi Kazuko, Lucy Knox, Bridget White Lennon, Sara Lewis, Elena Makhonko, Jane Milton, John Nielsen, Maggie Pannell, Carol Pastor, Keith Richmond, Rena Salaman, Ysanne Spevack, Marlena Spieler, Christopher Trotter, Sunil Vijayakar, Jenny White, Kate Whiteman, Carol Wilson, Jeni Wright and Annette Yates.
Photographers: Peter Anderson, Martin Brigdale, Nicky Dowey, Gus Filgate, Amanda Heywood, William Lingwood, Thomas Odulate, Charlie Richards, Craig Robertson, Simon Smith, Jon Whitaker and Mark Wood.
Picture agencies: Fotalia Page 6bl, 10bm, 21b, 27tm, 28bl, 75tm and 87br.